T0378054

Praise For Off-White

'The rise in antisemitism in recent years should concern us all. In a necessary exploration, Rachel Shabi asks the questions that few seem willing to address: why has antisemitism become such an Achilles heel for the left, why is there little attention given to right-wing antisemitism and how can progressives build more inclusive anti racist politics.'

Billy Bragg

'Rachel Shabi is deeply knowledgeable, across the territories of prejudice from the modern far-right to the near-historical left, and interweaves the personal and political with assurance, humour, passion and love. This is a challenging and nuanced book; an urgent read but also an enormously enjoyable one.'

Zoe Williams

'Rachel Shabi is gifted with a unique sensibility, embodying multiple identities and universal, non-negotiable human rights. Holding that together is tough, particularly in our times of competing injustices and public discourse filled with demagogic sound and fury... No one who reads this exceptional book will come away unchanged.'

Yasmin Alibhai-Brown

'Contemporary debates about antisemitism are often nasty, partisan and dishonest. Rachel Shabi's book is the opposite: thoughtful, fair-minded and humane. It offers a glimpse into what a smarter and more decent public debate might look like.'

Peter Beinart, author of *Being Jewish After the Destruction of Gaza*

'While you probably won't agree with everything in this timely book, it will force you to look at contemporary antisemitism, post October 7, in a deeper way… Shabi calls out antisemitism on the political right and left, and makes the case that fighting antisemitism is, at heart, a progressive cause.'

Kenneth S. Stern, Director
of the Bard Center for the Study of Hate

'Written in the context of Israel's war on Gaza, a sharp rise in recorded antisemitic incidents across the globe, and fierce debates over what actually counts as antisemitism, *Off-White* is essential reading for anyone who thinks our response to antisemitism requires better thinking and a better politics.'

David Feldman, Director of the
Birkbeck Institute for the Study of Antisemitism

'Shabi's book provides the language and tools needed to confront antisemitism head-on, not as a distraction, but as a central part of our fight against all forms of racism and injustice – including the fight for Palestinian liberation. It's time we made this struggle our own, and Shabi's work is the manual we need for the road ahead.'

Iyad el–Baghdadi,
author of *The Middle East Crisis Factory*

'The world needs the intellectual, values-driven insight of Rachel Shabi's *Off-White*… Shabi is unflinching in her bravery to lay bare uncomfortable truths, whoever they offend. The brilliance of *Off-White* not only unshackles us from toxic dogma but also paves the way to rehumanise and rethink how warring neighbours can finally live together.'

Lord Simon Woolley, founder of Operation Black
Vote and principal at Homerton College, Cambridge

OFF
WHITE

The Truth About Antisemitism

RACHEL
SHABI

ONEWORLD

A Oneworld Book

First published by Oneworld Publications Ltd in 2024

Copyright © Rachel Shabi, 2024

The moral right of Rachel Shabi to be identified as the
Author of this work has been asserted by her in accordance
with the Copyright, Designs, and Patents Act 1988

ISBN 978-0-86154-837-8
eISBN 978-0-86154-836-1

Typeset by Geethik Technologies Pvt Ltd
Printed and bound in Great Britain by Clays Ltd, Elcograf S.p.A.

Oneworld Publications Ltd
10 Bloomsbury Street
London WC1B 3SR
England

Stay up to date with the latest books,
special offers, and exclusive content from
Oneworld with our newsletter

Sign up on our website
oneworld-publications.com

MIX
Paper | Supporting
responsible forestry
FSC® C018072

Contents

Introduction

In early December 2023, a video about antisemitism went viral. Reflexively, I braced. And sure enough, it delivered everything I had come to expect. The politicised, polarised messiness. The bad-faith contortions and confusions. The dumbed-down, meaning-stripped binaries. In short, all the fuel needed to ignite the sprawling online dumpster fire also known as the modern debate around antisemitism.

The short clip came from a US House Committee on Education and the Workforce hearing entitled 'Holding Campus Leaders Accountable and Confronting Antisemitism'. This hearing took place amid alarm over antisemitism at American universities, including cases of Jewish students being harassed and attacked on campuses. It occurred in the context of a wider global spate of antisemitism: a Jewish woman stabbed in France, shootings at Jewish day schools in Canada, desecrations of Jewish buildings with hate-filled graffiti and swastikas across Europe, protesters screaming 'fuck the Jews' in Australia and a full-blown antisemitic riot in Russia's Dagestan. Countries everywhere reported the greatest escalation of antisemitism in modern times. It all followed the brutal rampage by Hamas on Israeli soil on 7 October, in which some 1,200 people, the majority Israeli civilians and including 71 foreigners, were killed and over 200 more taken hostage, including women, children and a nine-month-old baby. Israel immediately launched an unprecedented bombardment of the Gaza Strip. By the time that viral clip pinged onto my phone, tens of thousands, mostly women and children, had been killed or injured, the entire population terrorised and most displaced. In November, the UN secretary general António Guterres described Gaza as 'a graveyard for children' – some 13,000 of whom have been killed. The Strip was decimated, made uninhabitable. The scale of Israel's military response was so ferocious that in January 2024, the highest court in the world, the International Court of Justice, would find there was plausible evidence that Israel was violating the genocide convention in Gaza. By March, the court's president would warn: 'All the indicators of genocidal activities are flashing red in Gaza.'

But in early December at the House Committee hearing, the presidents of three of America's leading universities, Harvard, the University of Pennsylvania and the Massachusetts Institute of Technology, were each asked variations of an apparently simple question: 'Does calling for the genocide of Jews violate university rules or codes of conduct, yes or no?' Astoundingly, none of them answered with a categoric 'yes'. They resorted to evasive legalese, hesitant gestures towards 'context' and seemingly dispassionate distinctions. It was horrible to watch. It seemed to

confirm that Jews could not count on anyone to even recognise antisemitism for what it was, let alone condemn it,
and at a time when anti-Jewish hatred was spiralling. And
so, as is the way with social media firestorms, we were all
drafted into taking sides, and the news headlines played out
the debate day after day. In the end, two of the three testi-
fying university heads resigned.

All too predictably, however, a three-minute clip did not
accurately represent the proceedings of a hearing that lasted
over five hours. It reflected mostly that a trap had been set
by New York Republican congresswoman, Elise Stefanik,
in asking that particular question and that the three university presidents walked right into it. Stefanik had prepared
the ambush by suggesting that chants of 'Intifada', Arabic for
'uprising', at Palestine solidarity marches were equivalent
to calls for genocide. 'Intifada' is a long-used and common
slogan in Palestine solidarity actions, including in demonstrations across American campuses. Those university heads
botched a basic moral question that shouldn't require more
than one second of thought. And yet across those hours
of the hearing, we could also see the three thinking seriously about how to safeguard Jewish students and other
minorities, including Muslims also facing renewed threats,
while protecting free speech on campus. We learned that
action had already been taken, that they wanted to enable
students to communicate constructively across differences
and saw education as a key tool, helping young people
better identify, and thus avoid, antisemitic speech. Far from
dispassionate about the subject, these leaders came across as

caring deeply about their responsibilities to their students. Claudine Gay, the former Harvard president who resigned following attacks including racist abuse that dragged on for weeks, spoke during the hearing on why antisemitism had flared at universities. 'One of the things that has been laid bare over the last couple of months', she said, 'is how ill-equipped the community is and has been to deal with dialogue in moments of crisis. And instead, what is sub-stituted for that is the social-media-fication of dialogue. It is intemperate, it's ahistorical and just mean and it's a way of engaging that has been deeply socialised through social media and is reflexive for a lot of the students on our campus.'

She might as well have been talking about all of us. She might as well have pointed out that this is how the entire debate around antisemitism has been taking place and for far too long. Because that clip and the way it burned through our political ecosystem is typical of what we get wrong when we talk about antisemitism. It was a rerun of many similar controversies. It contained the hallmark features that have turned this issue into a convoluted pile-up, like an epic movie car crash, a snarled-up chaos of fire and smoke and spinning wheels and sprawling debris. It neatly revealed how antisemitism has become a 'Gotcha!' moment: a stick with which the right clobbers the left. It showed how claims of antisemitism are cynically invoked to silence pro-Palestinian voices and then attach to a broader culture war that strikes out against antiracism, 'wokeness', critical race theory, diversity, equity and inclusion programmes or just a generalised 'liberal elite'. It showed the supposedly progressive side tumbling into the traps set by the right, while often lacking the ability to recognise actual antisemitism. Many on the left could not see why the testimonies given by those university heads had been so hurtful and alarming and instead praised them for standing up for free speech in the face of enormous pressure. Yet again there was a wearying tendency to downplay antisemitism, to force it into competition with other axes of oppression, instead of building a tent that could hold us all in it together. As Claudine Gay, Harvard's first Black university president, faced escalating calls to quit, progressives claimed, not without merit, that she was being silenced and punished by a racist mob. Others bemoaned a hierarchy of racism: pointing out that Jewish communities, unlike other minorities, had the benefit of hearings and strategies and multiple condemnations of the bigotries they experienced, from politicians across the board and all the way up to the American president. And of course, many felt it was absurd and insulting to be debating the semantics of supposedly and hypothetically calling for a genocide of Jews, while genocide experts were sounding the alarm bells over the catastrophic situation actually unfolding in Gaza. When the Israeli defence minister could freely describe Palestinians in Gaza as 'human animals' and vowed to 'eliminate everything' in the Strip, when the Israeli army spokesperson stated it was focused on 'what causes maximum damage' and a defence official said Gaza would be reduced to a 'city of tents', it seemed surreal that pages of media coverage could be dedicated to the goings-on at

relatively safe American universities. From every perspective, wherever you stood, it felt like stepping into a hall of
mirrors, where the truth lay distorted in a dissonant muddle
of fact and fiction, impossible to unpack.

That clip and its aftermath were a dramatically scaled-up
version of a row we've been having for some time. Because
the truth is that the way antisemitism is talked about – on
air, in newspapers and by our leading politicians – has made
it entirely incomprehensible. The subject is a gnarled-up,
snowballing mess, sowing confusion and sparking antago-
nisms. The concerns of Jewish people take a backseat to
factional fights between different political tendencies. And
all that gets spewed up in moments of profound tone-deaf-
ness or through unbelievable missteps, of the sort we saw at
the hearing. As is often the case when it comes to racism,
our mainstream media and political class cannot be trusted
with the task of discussing it constructively, meaningfully
or safely.

It is not just the politicians though. In different ways
and to varying degrees, we are all bad at talking about or
understanding antisemitism. It doesn't matter who you are
or how you identify: Jewish or not, antiracist, educated,
whether you refresh your newsfeed regularly or skip past
to the recipe and fashion pages (no judgement). It doesn't
seem to matter whether we are members of political parties
or campaign groups, or none of the above. We all fall victim
to blind spots and biases. Sometimes it is just down to plain
old lack of awareness, which is not a crime. Or it might
be down to being low on bandwidth or interest, neither

of which is bigotry. It might be a reflex to being over-scrutinised or falsely accused. It might be confusion or not knowing where to start. The issue has been rendered indecipherable, densely unapproachable, requiring too much time and effort before yielding any clarity. As we shall see, confusion over antisemitism is actually built into the very mechanisms of this prejudice. But while accusations of antisemitism all too often appear to come down to being critical of Israel or being in the 'wrong' political camp, people grow bewildered yet afraid to ask about it, lest their questions are themselves misconstrued. When anyone from the UN secretary general to students and celebrities can be accused, what is the uninvolved onlooker supposed to make of it? And when the accusations seem factionally wielded to marginalise political opponents, the effect can only be to sow dread. People worry that spurious claims might one day be made against them. One leftist organiser I spoke with in the north of England, part of a group working in one of the most deprived parts of the country to build support networks and community cohesion, told me: 'I'm scared of it, I'm scared it will be used to ruin our reputation. I feel worried even saying this out loud.'

If people are feeling this way, something has clearly gone horribly wrong.

★★★

'If you had told me a decade ago that this is what I would be doing, I would have been shocked and so confused', says

Charlotte Fischer. For almost twenty years she has worked within British Jewish communities on social justice movements – on refugee resettlement schemes and campaigns for a living wage. Ten years ago, when it came to antisemitism, as she says, 'I wasn't thinking about it at all.' By 2018, she had co-founded a training programme in recognising and dealing with antisemitism and was taking it to progressive groups across the UK.

When she tells me this, I feel a flash of recognition. Antisemitism was not *my* beat, either. For decades, I have written about politics and current affairs, from anticapitalist protests to the Arab uprisings, from the UK's toxic immigration politics to pandemic profiteering, and 'What the hell is happening?' explainer pieces on Brexit commissioned by bewildered American editors. I reported on the Israel–Palestine conflict, spending years based in the region. That did sometimes include covering instances when voices critical of Israel were being decried as 'antisemitic'. But still, antisemitism itself? Not my beat. Sure, I would read the news items and reports, and follow the debates, but actually covering the issue was not something I thought about.

In the late 1990s and early 2000s, few of the Jewish progressives I knew were talking about it at length, either. Back then, we were not yet smack in the middle of the resurgent nativist populism that flared up with far-right wins across continental Europe and then exploded into mainstream politics with the rise of Donald Trump, Brazil's Jair Bolsonaro, Hungary's Viktor Orbán and Brexit Britain. Now the most powerful men in the world capitalised on fog-horning all the festering prejudices that people previously at least had the good sense not to express out loud. Inevitably, when the social guardrails around racism came off, antisemitism slipped in.

Immediately after Trump's election, synagogues and Jewish cemeteries were desecrated. Swastikas appeared alongside pro-Trump slogans. In August 2017, white supremacists marched through the streets of Charlottesville, chanting 'Jews will not replace us.' Trump, in his initial remarks on the confrontation between the white supremacists and counter-protesters, described 'very fine people on both sides'. Just over a year later, a truck driver walked into the Tree of Life synagogue in Pittsburgh. He opened fire and killed eleven people, in the deadliest attack on any Jewish community on American soil. Meanwhile, Viktor Orbán, now ensconced as the Hungarian prime minister, repeatedly attacked the Jewish billionaire George Soros, speaking of 'an enemy' that 'does not believe in working but speculates with money; does not have its own homeland but feels it owns the whole world.' Global leaders and media figures blithely amplified this antisemitic attack on a prominent Jewish philanthropist. And then various strands of the Covid-conspiracy-crazed far right used antisemitism as an online mobilising force, while high-profile figures with millions of followers spouted anti-Jewish hatred that acted as a force-multiplier in the extremist right recruitment pool.

With the far right in ascendancy across the world, Jewish people turned to leftist movements that had long been political heartlands – I'm using 'leftist' throughout as an umbrella for groups that might adopt the term, such as antiracist, social justice and human rights groups, trade unions or left parties – and found them not only lacking the language to speak to what was happening, but also often mired in ignorance over antisemitism.

Mere months after neo-Nazis paraded through Charlottesville, some of the coordinators of the Women's March against Donald Trump found themselves facing allegations of antisemitism over claims of their connections to Louis Farrakhan, the leader of the Nation of Islam, who has reportedly blamed Jews for slavery, and accused them of controlling the US government and causing degeneracy in Hollywood. Across the Atlantic, for the five years Jeremy Corbyn was Labour leader, the party floundered in the face of accusations of antisemitism, ill-equipped to deal with complaints. As American communications specialist Sharon Goldtzvik told me: 'We as progressives should be leading on the issue of antisemitism, but it has become a critical vulnerability, rather than a critical strength.' This Achilles heel is seized upon by the right wing, derailing progressive movements and thwarting efforts at social, economic and climate justice across the world. It is also undermining the Palestinian cause at a time when solidarity is most critical. It is dividing antiracist movements. It is helping an increasingly extreme right wing keep winning elections around the globe.

Part of the problem here is something that Charlotte Fischer mentions when we speak. 'The voices that I *did* hear talking about antisemitism, they weren't talking about it within a worldview that I share', she explains. 'They were broadly right-wing voices, so I tuned out. I tuned out of thinking about antisemitism as a modern phenomenon.' Fischer's criticism is directed at herself, for opting out of this discussion. Again, I relate. But I too have observed that if caring about antisemitism means making common cause with journalists or politicians who are, say, anti-union, supportive of privatisation measures in the NHS, critical of multiculturalism or scaremongers over immigration, many people with progressive sympathies, including Jewish people, simply don't want to join in. It is as though, just by talking about it, the political right had made the fight against contemporary antisemitism *their* issue, something that belongs to their camp, their box of priorities and concerns. And that alone was putting people off.

Our debate about antisemitism might as well be a lens through which we can perceive a political culture in crisis. Naomi Klein's latest book, *Doppelganger*, premised on her being chronically mixed up with Naomi Wolf, the liberal feminist icon turned conspiracy theorist and darling of the Trump-supporting MAGA faithful, explores the idea that politics is no longer driven by values or ideological beliefs. It is, instead, dominated by warring camps perpetually reflecting each other. 'All of politics increasingly feels like a mirror world', she writes, 'With society split in two and each side defining itself against the other – whatever one says and believes the other seems obliged to say and believe the exact opposite. The deeper I went, the more I noticed this phenomenon all around me. Individuals not guided by legible principles or beliefs but acting as members of groups playing yin to the other's yang – well versus weak; awake versus sheep; righteous versus depraved. Binaries where thinking once lived.' Klein writes about how the far right, using the language of the left, is hoovering up all kinds of reasonable fears and worries about the ravages of a people- and planet-crushing socio-economic system, but then spinning them out into wild conspiracies and hateful narratives. It is increasingly clear that the same dynamic is at play in our discussions about antisemitism. For instance, in Britain, when the Conservative party chairman James Cleverly stated in the week that the 2019 general election was announced, that 'Jewish friends of mine' would leave the country if Jeremy Corbyn 'got anywhere near the levers of power', the British left, with good reason, responded with outrage. But too often, protesting against the clear weaponisation of antisemitism has bled into a posture of indifference about antisemitism at best, and outright denials of it at worst. The left has ceded the space on antisemitism – responding to accusations of it, sure, but not taking up the fight against it as a left-wing cause. And the right has smartly and strategically filled that void. But then, just as Klein describes in *Doppelganger*, it misrepresented the issue, constructing a divisive narrative that allows antisemitism to fester while making it impossible to have a real conversation about it.

Like many other Jewish leftists I have spoken to, Fischer found that when she did start to talk about antisemitism, she lacked the language to do so. 'It was painful for me to realise that I didn't have an explanation, an answer to why something was antisemitic. I couldn't convince my colleagues of it.' Fischer didn't know how to respond to experiences of antisemitism within friendship circles or workspaces; she didn't know how to deconstruct instances of this prejudice. So along with her co-founder, she went on every antisemitism training course she could find in the English-speaking world and spent three years researching the subject, eventually setting up L'Taken, Hebrew for 'repair', which delivers training in how to identify and tackle antisemitism.

Accustomed to believing that until recently, antisemitism was a largely dormant racism, we have forgotten the tools to analyse it. We have forgotten that the dormancy itself is part of the cyclical nature of antisemitism – that things are fine until, all of a sudden, they aren't. Antisemitism doesn't seem to fit the 'story' of racism: of persistent structural disadvantage and bigotries premised on skin colour. And meanwhile discussions of antisemitism have isolated it from other racisms, despite the history of racism being a constant cross-pollination of bigotries, one influenced by the other, each directed against a different group, at different times.

When I mentioned I was writing this book, several of my friends reacted as if I had just said I planned to jump into a vat of hazardous waste. In recent years, every national conversation I've participated in about antisemitism has quickly turned toxic. When claims of antisemitism against the Labour party's former leader, Jeremy Corbyn, erupted in 2018, I was caught in the middle of a now familiar pattern of misunderstandings, mismanagement and distortion – accused by the right of supporting anti-semitism, accused by the left of participating in a smear campaign against them – while the party descended into a full-blown crisis. Talking about it sparked wearying accusations from the left that discussing antisemitism made one a 'Zionist shill', while the right raged about my supposedly 'downplaying' the issue. After Labour lost the 2019 general election and a new leader was elected, I appeared on a BBC radio programme in November 2020 to discuss the topic. I argued that while, yes, the antisemitism within Corbyn's Labour was real, his successor Keir Starmer's blunt, factional approach to the issue involved criticising and expelling opponents in the party which ended up making things worse. 'Well, what *do* you suggest then?' asked the presenter, and I could hear the puzzlement in his voice. I didn't blame him. I sounded like the Goldilocks of antisemitism. But in the years since, our discussion on the subject has only grown more polarised and incomprehensible. And in the middle of Israel's savage flattening of Gaza, the spectre of antisemitism and all the terrible confusion around it was raised in the most damaging way to try and stop people from protesting, from crying out against the atrocities – even, surreally, when those voices were Jewish, even when the cries were coming from Israeli Jews. Through all these years, as the issue kept dominating news headlines, it kept raiding my thoughts, taking up time, jangling my nerves. So I did what writers often do. I tried to write my way out of the despair.

And just as listening to the full, over five-hour US hearing with those university heads helped me tune out all the confusing noise and figure out what had happened, so too researching this book has helped me see how things have gone so wrong. Leaning into the task of investigating what I had avoided for so long, I found that there were distinct, identifiable themes. I realised it was possible to pull each contributing factor out of the tangle and deconstruct it, so that the moving parts of this chaos start to make sense. I saw that, all too often, the left has forgotten to apply to antisemitism the frames of analysis already available within our movements. And I'm more certain than ever of the urgency of untangling the mess of our antisemitism conversation. I am more convinced that a true understanding of what has gone so wrong with this discussion – and how to put it right – will not just fortify the left, consolidate our antiracist endeavours and yield inclusiveness, moral clarity and cohesion. It will help us make sense of the alarming, divisive and destructive rightwards shift of the world we are all in – because only then do we stand a chance of changing it.

ONE

The Colour Chart Conundrum

'Of course you're not white, you're Iraqi for God's sake!' a friend tells me. Not out of the blue, I mean; I asked him. 'You're Iraqi and Jewish, you can never be white', he says. Which is true, but also not really true – because if, right now, I tried to tell you that I'm not white, you might reasonably suggest I take a good look in the mirror.

Born in Israel, raised in Britain and having inherited the features of light-skinned Iraqi-Jewish parents, I read as white in most of the ways that matter: white while not being stopped by police or tailed around stores; white while not negatively stereotyped, assumed to be lazy, stupid, aggressive or threatening; white while not facing poorer outcomes in classrooms, offices or the housing market; white while avoiding people's inexhaustible biases based on skin colour. What I experience daily is exactly the definition of white privilege described by British journalist Reni Eddo-Lodge in the bestselling *Why I'm No Longer Talking to White People About Race*: 'An absence of the negative consequences of racism. An absence of structural discrimination, an absence of your race being viewed as a problem first and foremost.'

So then I'm white, right? Yes. But also, not exactly. Or yes, *until* it's a no. Not quite knowing how to explain, I have sometimes used the term 'white-presenting', although to me, this feels laboured and could easily sound like equivocating, like I'm angling for a hall pass that gets me out of whiteness. Honestly, it would be much easier – and really, what's the problem? – to go with 'white'. Why not just say it?

I'm not the only one feeling this ambivalence, the reluctance and the hesitation. British Jews who are coded white and benefit from that don't necessarily describe ourselves that way, even though we know that self-definitions don't actually define whiteness. You don't get to choose. And some people, including Black Jews, never have that option. Still, we stumble over the question, unsure what to say or which box to tick.

Ask Jewish people in the UK about identity and what's striking is the 'Yes, but …'. They are white, but the kids at school used to throw coins at them. White, but called 'Yid', 'Towel-head' and 'Sand n-word' at school – that last one is a cousin, who is also 'randomly' stopped at airport security. White, but colleagues assume they're good with money, or suggest fundraising roles. White, but the neighbour approvingly comments that their young child so far has a small nose. White, but outside of big cities, still asked: 'No, but where are you really from?' Assumed to be white, but, while viewing a flat a few years ago, they're told by one of the building's residents that the place was previously occupied by 'terrible neighbours, Jewish people, you know what they are like.' This property-hunter (who bought elsewhere) now tells me: 'How can I not feel a racialised minority? That doesn't mean to say I think I'm Black, or face the everyday racism and structural discrimination that a Black person faces. I don't for a minute think that. But I'm not white in the sense of the majority British population, of course not.' (Throughout this book I have anonymised those who have spoken with me about personal experiences, so that they might do so freely.)

Chances are that when people think 'Jewish', the person they have in mind is of European-Jewish origin: German, say, or Polish, Hungarian, or Russian. European Jews are the majority globally, but we are too quick to overlook millions of Jews with Middle Eastern and North African heritage, Black Jews, and Jews of other ethnic backgrounds. One British Black Jewish woman tells me that her identity carries with it experiences of what she describes as a 'constant and soul-destroying erasure' and asks: 'In this day and age, why are we still doing this?' Meanwhile, even amid European-Jewish communities, more likely to have been folded into white majorities across the West, there is a lingering ambivalence over whiteness, the sense of this being a category error. White Jews aren't not white. But we aren't really *white* white either. We are off-white.

American-Jewish progressives I speak with are more likely to unreservedly self-describe as 'white', in a country where racism was historically imposed and remains embedded in a strict binary of black or white, with Jewish people long ago placed on the white side of it. The whitening happened more recently and took a different path across Europe, where Jews have for centuries been the racial 'other', the outsiders and the foil for white Europeans. But everyone ended up in more or less the same place in the postwar period. Western societies welcomed Jewish people into whiteness, ushered us in to help maintain it as a social construct. After all, what is the dubious 'Judeo-Christian' tradition of shared values, the one invoked by Western politicians from the 1950s to the present day, if not a way of signposting Jewish people's absorption into the dominant Western culture, following the history of violent European antisemitism culminating in the Holocaust? These references to a supposed shared heritage effectively align Jews with whiteness while other minorities, with their implicitly inferior values, are excluded. So now, according to the construction of racial theory in the contemporary world, we pass as white, those of us with light skin and 'good' passports and all the benefits that come with both.

The common parlance is of Jewish people having been 'absorbed into whiteness'. Yet we frequently glide over the 'absorbed' part, a process of being separate at first and subsequently soaked up into the defining majority. And that's a problem. Because it might sound like equivocation, but there is a difference and it matters. Jewish whiteness feels contingent and attenuated. It is hard to trust.

This may be why many of us are messy about our whiteness. We know other minorities don't ever have the option to pass, to hide in plain sight and duck out of prejudice, and the not-quite caveats are hardly a major gripe. In fact the fussing might seem obtuse in the face of the all-day, every-day freedoms of whiteness. But still it squashes parts of our identity. Presenting Jewish people as *basically* white closes off opportunities to talk about those experiences of being racialised and othered – and the sharp realisation that, for many, whiteness is not so unconditional.

'People are really still antisemitic?'

In November 2016, Carin Mrotz was a month shy of becoming the director of Jewish Community Action, a racial and economic justice organisation in Minnesota. One day that month, she was scrubbing a giant red swastika that had been spray-painted onto a garage door in the state's largest city, Minneapolis, with a friend and Black organiser, Wintana Melekin, who had offered to help. A few years later, Mrotz wrote about the incident for online magazine *The Forge*. She explained that the pictures documenting their clean-up and posted on X (then Twitter) swiftly gained attention from the far right, who besieged both women online with racial insults and violent threats. Mrotz recalled that her friend Melekin was stunned by the nature of some of this abuse: 'People are really still antisemitic?' she asked. 'I thought you all were just regular white people now.' Mrotz replied: 'I think a lot of us did, too.'

That's the trouble with antisemitism. It thrives when others don't see how it still could. It can even take its targets by surprise. Writing on racial identity, the American sociology professor Robyn Autry observes: 'The fact the Jewish people themselves may disagree over whether they are a racial or ethnic group does not undo their long history of being categorized and marginalized as such.' Her words point to something we easily overlook: that Jews have been othered for longer than we have been welcomed into whiteness. That's hard to shake off. And it's especially hard when white nationalism, infused with an ideology of antisemitism, is politically resurgent across the West.

That hateful Nazi symbol that Mrotz and Melekin were scrubbing out in Minnesota was just one of a series of antisemitic incidents across America following the election of Donald Trump in November 2016. Amid bomb threats, desecrated Jewish cemeteries and vandalised synagogues, the run-up to and immediate aftermath of that US election saw a spike in incidents of harassment of Jewish people in America, including schoolchildren. In May 2016, graffiti posted in Denver, Colorado read: 'Kill the Jews, vote Trump.' In November, an attacker in Florida told his victim: 'Trump is going to finish what Hitler started.'

And across Europe, far-right parties with antisemitism at their core have been gaining political power. Formed in 2013, the radical right Alternative for Germany party (AfD), which has an antisemitic and anti-migrant worldview, was, by early 2024, polling at second place for the German federal elections slated to take place before October 2025. Marine Le Pen, the French presidential candidate of the National Rally, a rebrand of the National Front party rooted in fascism and with neo-Nazis and antisemites among its ranks, made it to the second round of France's presidential elections in 2022. She received over forty per cent of the vote in a run-off with Emmanuel Macron. Polls suggest that had the elections been held in 2023, she would have won outright. The Freedom Party of Austria, which has historic connections to former Nazis and current appeal to antisemites, is also rising in the polls, hitting figures of around thirty per cent by late 2023.

Our understanding of contemporary racism is that it is centuries-old, systemic and structural, baked into societies and targeting people of colour in order to subjugate, segregate, colonise, enslave and kill them. Antisemitism, with its history of deadly persecution, doesn't quite fit a contemporary understanding, not least because, by and large, Jewish people today don't face that kind of structural racism: we don't have entire systems, institutions, security forces and other state bodies discriminating against us. (Yes, there are caveats; we'll get to them.) Bringing antisemitism into the frame doesn't – or really shouldn't – mean diluting or distracting from the realities of ongoing racism against Black, Muslim, Asian or other communities. But it does involve integrating an additional account, another historical layer that usually gets parcelled into separate fields of study. The not-white experiences of Jews are vital to our understanding of the ongoing structures of racism. And that means revisiting the origins of different racisms, to map them in connection with each other. Pulling antisemitism into the frame of antiracism is about much more than deepening our understanding of this ancient hatred. By looking at the history of Jewish not-whiteness we could open up a more meaningful understanding of whiteness itself – how it is constructed, how it marginalises people, and how fragile it is as a category. All of which gives progressives and antiracists more tools to fight with – and God knows, we're going to need as many as we can get.

England: the first and the worst

In Britain, the nation's history of antisemitism is, much like its broader history of colonialism and oppression, poorly understood and barely acknowledged. When it comes to narrating its own past, Britain prefers to present itself as a sort of white saviour state, swooping in to save the day. So a civilising rescue mission is rolled out as the moral pretext for Empire and colonialism. The country's vast and terrible involvement in slavery is camouflaged by a myopic focus on its role in abolition. As the Trinidadian historian Eric Williams once remarked: 'The British historians wrote almost as if Britain had introduced Negro slavery solely for the satisfaction of abolishing it.' In similar fashion, British antisemitism gets a weirdly sanitised treatment with a prevailing narrative casting the country as the 'good guy', what with the Brits defeating Hitler and saving 10,000 Jewish children through the Kindertransport. This story itself has a few glaring omissions. The adults – and all the other children – left to perish in Occupied Europe after Britain largely shut down official migration routes go unmentioned. So do the 30,000 Jews interned on the Isle of Man and elsewhere around the UK, on suspicion of being 'enemy aliens'.

In reality, as historian Geraldine Heng explains in her book, *England and the Jews*, when it comes to antisemitism: 'England was the first, and England was the worst.' This particular iteration of historic villainy came during the Middle Ages, by which point Christianity all across Europe was falsely charging Jewish people with Christ's death. From its early days, Christianity had essentially needed to vilify Judaism, as wrong-headed at best and actually evil at worst, in order to ensure its own spread and eventual dominance. And since the Church held social and political power for centuries, the othering and demonising of Jewish people was structural in its impact. Medieval laws limited the freedoms of Jewish people, from the work they could do to the clothes they could wear. But then England upped the stakes and invented the blood libel, a dangerous con-spiracy theory that accused Jews of ritualistically torturing and murdering children in religious ceremonies. It began in Norwich in 1144 when a twelve-year-old boy, William, was found dead, his body mutilated. Nobody could figure out what happened but Thomas of Monmouth, a Benedictine monk, claimed that he was last seen going into the house of a local Jew. With zero evidence, it was decided that the boy had been tortured and killed by the Jewish commu-nity, his blood used in the performance of religious rituals. Subsequent iterations of the blood libel introduced the idea that blood was extracted from victims in order to bake matzahs (unleavened flatbread) for Passover. It's at this point in the story that Jewish narrators will explain that, aside from anything else, this could not possibly be true because blood isn't even kosher for crying out loud.

But reason be damned, the blood libel spread fast and hard. By 1255, when a young boy, Hugh, was killed in Lincoln, the king himself got involved. Henry III arrived in the cathedral city calling for ninety random Jews to be taken to the Tower of London. Nineteen were executed. This turbo-boosted the blood libel conspiracy, spreading now with the royal seal, travelling from mouth to mouth and passing through literature from Geoffrey Chaucer's *Canterbury Tales* to Christopher Marlowe's *The Jew of Malta* and variously authored ballads about 'Little Saint Hugh', despite him never being officially canonised.

Heng writes that in the European Middle Ages, Jews were 'the benchmark by which a variety of racial others were identified, measured, scaled and assessed as modalities of racial form worked, with a near-monomaniacal attention, to congeal Jews as figures of absolute difference.' Other professors of Jewish history share this view. The historian Christopher Browning, who specialises in Holocaust studies, has written: 'The broad and pervasive anti-Jewish stereotype of the Middle Ages had all the functional features of racism, but without a theory of race.' Before anyone was even talking about race, Jewish people were treated as a different species with negative physical features and character traits. And back in medieval England, long before 'antisemitism' was coined, the key twist in this form of racial hatred took hold.

Jews probably arrived in England after the 1066 Norman Conquest at the invitation of William the Conqueror, settling there as 'property of the king'. They weren't allowed to own land, but they *were* permitted to lend money with interest, at a time when Christians were forbidden from doing so by the Church, which viewed usury as immoral. Jews could collect debts, and the Crown could take its share in taxes. Scaled up, this is how Jews so often ended up as moneylenders: they weren't allowed to do anything else and it became a convenient arrangement for those in power. But since the Church had decreed that moneylending was evil, the arrangement also automatically attached negative traits onto Jewish people. Rulers took a fat cut of the profits, while Jewish people would take the flak for any economic-anxiety-fuelled rage that might otherwise be directed at the Crown. One of Britain's most deadly instances of antisemitism was the massacre at Clifford's Tower in York in 1190. The city's entire population of Jews, some 150 people, were killed by angry mobs egged on by noblemen seeking to wipe out debts owed to Jewish moneylenders. This is an essential facet of antisemitism: it sets up a scapegoat. Unlike other kinds of racism, the one directed at Jews is not just about subjugation. Instead, it positions a minority with just enough status that, in times of crisis, they can be the buffer, the punchbag. It's this peculiarity that makes antisemitism prone to falling off the antiracism radar. This racism is *not* about socio-economic disadvantage – even though that can be a feature of it. And so, while frequently impoverished like other minority groups, some Jews were privileged by those in power, allowed enough money and status precisely so that the Jewish community in its entirety could be vilified and exploited when necessary.

In England in the Middle Ages, Jews were not treated as regular folk. They were forced to wear badges and keep to themselves; forbidden from marrying or even eating with Christians, banned from praying too loudly in synagogues. Special registries tracked Jewish assets while the king extorted this community in a medieval equivalent of having the tax office impose constant sky-high rates on one minority. Comprising only 0.25 per cent of the population, Jews provided ten per cent of the Crown's revenue.

Yet despite being such an important income source, when push came to shove, England's kings were not on Jewish people's side. This Jewish community was expelled in 1290, another trendsetting moment as 'the first permanent forcible expulsion in Europe', as Heng puts it. There was a clear cash incentive here too, since all Jewish assets went to the Crown. At the time England was strapped for cash – Edward I had been a terrible spendthrift over wars waged abroad. Fast forward to 1656 and we see that inviting Jewish people back to Britain was also financially motivated. Ruling at that time as Lord Protector of England – the head of state – Oliver Cromwell saw that the Jewish community in Amsterdam, mostly descended from those fleeing Christian-dominated Spain and Portugal, had helped to turn the port city into a thriving hub. Why not bring them back to Britain and have them do the same thing?

Other parts of Europe followed England's lead in expelling their Jewish populations whenever they needed a quick cash boost or a political outlet for a dissatisfied population. After the Christian Reconquista in Iberia in the late fifteenth century, which recovered parts of the peninsula that had been under Muslim rule and known as Al-Andalus, Spain adopted a militant approach to its Jewish population. The country had allowed its Jews to stay, on a 'convert or die' basis, but this had the unforeseen consequence of giving now-Christian Jews, so-called *conversos*, access to respectable official jobs. That couldn't happen. Long before people thought in terms of 'races', the subtext was there: Jewish people could become Christian, but this didn't make them 'white'. Spain came up with a kind of early prototype of the one-drop rule, the American legal definition used to maintain white power by racially discriminating against anyone with even one Black ancestor. The Spanish version was invented in Toledo by a local governor in 1449, termed *limpieza de sangre*, 'cleanliness of blood', and spread from there. They were pretty obsessive about it, as a way of rumbling those supposedly morally inadequate, God-killing Jews. Later extended to apply to Muslim converts, this blood purity rule is cited as the first example of legalised racism. For Spanish rulers, it gave them a tidy pretext for later kicking out both Muslim and Jewish communities in 1492.

Racism doesn't translate word for word, pigment for pigment. It targets different minority groups in different ways, but it echoes as it travels, morphing and adapting to the requirements of those in power. That Spanish need to sift and silo people in order to maintain supremacy journeyed across the Atlantic at around the same time, influencing the creation of a 'Black race', conjured up specifically to justify the African slave trade. Ella Shohat, a professor of cultural studies at New York University, has written about the 'two 1492s', this date marking both the beginning of the Spanish expulsion of Jews and Muslims from Iberia and Christopher Columbus's first transatlantic voyage of discovery, under the patronage of Spanish monarchs, the beginning of the conquest of the 'New World'. Shohat explains how the purity rules invoked to expel unwanted 'others' when successive Spanish monarchs reconquered Al-Andalus then prepared the ground for colonial racism and slavery elsewhere. 'The campaigns against Muslims and Jews, as well as against heretics and witches', she writes, 'made available an entire apparatus of racism and sexism for "recycling" in the newly raided continents.' This is why, in Shohat's analysis, those racisms are joined together, twinned in history, forming, as she puts it elsewhere, 'a transoceanic drifting of tropes'. In her words: 'Antisemitism formed an especially integral part of the European ideological system then projected outwards against Europe's external others – the indigenous peoples of Africa and the Americas.'

Portugal started the trade in slaves during the mid-1400s, with Spain following shortly after its colonisation of the Americas in 1493. Britain and its American colony joined in the enslavement of Black people during the 1600s. In *How to Be an Antiracist*, Ibram X. Kendi describes the invention of 'Black' to denote a group of people who could be brutally enslaved. It all began with the Portuguese prince Henry the Navigator, who launched the transatlantic slave trade by sending ships to West Africa. These ships returned with enslaved people whom he put up for sale in the first slave auction back in Lagos in 1444. Less than a decade later, the prince's biographer Gomes de Zurara was tasked with retrofitting slavery as a noble cause. So he grouped enslaved African people into a single 'race' and depicted them in negative terms: they were 'like beasts' and 'knew only how to live in bestial sloth'. As Kendi writes: 'From the beginning, to make races was to make racial hierarchy.' This hierarchy-making enabled 400 years of the transatlantic slave trade, during which over fifteen million African people were enslaved. Untold millions died during the forced march to the African slave ports and some two million more on ships during the 'Middle Passage', the journey across the Atlantic in the most inhumane conditions, chained and packed together and then tossed overboard when this grotesque torture killed them. It is a deep, long legacy of death, violence and misery that continues to underpin structural racism today.

Britain and America grew wealthy from the forced labour of enslaved people on plantations that yielded high-value crops: tobacco, sugar, cotton. Such incredible financial gain was only ever possible through slavery. But here, again, is that vital distinction between anti-Black racism and antisemitism, both unleashed by the powerful, each with a different purpose. Jews were racialised by European

Christians to be scapegoated, which led to endless persecutions, pogroms and, ultimately, mass genocide. Black people were racialised into a category specifically invented to subjugate them, so that their enslavement could enrich those who thought of themselves as 'white': European Christians. As populations mixed during the period of slavery, white Americans worried that 'impurity' (there it is again) would weaken or threaten white power, so they came up with the one-drop rule, first used in the state of Virginia during the 1660s. 'Black blood', even just one drop of it, would contaminate – no matter how far back in your ancestry, it would consign you to the subordinate group.

While US slavery officially ended in 1865, racism persisted with Jim Crow segregation laws rolled out from the late 1870s so that newly free African-Americans could still be controlled and subjugated. These laws enforced racial segregation everywhere: in schools, universities, restaurants, clubs, all public buildings and spaces, even when it came to riding on buses, walking through parks or using public water fountains. Jim Crow suppressed the Black vote at state and national elections and inevitably impacted the workplace, with companies refusing to hire Black people and unions passing laws to exclude them. It was legalised white supremacy. Meanwhile in Europe, racism enabled colonialism and the looting of other people's lands and resources. Jump to the twentieth century and you can see how modern racists drew inspiration from old-fashioned racists, again and again. When the Nazis were looking for a way to isolate, persecute and then annihilate Jewish people, they turned to US definitions of race, because America had managed to be both democratic and racist. Nazi Germany wanted to know how to do just that. Nazism didn't end up adopting a one-drop rule for antisemitism, but still located 'purity' in blood: having a Jewish grandparent was enough to condemn you to the death camps.

The parallels across different types of racism tell us something so obvious that it kind of fades into the background. Racism and antisemitism, invented and propagated in different forms across the centuries, are tools used by those in power to maintain their power. That's why there are so many similarities in this business of race-making across different minority groups. And it is also why Jewish people don't necessarily see themselves as neatly fitting into the white people camp: historically, we weren't sitting on those race-creating committees or calling the shots.

The bullshit science bit

By the time we get to the era of modern racism, the commonalities become more blatant. A sort of racist heyday came about through the entirely bogus but widely influential field of scientific racism which kicked off during the Enlightenment in the late seventeenth century and which set its sights on both Black and Jewish people, among others. Jewish minorities across Europe were emancipated during the Enlightenment period which spanned hundreds of years. By the early 1900s, Jewish people across most of Europe had been granted equal rights of citizenship. Up to this point, Jews mostly lived in ghettoes or urban slums, and had to abide by senseless legal restrictions. While emancipation in some parts of Europe eventually dissolved those ghettoes, it did not stop the persecution. Because as we know, you can have the same legal rights as everyone else and still be targeted. In fact, this was the focus of scientific racism: it was concerned with finding ways to discriminate despite the unfolding principles of reason, liberty and egality.

It's worth just gently noting here that none of this was happening to Jewish people living across Arab and Muslim lands at around the same time. While European Jews were fleeing from pogrom to pogrom, Middle Eastern Jews for the most part lived peacefully and stayed put. Jews in Iraq could date their community to over five hundred years before Christ and accounted for one-third of Baghdad's population by the First World War. Jewish people living under Islamic rule were generally respected alongside Christians as '*Ahl al-Kitab*': monotheistic People of the Book. They had a distinct status on religious grounds, but they were mostly not persecuted because of it. Jewish communities in the Middle East were an integral part of the Arab world, woven into the fabric of its communities and societies.

But back in Europe, scientific racism, invented by white European men, was about creating biologically distinct races with – surprise! – white European-heritage men coming out on top (white women came in second). They invented an entirely bullshit field of science as a way of 'proving' their own superiority. Not only intellectually superior, white people were, according to this sorting system, also morally superior, more civilised, harder-working, better-looking, just better in every conceivable way. So, for instance, we have the Swedish biologist Carl Linnaeus, who was the first to classify humans into distinct and fixed sub-species in the mid-1750s. For him, there were Europeans (white), Africans (black), American Indians (reddish) and Asians (tawny). Each variety of human had different physical attributes and temperaments such as 'wise' or 'sluggish', 'sanguine' or 'lazy'. Just take a wild guess at which of his human 'species' Linnaeus put at the top of the chart. Then there was the 'science' of measuring skulls, craniology, pioneered by Samuel George Morton, which made the claim that white people had the largest skulls, ergo they were the most intelligent of all. Black and Jewish people were filed in different categories, but since these were bogus categories invented by bullshit science there was slippage between the two. And this blurring itself drew from medieval times when black skin colour was seen as evil and demonic and was often associated with the other 'other' deemed to be devilish: the Jew.

In his book, *Hybrid Hate: Conflations of Antisemitism and Anti-Black Racism from the Renaissance to the Third Reich*, the historian Tudor Parfitt explains that for centuries, Jewish people were associated with the colour black, seen as of dark colour and having Black African traits. But he also writes that at the same time, Jewish people were seen as completely indistinguishable from white people. That, of course, is what led to those medieval English 'Jew' badges and the yellow star of the Third Reich. While there was a long tradition of seeing Jews as Black, it was, as Parfitt writes: 'in the context of the overarching caveat that the general concept of Jewish colour was chronically unstable'. In other words, for as long as Europeans have tried to 'other' Jewish people, they have been unable fully to categorise them. And this in itself stirred suspicions over the reliability of Jewish people since they were confounding classifications, sometimes passing as white, thus potentially up to no good as the enemy within.

This medieval entwining of Black and Jewish people – both considered to be aggressive, hostile and brutish with ugly, freakish features – was given a reboot in the era of bullshit racial science. As Parfitt explains: 'The linkages between Jews and Blacks, embedded as they were in the cultural landscape of medieval Europe, became more pronounced during the period of the Enlightenment as both were scrutinised anew. The precise interrelationship of Jews – whether they were perceived as dark or pale – and Blacks, would preoccupy some of the finest minds among European and American thinkers for the following two centuries.' For those fine minds, this was a time for charts and tables. The labelling and classifying started with the natural world and then moved through to people, ranked in preferential order.

As professor of Sephardic studies at the University of Washington, Devin E. Naar, explained in *Jewish Currents* magazine in Spring 2019, also among those doing the sifting and sorting was the German philosopher Immanuel Kant who, across several works written in the 1770s, put white men at the top of the charts, effectively marking them a ten out of ten, no notes, what with their Christianity and rationality and all-round Western superiority. Black people, 'the Negroes of Africa', came bottom of the list, billed as 'lazy, indolent and dawdling'. Then he placed Jewish people in between these two invented poles while describing them as a bigger problem that, while living in Europe, could cause trouble from within. It's a double whammy of the oldest conspiracy – shadowy internal troublemakers – wrapped up in the newest bullshit science.

Then there was the British philosopher Houston Stewart Chamberlain, who in 1899 wrote *The Foundations of the Nineteenth Century* and who inspired various European politicians including one Adolf Hitler. Chamberlain placed the 'Aryan race' at the top of the human league tables and saw Jewish people as racially impure, a 'half-caste'.

Filing Jews as Black people had little to do with skin tone, since Jewish people appeared in shades across the colour chart spectrum, which confused the hell out of the scientific racists, just as it had the medieval racists before them. Unable to call upon the colour chart of racial classification, those esteemed men of science put the blackness of Jews down to, well, vibes. Writing in the early nineteenth century, the British anthropologist Robert Knox held that Jews were of negro origin. He thought Jews had black blood. He, like other 'rational thinkers' of this time, had taken a look at the ancient Egyptian and Middle Eastern artefacts discovered in archaeological digs of that period, and deemed that the statues showed negro and Jewish faces. To Knox, according to Parfitt, it proved that Jews were 'different and apart and were associated with the dark races of man'. Like I said: vibes. This was echoed by the German antisemite Wilhelm Marr, credited with inventing the term 'antisemitism' and a vicious anti-Black racist (he visited America and came back supporting slavery). As Parfitt describes it, Marr 'argued that the despised blood of the negro flowed freely in the veins of Jews'. Other observations made during this period were to compare Black and Jewish people to apes and goats, respectively, to describe both peoples as physically and spiritually ugly but sexualised, each with a distinctive bad smell, thick lips and 'woolly matted hair' according to a Bavarian writer who came upon Polish Jews in Vienna in the 1780s. Jews and Blacks were hated for different reasons, but the terminology with which they were denigrated is strikingly similar.

Scientific racism went to work in different ways across different countries. In the US, it translated into Jim Crow. It also at various points demonised Jews and others deemed not-quite-white, including Irish and Italian migrant communities. Right into the twentieth century, racism ensured that US-bound Jewish migrants – considered morally, physically and intellectually inferior – could be met with hostility, amid fears that they would somehow weaken American society.

Scientific racism was the self-fulfilling, self-justifying pretext for European colonialism across Africa and the Middle East. But in Europe itself, it compounded long-standing hatred of Jewish people. It became an actual ideology with a name and it was antisemitism's most vicious phase. Black Europeans at this time were horribly discriminated against. But larger in number, reviled as Christ-killers and vampiric blood-drinkers for centuries, Jewish minorities across Europe were the shadowy internal other, the outcast, the scapegoat – the not-white. They were dehumanised and derided as filthy, 'Asiatic', 'Oriental', scheming, rootless, parasitic, disloyal and greedy. At the same time, they were held responsible both for the ills of industrial, metropolitan capitalism and for the looming evil of socialism because, of course, Jewish people were behind every dastardly plot to tear apart the very fabric of society. Here we find one of the paradoxes of antisemitism: it is a contradictory, catch-all prejudice. Jews can be Asiatic and ugly-featured and yet at the same time white-passing and hiding in plain sight. They can be wealthy puppet-masters but also impoverished degenerates. This bigotry is so scattergun, so all over the place, that it makes it hard to grasp. And this multi-pronged prejudice has been going on for centuries, with all that so-called science building on those older anti-Jewish conspiracies.

These newly rational white Europeans hadn't forgotten that Jews were supposedly responsible for deicide too. As George L. Mosse notes in *Toward the Final Solution*: 'Anti-Jewish riots in Europe remained largely traditional up to 1918, whether in Russia or in the West.' But now on top of those habitual riots, countries across Europe saw distinct antisemitic flashpoints, each substantial on its own and together feeding an overall sense of precariousness for Jews across the continent.

In Britain, antisemitism blew up during a debate on Jewish emancipation that was sparked by the 1753 Jewish naturalisation law, pithily dubbed the 'Jew Bill'. This law allowed Jewish people who had lived in the country for three years to apply to become British subjects, although it was repealed a year later due to public outcry. The usual conspiracies popped up with accusations of, among other things, ritual murder and plotting to take over St Paul's Cathedral and turn it into a synagogue.

A century later, there were accusations that Jewish global finance – what else? – was behind British involvement in the Second Boer War of 1899–1902. And antisemitism was all over the anti-alien movement which ran from the 1890s right up to the 1905 passing of the Aliens Act, which ruled that 'undesirable immigrants' would be denied entry to Britain. The migrants that so worried the anti-alien movement were Jewish arrivals fleeing Eastern Europe, around whom swirled all the racial imagery that we see in the modern-day scapegoating of migrants and refugees. A Conservative MP, Sir William Marriott, visited the East End of London, home to many of those new Jewish arrivals, and said: 'There are some streets you may go through and hardly know you are in England'. The editor of the *Clarion*, a socialist weekly newspaper, said of an afternoon spent in this London neighbourhood that it felt like 'we were in a foreign country'. A local midwife described their Jewish neighbours as 'unpleasant, indecent people' who had turned the area into a 'seething mass of refuse and filth'. It's not a million miles away from the Conservative MP Paul Scully describing the East End's Tower Hamlets as having 'no-go' areas now that it's mainly populated by South Asian Muslims (he later apologised).

Right-wing campaigns against 'aliens' – everyone knew this was code for 'Jews'– drew connections with disease and crime. Meanwhile the left fretted over migrant workers depressing standards and wages for the working class. Yes, all the fearmongering themes that currently populate Britain's immigration debate were previously road-tested on Jewish people. Racism is largely an unoriginal business.

One of the better-known antisemitism scandals arose in France, where a Jewish artillery captain, Alfred Dreyfus, was wrongly convicted of spying in 1894, amid a storm of antisemitism that saw him paraded in front of a crowd yelling 'Death to Judas, death to the Jew.' The Dreyfus affair reverberated for decades; it divided France and shocked Jews around the world, not least because French Jews were by then considered pretty integrated. Another crisis point occurred in 1903 when a Russian publication, *The Protocols of the Elders of Zion*, spread far and wide. It was an antisemitic conspiracy accusing Jews of secret plans for global domination. Editions were printed across Europe and in 1920 the US car magnate Henry Ford serialised the *Protocols* in his antisemitic newspaper *The Dearborn Independent*. This paper was incredibly popular, spewing out antisemitism across eight years and at one point selling almost half a million copies weekly. Both Hitler and his head of propaganda Joseph Goebbels were big fans – of Ford and of the

Protocols. And Ford is apparently a big name in the world of online white supremacists today.

The sort of racism that nowadays targets refugees from Africa and the Middle East was aimed at Jews for centuries prior to the Holocaust. It was even in evidence on the eve of the Second World War against Fascist Germany. In July 1938 in the French resort town of Evian, delegates from thirty-two countries met to talk about helping Jewish refugees who were trying to flee the Third Reich. Everyone expressed sympathy, but Britain and America, alongside every other country aside from the Dominican Republic, rolled out the reasons it was impossible for them to take in more refugees.

All of this might help to explain why British Jews can have a hard time with the idea that they're white, without caveats. Even before we get to the horrors of the Holocaust, antisemitism was tightly woven into the fabric of societies spanning across the continent. It was unleashed by religious and ruling powers, from the Catholic Church to the Russian Empire, from British parliamentarians to Viennese aristocrats. It was everywhere. The Holocaust wasn't a blip, but a grotesque culmination in a landscape saturated with antisemitism. It was what happened when those ideas of racial purity, amplified by religious scapegoating and scientific racism, got state power and a state machinery dedicated to putting them into practice.

After the sickening scale of the Holocaust became clear, scientific racism was swiftly sidelined. Nazi Germany had shown the world where that kind of thinking could lead.

This too-late realisation accelerated the absorption of Jewish people into whiteness in both Britain and America. But in the postwar years there was also growing awareness of the parallels between different racisms. This was not an attempt to give the Holocaust a sort of #AllLivesMatter spin, or to erase the specificity of the antisemitism that led to the state-sponsored, industrialised murder of six million Jewish people. It was instead a recognition of the fears and fates shared by different peoples first deemed not-white and then dehumanised and persecuted for it. As Mosse wrote: 'Who knows but that 6 million Jews might not have been joined by as many blacks had these lived in the midst of the peoples of Europe.'

After visiting the Warsaw ghetto in 1949, the African-American intellectual W.E.B. Du Bois wrote of no longer seeing the problems of slavery, segregation and Jim Crow in the US as separate, or unique. Racism was not, he wrote, 'solely a matter of colour and physical and racial character-istics, which was a particularly hard thing for me to learn, since for a lifetime the colour line had been a real and efficient cause of misery'. For Du Bois, the Warsaw ghetto 'helped me to emerge from a certain social provincialism into a broader conception of what the fight against race segregation, religious discrimination and the oppression by wealth had to become if civilization was going to triumph and broaden in the world.'

What the trajectory of racism through history keeps showing us is that racism itself creates race – and not the other way around. As the American author and journalist

Ta-Nehisi Coates put it in his book, *Between the World and Me*: 'Race is the child of racism, not the father.' By 2000, science confirmed what was already plainly true, when the Human Genome Project found all human beings are 99.9 per cent the same at a DNA level. Scientific racism was scientifically proven to be bullshit. All race is fiction, including 'whiteness' – which explains why the category is so moveable and unstable. Whiteness isn't real; it's a giant power play. Now that doesn't mean we can skate past our understanding of it as the mechanism by which structural racism is maintained. We need that frame of comprehension, especially and as long as the violence and misery unleashed by racism surrounds us. Race isn't real, but racism definitely is. We need to hang on to this understanding of whiteness as part of the analytical framework of racism, but then build on and expand it, just as Du Bois did, to create a broader conception of what the fight for equality must become.

Category error

The history of Jewish people in the West, persecuted, killed and then, finally, absorbed into white majorities, is not only a story of antisemitism. It is itself a story about the fakery of whiteness. That we can't agree on whether or not Jews are white does not tell us that Jewish people are hard to categorise. It tells us, again and again, that racial categories are specious. Even in America, where the whitening of Jews has been so successful, this speciousness runs through the story. As James Baldwin wrote in 1984 in his essay 'On Being White and Other Lies', no American was 'white' before they came to America: 'It took generations, and a vast amount of coercion, before this became a white country.' He added: 'It is probable that it is the Jewish community – or, more accurately perhaps, its remnants – that in America has paid the highest and most extraordinary price for becoming white.'

Baldwin explains that the Jewish community came to the States from countries where they were not white; they came *because* they were persecuted as not-white – but that the price of whiteness was to opt into anti-Black racism. In other words, to halt the othering that spawned antisemitism, Jewish people had to other others. These conditions of integration come across in several accounts of American-Jewish history. In her book, *Bad Jews: A History of American Jewish Politics and Identities*, Emily Tamkin writes: 'Precisely because race is a construct, the boundary between "white" and "not white" is slippery and inconsistent. And so there was a perceived benefit, if not tangible then emotional, to these American Jews discriminating against other immigrants and against Black laborers and customers. So long as they could discriminate, they could prove, if only to themselves, which side of the boundary they were on. They could prove that they were not *not* white.' The historian and Jewish studies professor Eric L. Goldstein explains in *The Price of Whiteness* how becoming 'white' was not linear or unqualified. It was a constant battle against prejudice and conspiracies, a battle to preserve culture and religion and a battle also filled with revulsion at the racial rules of white America.

But the absorption was successful. Now integrated, American Jews are relatively safe, secure and thriving. In the postwar period, this community was afforded privileges to speed along their advancement and then held up as a 'model minority' in order to shame other racialised groups, mostly African-Americans (who, of course, were not given the same perks and pathways to success in the first place). One material example is the American postwar GI Bill, officially known as the Servicemen's Readjustment Act of 1944. This law provided returning soldiers with education grants, government loans, housing and other financial benefits – all available to Jewish but not African-American veterans, who continued to face segregation and violence despite their service. The process of Jewish integration is so completely an all-white-American success story that it's hardly any wonder that American Jews locate themselves on the white side of history.

The trouble is that America, with its large and established Jewish community, tends to set the tone for Jewishness and the Jewish experience beyond US borders. It does this so comprehensively, in fact, that many first-time visitors to Israel, the only country with a larger Jewish population than America, are surprised to find that it does not culturally resemble a Jewish-resident-heavy suburb of New York. Israel's Jewish population is predominantly from the Middle East so, no, it does not look like Brooklyn. America's sheer expansiveness and cultural dominance gives it a global foghorn – and that extends to its appraisal of racism, antisemitism and how we understand the experiences of racialised minorities.

'It's not about race'

In late January 2022, actor and TV personality Whoopi Goldberg was discussing a much-loved, award-winning graphic novel about the Holocaust – Art Spiegelman's *Maus*. As co-host of *The View*, a US talk show, Goldberg was talking about the news that a Tennessee education board had banned the book, on the grounds that it features nudity. Debating the rights and wrongs of the ban, she stated that the book's theme, the Nazi genocide of Jews, 'wasn't about race. No, it's not about race.' She expanded that it involved 'two white groups of people'.

It came up again when Goldberg subsequently appeared on *The Late Show*, a popular American talk show, explaining how the Holocaust could not have been about race. By this point, commentators were bleakly pointing to the epitaph from *Maus*, the book that had prompted this discussion, which carried a quote from Adolf Hitler: 'The Jews are undoubtedly a race, but they are not human.'

Goldberg apologised, repeatedly, but her thought process – how can this be about race, when Jews are white? – isn't really so unusual. Nor, as Robyn Autry wrote in her appraisal of the incident, is it surprising that 'an American, perhaps especially a Black one like Goldberg or myself, would think that race is about skin color given how it plays out in our lives'. Autry explains that as a graduate student of racial violence and collective memory, she had gained a wider understanding of how 'racial difference varied wildly across societies and how those ideas could morph within the same society over time'.

Speaking on *The Late Show*, Goldberg tried to talk us through her thought process: 'I feel, being Black, when we talk about race, it's a very different thing to me', she told the host Stephen Colbert, acknowledging that other people didn't see it the same way and were upset by her comments. 'I thought it was a salient discussion because, as a Black person, I think of race as being something that I can see', she said. If a member of the violently white supremacist Ku Klux Klan 'is coming down the street and I'm standing with a Jewish friend … well, I'm going to run. But if my friend decides not to run, they will get passed by most times because you can't tell who is Jewish, you don't know …'

Goldberg was derided and denounced in the sensationalised outrage economy of the social-media-fuelled news cycle. She did get it wrong. The Holocaust *was* about race. Jews, especially religious ones, are frequently visible and targeted for it. Violent white supremacists are going to find a way to attack Jews, not least in synagogues – as we have seen in recent years. Antisemitism absolutely racialised Jewish people in physical terms: hooked noses, curly dark hair, beady dark eyes, dirtiness and smelliness – stereotypes that circulate to this day.

But rather than teasing out the specificities of different racisms, the media spectacle mostly involved yelling at an

African-American celebrity, while using her comments to attack 'wokeness' and critical race theory and to denounce antiracists in general, using their presumed lack of awareness as fuel for attack. In short, no one was interested in having an honest discussion over a complex issue. The scale of the outrage reached a point where Goldberg simply shut down. I'm pretty sure that, in the face of such an onslaught, I would, too. 'Don't write me anymore', she said on *The Late Show*. 'I know how you feel, okay, I already know, I get it. I'm going to take your word for it and never bring it up again.' We need time and space and generosity to talk about different types of racism. Instead, Goldberg was silenced in a media furore with ugly racist undertones and this necessary conversation could not take place.

An eerie parallel of this scenario emerged in the UK in April 2023. The Labour party's Diane Abbott, Britain's first black woman MP and herself the target of endless racist abuse, wrote a letter to the *Observer* newspaper casting doubt on the idea that Irish, Jewish and Traveller people all suffer from racism. 'It is true that many types of white people with points of difference, such as redheads, can experience this prejudice', she wrote. 'But they are not all their lives subjected to racism.' There it was again: the idea that Jewish people were 'white' and the prejudice against them was not actually racism. Abbott apologised in full, claiming that a mistake had occurred with an earlier draft sent to the newspaper in error (an explanation that did not, in truth, shed much light on the matter). Still, I watched with incredulity as the media storm over the issue almost exactly mirrored the furore over Whoopi Goldberg's comments a year earlier: the outrage that a left-wing politician could be so offensively ignorant about anti-Jewish racism on the one hand; the anger that Abbott, who has faced an intolerable amount of racist abuse, seemingly wasn't allowed to talk about anti-Black racism on the other. Worse, despite speedily withdrawing her comments, Abbott was suspended as Labour MP.

In the subtext of some of the progressive left's reaction to such incidents is the worry that talking about how some 'white' people experience racism might take away from the deadly urgency of confronting systemic anti-Black racism. But as Alana Lentin, a professor in cultural and social analysis, points out when we talk: 'That assumes we are in a state of zero-sum racism with a finite, set amount of racism to go around. The fact of the matter is that, unfortunately, there is plenty of racism to go around.' She suggests a better approach, if we're going to build antiracist coalitions, is to 'look at the construction of blackness as so powerful and so flexible a force that it can leak out beyond the confines of a black-white binary'. It is so necessary for racism to exist as a system of division and oppression that it flexes to fit different groups, contexts and countries. That's what we see in the history of racism. That's what Du Bois alluded to in his essay on visiting the Warsaw ghetto.

Thinking about it in those terms allows us to look at the broader picture without competing for attention or taking away from the experiences of any minoritised group. A comprehensive snapshot – if anything an understatement, both because of the research methods and because experiences of racism are notoriously under-reported – was recently provided by Britain's largest audit of race inequality for over a quarter of a century. (It was a comment piece about this audit that Diane Abbott's letter was responding to.) The Evidence for Equality National Survey, published in April 2023, showed levels of abuse and discrimination were 'strikingly high' across minority ethnic groups in Britain. Groups coded 'white' were among those topping the lists: Gypsy, Roma and Traveller (GRT) communities and Jewish people were in the top three categories most likely to experience some form of racist assault. Both minorities also featured in the ranks of people likely to experience discrimination in institutional settings, such as in housing, employment or education, or from the police. Different minorities – such as Black Caribbean, Other Black, Bangladeshi and Black African – faced the worst outcomes across most of those settings, a reality confirmed by multiple reports on the effects of racism in the UK. But the Evidence for Equality authors noted in media interviews that the results gave unprec-edented insights into the experience of GRT and Jewish communities. The sheer volume of racial assault experi-enced by Gypsy and Traveller people exceeds that faced by any other minority group, while the GRT community suffers the highest level of socio-economic deprivation and widest gaps in health and education. Meanwhile, it is not true that British Jews are uniformly well-heeled, well-housed or well-employed.

Broadening out this racialising process taps into different parts of my identity. It's true that in the UK, I freely float along as white. But, just as my friend pronounced, there's a parallel narrative in which parts of my background don't fit the category. First, through my parents whose formative years in Iraq shaped them. While my parents lived there, Britain controlled Mandate Iraq by imposing puppet rulers in an at-a-distance colonial set-up. The 1917 Balfour Declaration, in which the British pledged to establish a 'national home for the Jewish people', set the creation of Israel in motion. Israel's founding in 1948 unleashed a catastrophe, or *Nakba*, upon the Palestinian people, upwards of 700,000 of whom (eighty per cent of the population at that time) fled or were expelled. At the same time, it forced a nationalist wedge between the hyphenated identities of Arab-Jews like my family in Iraq, rupturing a 2,600-year-long presence in that country and making a mass exodus to Israel all but inevitable in 1951.

Arriving in the new state of Israel, Arab-Jews were called '*Mizrahi*' (Easterners or Orientals) and deemed inferior by the European-Jewish or '*Ashkenazi*' elite that established the nation. Those Zionist leaders of the new state had internalised the racial superiority complexes of late nineteenth-century Europe and cast Mizrahi Jews as backward, uncivilised, uneducated ... all the classic racial epithets of colonialism. Such prejudices poured into the foundations of the Israeli state, into the unequal, discriminatory and culture-stripping treatment of Mizrahi Jews, so that the original appraisal of inferiority became a socio-economic reality.

Mizrahi Jews were pejoratively called '*Schwarz*' (German and Yiddish for 'Black') by their Ashkenazi compatriots, while the ruling elite was openly scornful. As the historian Tom Segev chronicles in his book *1949: the First Israelis*, Israel's first prime minister David Ben-Gurion said: 'The ancient spirit left the Jews of the East and their role in the Jewish nation receded or disappeared entirely. In the past few hundred years the Jews of Europe have led the nation, in both quantity and quality.' By the early 1960s, Ben-Gurion was considering the idea of segregating Mizrahi and Ashkenazi children in schools. 'The danger we face is that the great majority of those children whose parents did not receive an education for generations, will descend to the level of Arab children', he said of the Mizrahi population. 'In another 10–15 years they will be the nation, and we will become a Levantine nation.' My mother to this day remembers the humiliation of being sprayed with DDT pesticide on the plane from Iraq to the nascent Israel.

Mizrahi Jews often internalised all that disdain, hiding their Arabic language, music and culture; lightening and straightening hair and changing names. The Israeli Black Panthers, a Mizrahi mass protest movement during the 1970s, took their name in a conscious tribute to the African-American revolutionary party, but also as a reclamation of the 'Black' pejoratively used against them. Seeking socio-economic justice for the disadvantaged Mizrahi community, the language they used was of 'Ashkenazi oppressors' and 'racist policies'. It is not coincidental that the Panthers were the first Israeli group to make contact with the Palestine

Liberation Organization (PLO), recognising the Palestinian struggle for self-determination and explicitly linking that to the Mizrahi cause. Crushed by the state, this protest group's impact was short-lived. By the late 1970s the right-wing Likud party, led by the Polish Jew Menachem Begin, cynically tapped into the Mizrahi population's grievances over discrimination at the hands of the Ashkenazi elite to win votes. To this day Likud, currently helmed by Israeli prime minister Benjamin Netanyahu, is reliant on this key support base.

When I was growing up in a small town in the UK during the 1980s, the Shabi family of Iraqi parents and their Israeli children showed up as foreign, other: guttural accents, non-Anglo looks, strange culture, hummus and falafel in the school lunchbox (cool now, mortifying then). My parents were of the migrant generation that didn't like to dwell, or maybe they were jaded at having done the whole deemed-inferior-migrant experience once already. In the UK, they went into full integration mode, raising children to speak only English, dropping our native Hebrew and their native Arabic (the language they loved most and maintained between them). After taunts at school, I grasped that speaking idiomatic and unaccented English was essential and learned to approximate that, using music radio as a teaching aid. Looking back, I wonder if my sense of not fitting in was about antisemitism (for other family members, it certainly was), or more to do with being a migrant child of Iraqi parents. Hyphens in an identity make it tricky to know which bit people are reacting badly to.

But sometimes reverse experiences can shed light on what's been missing all along. Reporting across the Middle East, decades later, I was often assumed native to the region. In Cairo, the Egyptian journalist I worked with around the 2011 revolution stopped fretting so much about me stepping out alone because he thought I blended. When I first landed in the Tunisian capital to report the country's first free election after the 2011 revolution, the border security official glanced at my passport and asked: 'Are you related to our poet, al-Shabbi?' Beloved throughout the Arab world, the early twentieth-century Tunisian revolutionary poet Abu al-Qasim al-Shabbi was having a revival during that period across the Middle East. There's a street named after him in Tunis. Meanwhile, Middle Eastern friends or colleagues sometimes half-jokingly pronounce my name 'Sha'abi', using the Arabic elongated, guttural 'ayn' vowel instead of the short 'aleph' for the English 'a', turning the name into a word meaning 'of the people'. Certainly I, a walking left-wing cliché, enjoy being thought of as possibly related to a revolutionary poet, or perhaps named Rachel Of-the-people. Many individuals have the sort of arrangement of features that allow them to blend across different countries and continents – there is nothing unique about this experience. But for me, there is a sense of affinity and belonging evoked in the Middle East through having a familiar look and surname, things that often elicited the opposite reaction back in Britain.

Rifling through the past, looking for potential migrant battle scars feels icky. It was so long ago. It seems like navel-gazing. I've done the therapy, made peace with the past, forgiven the younger, flailing me, so out of depth and ill-equipped, lacking the social codes I didn't even know I needed to know. It is all energy I'd rather turn elsewhere, not least to the ceaseless inequities and injustices of our fast-burning planet. I don't want to take space, yet do sometimes bristle at the thought of not being offered the space I didn't want to claim in the first place.

It's an odd, convoluted reaction, but maybe this gets at the ambivalence so many Jewish people can feel about being called 'white' in such an unqualified way. It's hard to shake off a sense of not-whiteness that's so deeply embedded in the Jewish experience. On top of which, it feels like the actual forming of racial categories (and not just the everyday practice of living, maintaining and reproducing them) ought to be one of the defining features of whiteness. While an essential frame for analysing racism, 'white' is clearly not the only way in which to understand it. And only seeing racism in this way can flatten out the sense of paper-thin conditionality that feels ever-present for many Jewish people; a visceral sense that we belong just fine, right up until we don't. Now, personally I don't believe that any of this is temporary, or that Jewish people will be cast out of whiteness anytime soon. But then again, my ancestors didn't spend hundreds of years running across Europe to escape antisemitic violence. I do not carry that generational trauma and anxiety about conditionality, perhaps in no small part because my Iraqi ancestors stayed put for over two thousand years. In any case, mine is a rational response;

I do not experience that flood of anxiety that I have seen overwhelm others. And rationality won't convince those who still suffer prejudice, or have family lines wiped out by the Holocaust, to stop worrying that things can turn at any time.

One Jewish socialist I spoke with said that the requirement to avow her own whiteness felt like an evisceration, something she instinctively rails against given the long European-Jewish history of erasure. And a young British leftist told me that antisemitism, when it appears in her world, feels visceral precisely because it hits the nerve of conditionality. 'That can only happen to a community that doesn't have a stable or secure attachment to privilege, which, rational or not, is a deeply held, generationally carried feeling, an anxiety over perennial uprootment that we can't call a white experience.'

Sometimes just being able to articulate this within progressive left spaces, safely, without dismissal, disbelief or bad faith, is all it takes. But bad faith abounds, just as it did in the media fray over Whoopi Goldberg and Diane Abbott, because that's the only kind of discussion currently on offer. And everyone gets battered by it. Examining the subject of Jews and whiteness, I have come across various impatient appraisals, from Jewish and non-Jewish interviewees alike. Among them are that Jewish people who think they aren't white, don't really understand what white privilege or structural racism mean; that Jewish people are claiming non-whiteness because they want a piece of the identity politics pie; that Jewish people, in their reluctance to discuss their own whiteness, are displaying the stock denials of regular white people. All of these are probably true in some cases. But we don't always need to foreground these aspects in our conversations to such an extent that our understanding of 'whiteness' and Jewishness gets lost.

Meanwhile, we could add another important ingredient to the overall confusion: that experiencing racism clearly doesn't inoculate against holding racist beliefs. That much is evident in the experiences of Mizrahi Jews who faced discrimination and derision from the Ashkenazi ruling class. It is manifest in Israel's decades-long occupation of Palestinian territories, with all the daily violence, killing, segregation, dispossession and humiliation that it entails. We see it, too, in the experiences of Jews of colour. In 2021, a year after the brutal murder of Black American George Floyd by a white police officer sparked global protests and a reckoning with racism, the Board of Deputies of British Jews published a report on racial inclusivity. Chaired by the British political journalist Stephen Bush, the commission's report highlighted the way Jews of colour experience racism and prejudice within the Jewish community: through racial profiling by synagogue security, feeling unwelcomed and underrepresented in those spaces, and in the assumptions of Ashkenazi-white-Jewish as the default across Jewish media. The 2023 documentary *Rabbi on the Block*, directed by Brad Rothschild, looks at the social justice work of its protagonist, Black rabbi Tamar Manasseh, who speaks about the endless prejudices and micro-aggressions she experiences. 'There's always this question of, "How did you become

Jewish?" Everyone wants to know and I never answer it',
she says, adding that sometimes people in Ashkenazi synagogues rush over to take selfies with the Black Jew. 'It is
very *National Geographic*-esque', she says. One Black Jewish
woman I spoke with told me that, as well as navigating
prejudices within the British Jewish community, she found
showing up in leftist spaces difficult. 'When you straddle
multiple identities, it just becomes too emotionally taxing',
she said. It's as though people expect her to pick a side of
her identity, not quite comprehending that one is not sec-
ondary to the other.

It often feels impossible to contain all these contradictions
around Jewish identity within progressive spaces. Navigating
the subject of Jews and whiteness is confounding, because
several conflicting things are true at the same time: most
Jewish people are mostly treated as white but, until recently,
were not-white; benefit from whiteness (aside from Jews of
colour) and uphold racism, but also experience prejudice
and discrimination. And we crave certainty. Weirdly, we're
more comfortable with race–identity binaries, even though
those binaries are made up. Maybe the value here isn't in
whether or not Jewish people self-identify as white, but of
what 'whiteness' really means in its capacity to maintain
racism. All racism. It's not as though our current approach
is creating informed and resilient coalitions, is it?

Just as author and academic Emma Dabiri writes in *What
White People Can Do Next*, coalition-building ought to be
about 'the identification of affinities and points of shared
interest that exist beyond categories that were invented to

divide us, invented in order to more effectively oppress us'. So we're going to have to make peace with that state of ambiguity about Jewish people and whiteness. Get beyond the boxes. Embrace the complexity. Because apart from anything else, cleaving to a categorisation system imposed by racism itself is simply absurd.

TWO

Whose Privilege Is It Anyway?

One summer evening in 2019 as I loitered in the kitchen of a house party in London, the subject of anti-Jewish racism came up. It often did back then, derailing dinners, disrupting drinks or just generally bursting into social occasions. In those moments, it felt like dealing with an explosive liquid spill, where you think you've mopped up the worst of it but then turn around and find congealing wet splodges across a back wall, or quietly pooling inside a cutlery drawer. It was months before the December snap election and antisemitism within Labour, under its then leader Jeremy Corbyn, was dominating the news. In as much as it is possible to swiftly surmise this painful, convoluted and fractious period, it went like this: between 2015 and the end of 2019, while Corbyn was party leader, Labour was riven by mounting accusations of antisemitism and it became a topic of endless debate. The issue raged on and on, punctuated by accusations, claims and counterclaims. In our unedifying pundit media economy, everyone had to have an opinion – and still does. The entire affair was characterised by misunderstandings, mismanagement, factionalism and distortion. Broadly, much of the Corbyn-supporting left minimised the problem, while the right hyperbolised it. That said, in October 2020, the Equality and Human Rights Commission, which had launched an inquiry into the issue, found 'specific examples of harassment, discrimination and political interference' in Labour's handling of antisemitism and that the issue could have been dealt with more effectively 'if the leadership had chosen to do so'. While all this was playing out, it was excruciating to be both Jewish and left-wing, trying to speak both to the real problem of antisemitism and to the way it had been cynically mobilised in politics. Whatever your view, the subject remains acrimonious and polarising – not unreasonably, but so much so that anyone who thinks I've just misrepresented the matter, with even one word out of place, will probably want to bin this book immediately.

So going back to the discussion in the kitchen of that party, one young Labour campaigner, let's call him 'Bob', took the view that the media focus on Labour's antisemitism was hypocritical, given that the Conservatives in government had a much worse track record when it came to racism. Instances of Conservative bigotry were widespread, he said; the party was bursting at the seams with it. This was not a wild claim. The Conservatives were (and are still) embroiled in accusations of Islamophobia running rife through the party, with multiple instances of it among sitting local councillors and standing parliamentary candidates. The then prime minister Boris Johnson seemed to trade in a sort of upper-middle-class, just-joshing-but-actually-odious racism, from referring to Black people as 'piccaninnies' with 'watermelon smiles' in an article in 2002 (for which he apologised during a London mayoral contest debate in 2008), to comparing Muslim women who wear burqas to 'letter boxes' in 2018, when he was foreign secretary (initially refusing to apologise for this comment, Johnson did so during the election campaign of 2019). And the Windrush scandal in 2018 exposed the racism that underpinned the government's hostile environment policy designed to deter immigration. Caught in its net, thousands of British citizens, mainly of Caribbean origin, were deemed to be in the UK illegally. They were denied jobs, healthcare and housing and were, in some cases, deported. At least fifty have died before seeing any redress from the government.

Bob was pointing out that antisemitism in the party could not be considered of the same magnitude as the racism emanating from the sitting government. All of which I agree with. In fact, I appeared on a Sky News politics show, *All Out Politics*, during that year's December election campaign saying pretty much the same thing: when it came to racism, the Tories were demonstrably worse. But there was a disturbing plot twist in the kitchen that summer. Bob thought that antisemitism had come to dominate the news because those raising concerns about it were 'white people using their privilege'.

By then, I had heard this formulation several times, as had many Jewish leftists caught in the crosshairs of the antisemitism row. Before we discuss the media attention that different kinds of racism do or do not receive, depending on both the type of racism and the source of it, we really should examine this business of Jewish people 'using their privilege'. What does it mean, exactly? What 'privilege'? If it's the idea that those perceived to be economically secure cannot face racial persecution, well, we know that's not the case, across all types of racism. When it comes to antisemitism specifically, we know that historically it has targeted Jews as wealthy and powerful, regardless of whether or not they were. Indeed, that is one of antisemitism's defining mechanisms. So yes, attributing the voluminous media coverage of antisemitism to one of the operational premises of antisemitism does in itself set alarm bells ringing. But a wider problem here is that claims of 'privilege' are the inevitable result of Jewish people being predominantly cast as white. Or to put it another way: if Jews are regular white people, they're going to behave in the manner so often catalogued within antiracist discourse as the way regular white people behave: prone to expending their power and privilege on centring their own issues, oblivious to this dynamic existing in the first place. And so, in raising concerns over antisemitism, Jews were seen as taking up space and jostling out more pressing or deserving issues, not least those concerning structural racism. Echoes of this sentiment could be heard across the Atlantic around the same time within the anti-Trump Women's March. This spontaneous grassroots movement, one of the largest protests in history, erupted across America and around the globe on the day after the inauguration of Donald Trump as president in January 2017. Drawing millions of supporters, the organisation was a year later rocked by accusations of antisemitism. Just as had been the case with Labour, it split supporters. Just as we had seen in the UK, antisemitism became a political attack line. And just like the rupture in Britain's main opposition party, the US iteration carried some of those assumptions that it was only gaining traction because of 'privilege'.

In October 2022, the Jewish-American comedian Amy Schumer skewered a particular aspect of this phenomenon in a sketch where she plays a participant in workplace harassment awareness training. As she is invited by the facilitator to roleplay various, potentially discriminatory workplace scenarios, she experiences repeated and glaring antisemitic comments which, to her growing frustration, nobody calls out. Finally, a Black colleague does name it, standing up to say: 'Wait a minute! That is super antisemitic!' At which point Schumer apologises profusely: 'No, no, no that's OK, don't worry about it, especially you of all people … It's nothing like what Black people have to go through.' Whatever one might think of Schumer – her comedy or her politics – what she taps into here, in not wanting to barge past a person of colour while raising racism complaints, is a sentiment I've heard in countless conversations with Jewish progressives. There's a reticence over flagging antisemitism while systemic racism is so salient and harmful. But the hesitation is also down to the dynamics Bob had pointed to: that our media and political conversation *does* routinely barge past other complaints of racism. Other types of racism really do have a different weight and often elicit a lesser response. We are not simply imagining this double standard. And our mainstream politicians *do* talk about antisemitism – and the need to combat it – in a way that happens less frequently with anti-Black racism, say, or prejudice against Asian communities, or Islamophobia. Pointing this out is not unreasonable. More than that, it is necessary. It's just that Jewish 'privilege' is a particularly inadequate explanation for why it is happening.

Looking back at the Women's March and Labour under the leadership of Jeremy Corbyn, what's striking is how easily antisemitism ruptured these mass movements. Forged in different circumstances, with different trajectories and aims, these movements inspired millions of progressives who felt let down, ignored by or disconnected from mainstream party politics. Both Corbyn's Labour and the Women's March held extraordinary potential, promising the social and economic change yearned for by many, especially while mainstream politics keeps failing us and the planet. To watch both movements riven by the same weakness was dismaying. To see such fissures draw such extreme media attention, thus escalating the tensions, was mortifying. And to then contend with the assumptions, within progressive camps, that antisemitism was getting special attention because of 'privilege' was a devastating twist of the knife.

The privilege is part of the MO

Few aspects of our antisemitism conversation illustrate the gnarled-up messiness of it so much as discussions over the current political spotlight on this racism and why it is happening. There's so much going on with this topic and it is all inconsistent, not least in the erroneous assumptions over 'privilege' and the accurate appraisals of antisemitism generating more political airtime. We're going to have to break it down and examine each aspect, piece by piece. Therapists describe this sort of dissection as a process of peeling off and examining each layer of hurt and confusion, much as you would peel away layers of an onion, to get to the core truth. This metaphor annoys me, because I don't know any cook who would actually prep an onion in this way, but let's just go with it for now.

The first layer should be obvious: when Jewish people raise concerns of antisemitism, it sure as hell does not feel like a privilege. Over the many discussions I've had with leftist Jews in both Britain and the US, there is a common thread of fear, discomfort and alienation in speaking up about antisemitism. The conversations that stay with me are the ones with British Jews who live beyond London and outside Jewish communities. As antisemitism hit the UK headlines, Jews across the country felt this issue crash into their lives unexpectedly: at work, down the pub or within political organising spaces. Suddenly, they were not just regular friends, colleagues or fellow campaigners, but first and foremost Jewish. 'To be critical of Labour on antisemitism just marked you out', explains 'Mark', a man in his mid-forties who lives in the north of England. He had not previously mentioned or been asked about his Jewish identity in work or social circles. But when he spoke about antisemitism, he says, he was often assumed to be right-wing – even among those who had known him for decades. 'It was very frustrating, upsetting and more than anything, humiliating', he recalls now. 'You had to do this routine of explaining that you cared about other issues and other racisms, you were being asked to prove you were the right kind of socialist before you might get a hearing.' He felt like he was having to establish he was a good person before he was even allowed to raise the issue. 'And there's only so many times you can do that before you either go slightly deranged, or just wash your hands of the whole thing.'

Even Jews who do self-identify as white-with-all-the-benefits get unsettled by the idea that to voice concern over antisemitism is to use privilege and distract from more important issues. There's a keen understanding that the perception of privilege is built into antisemitism. As we have seen throughout European history, Jewish people had to be first elevated to be then reviled, so they could act as a buffer community between the ruling powers and the masses. That is the MO. Antisemitism is first and foremost a conspiracy theory about power, who holds it and who uses it to dominate everyone else. If Jews are a secret, shadowy elite ruling the world, then pretty much by definition they would have to be privileged.

In 2020, white nationalists helpfully spelled this all out for us when they created a Twitter (as it was then known) hashtag #jewishprivilege to spread antisemitic conspiracies about Jews ruling the world. The hashtag was attached to an article in *The Sun* newspaper, on how Ghislaine Maxwell, the convicted sex trafficker and former accomplice of sex offender Jeffrey Epstein, was receiving prison perks after adopting her late father's Jewish faith (she got kosher food and was excused from work on the Sabbath). #Jewishprivilege ran alongside pieces about the cryptocurrency exchange founder Sam Bankman-Fried supposedly walking free after charges including fraud and conspiracy (he was eventually jailed for twenty-five years). Overnight, this hashtag was reclaimed by Jewish people who used it to describe experiences of anti-semitism. There were hundreds of posts in this vein, including from the Jewish-American comedian Sarah Silverman, who wrote: 'My dad getting the s★★★ kicked out of him everyday at school 4 being a k★★★, to kids in NH [New Hampshire] throwing pennies at me on the bus, to pastors in Florida calling for my death and telling their congregation that knocking my teeth out and killing me would be God's work. #Jewishprivilege.'

This white supremacist hashtag tells us how 'privilege' is still a live motif for virulent anti-Jewish racists. And the fact that it is a key theme amid far-right circles explains why Jewish people feel uneasy about it. Obviously, I'm not issuing a catch-all prohibition on the word. I doubt Jews will take offence over 'privilege' in a conversation relating to, say, well-paid jobs or fancy houses or multiple other contexts, including those to do with the benefits of whiteness. But using that term within progressive spaces specifically to explain the attention given to Jewish experiences of racism is going to be unsettling.

Please, no Jews in the news

You may have noticed that your Jewish lefty allies within movements on both sides of the Atlantic were not actually talking about antisemitism at all until pretty recently. And that's because politics changed (which, again, you probably noticed). Antisemitism suddenly became real, overt and violent. That much was evident in the rise of far-right politicians across Europe, all amplified by the election of Donald Trump as US president. Back when Britain did Brexit and the US did Trump, there was bewildered shock at this resurgence of reactionary politics (although bigotry had long been bubbling under the surface). It seemed like a nativist blowback, a chauvinistic reaction to progressive social advances. Left-wing movements were consumed with worry over the consequences of these stark rightward shifts, in particular for vulnerable minority groups and for our hard-won collective rights.

And running through all those reactionary views, gushing out into our politics like sewage from a burst pipe, was the oldest racism. Trump's presidency emboldened white supremacists, for whom hating Jewish people was an ideological trump card. In Britain, the Brexit shock seemed to give people permission to say out loud all the racism and xenophobia that had for a time been socially unacceptable – and, inevitably, antisemitism was in there, too. Alarmed, Jewish people turned to progressive circles but found obliviousness at best, and antisemitic stereotypes at worst – which of course, only fuelled the fears. All of that got expressed at speed in the middle of a period of political tumult on both sides of the Atlantic. Few of us within leftist spaces had either the clarity or the tools to tackle the confusions and seemingly competing claims. Things spiralled and fell apart.

In different ways, we forgot the foundational left politics that drew us together in the first place, our shared belief in a more inclusive, caring, just and equal society. And so communities that might have united against the divisive politics of the far right, which had so alarmingly been injected into the political mainstream, were instead torn apart.

Strikingly, both British and American Jews have told me that, when it came to it, they felt ill-equipped to have these conversations about antisemitism. As a result, progressive Jews started to teach themselves in order to be able to effectively and impactfully discuss antisemitism within wider movements – and this has taken a while. It's reasonable to assume, then, that those initial concerns over antisemitism may have been expressed clunkily, coming across as garbled, confused or uncalibrated. 'We didn't know how to play it and part of that is on us, because we don't know where to put ourselves', one British Jewish community organiser told me. 'There is a real need to give antisemitism room, but also to give this its rightful attention. So it becomes a messy conversation, because antisemitism doesn't operate in the same way as other racism and you end up feeling guilty and wondering if it is minor.'

Another factor is that for decades, British Jews deliberately did not centre antisemitism within progressive movements. It just wasn't the thing to do. In more mainstream contexts, even Jewish communal groups were silent on the subject, thinking that it would draw the wrong kind of attention, making vulnerable a minority that just wanted to keep their collective heads down. Tony Kushner, professor of history at the University of Southampton, focuses on modern British Jewish history and representations of the Holocaust. He told me that for the most part, the approach from British Jewish communal groups and newspapers was: 'Softly, softly, in the background, stay at home, make yourself less visible and more respectable.' The guiding principle, he adds, was to 'avoid British Jews in the news'.

By the early 2000s, Jewish leftists within racial justice spaces would be no more inclined to discuss antisemitism than they would, say, the idea of Britain leaving the European Union. It just wasn't on anyone's radar. One campaigner in her late sixties tells me of leftist organising during the 1980s and 1990s: 'It was just so much worse for Black people, so it was absolutely right to focus on that.' Back then, she says, 'You weren't in antiracist groups to talk about Jews, unless it was Jews of colour.' 'Sarah', another Jewish woman, explains of the same period: 'We were brought up not to feel victim-y. We were lucky to be in this country and should just be grateful … If you were left-wing in the 80s, it was about racism against people of colour and you didn't really feel you could put yourself in that category.' This Jewish Londoner still feels reticent about mentioning antisemitism. 'I still can't talk about it with some friends', she tells me. 'It's like people feel we are just bellyaching, we are not really oppressed, why are we making so much fuss.'

Coming across antisemitism in progressive spaces – even if it is just casual ignorant comments – is, for many Jews, a reason to panic. One socialist in her late twenties recalls being told, while at university, that antisemitism was not

really racism because Jewish people are economically privileged. 'I felt physically slapped in the face, that someone
could express such a dangerous stereotype', she now says.
Explaining this reaction she adds: 'I unadulteratedly move
through the world as a white person, I obviously don't
think there is going to be another genocide against Jews
in my lifetime. But I don't know how to live as if I know
that.' As Sarah, the Jewish Londoner, reflects: 'We know
in our lifetime that people can be urbane, sophisticated,
highly educated, enjoy classical music and then it can all
just disappear. Deep down we know it can go in a blink.
And that's what makes it different. You are almost waiting
for it. However wealthy, however many Nobel Prizes, you
just know it can go. It is such a deep-rooted fear.' Carin
Mrotz, the former director of Jewish Community Action
in Minnesota, describes her mother's reactions in similar
terms. 'My mum would hear an antisemitic slur and in the
next moment think, "We are going to get deported." The
urgency in the way we react is not to a current threat, but
to a future threat implied by the current comment and
which is invisible to everyone else.'

These women are tapping into something that might
seem odd when it's coming from a minoritised community
that in the present day is relatively well represented, established and secure. It can seem bewildering, not to mention
disproportionate, if you are not the one feeling triggered. I
imagine this fear of a future threat might even seem downright absurd if you are navigating the present, daily threat
of race hatred from the moment you step out of your front

door. Still, this anxiety happens precisely because, so often in European-Jewish history, everything was just fine right up until the moment it suddenly was not. Antisemitic violence operates in cycles by its very nature, with some Jewish people elevated in status precisely so that the entire community can be used to deflect attention from the powerful when necessary. That is why the history of antisemitism in Europe cycles between periods of calm and episodic persecution. 'Things are good and then it all comes crashing down', says the late-twenties socialist. 'That is not a blip, that's how it works.' If a group of people have been racialised to near-extinction within living memory, the notion of contingency is probably going to feel urgent and real and proportionate. For many Jewish people, antisemitic language can be unbelievably triggering. And that can be confusing when contrasted with the experiences of other minorities, living with the continuous and overt material realities of everyday racism.

So what can we, in progressive spaces, do? It's a question that Mrotz and others are now thinking about. 'We need to sit down and explain why Jewish people are freaking out', she says. 'To acknowledge that people may not be facing a threat, but that the thing they are bodily experiencing is real and that we are not going to gaslight them about it.' This sounds almost pastoral in nature, so I take the question to rabbi Lev Taylor, who at that time was looking after a reform synagogue in Essex in the east of England. (His X bio reads: 'Love Torah. Hate capitalism.' He is my kind of rabbi.) Taylor tells me that, during the height of what became Labour's antisemitism crisis, he was working in a Holocaust survivors' centre in London and an elderly resident asked him if she needed to pack her bags. 'I told her, "Of course not"', he says, recalling his acute sadness that a vulnerable member of the community was feeling this way. So what does he do if one of his congregants is having a trauma response? 'In the moment, the conversation has to be about making them feel safe, being a calm presence', Taylor says. 'It's about recognising that they feel afraid, but that you don't feel that way, which means that you are able to hold their feelings.'

This compassionate presence is sorely needed in our progressive spaces, where people often show up in different kinds of pain. We are all hurting in some way from the experience of living within atomising, harmful, exploitative and injustice-laden societies. Knowing that the system is viciously destructive is, after all, why we want so desperately to change it. But it's a lot. It's coming at us all the time. And sometimes Jewish responses to triggers are occurring while obviously disenfranchised minorities are actively unsafe. During the Corbyn years, you would see media reports of British Jews feeling anxious that they might have to leave the country should he be elected as prime minister. But at exactly the same time, another group of people *were* being forced to leave the country. Over 160 British subjects from Caribbean countries were detained or deported as a result of the Windrush scandal. It was a visceral and profound injustice, snatching away a sense of security and belonging and any assurance of being afforded the basic rights of citizenship. Understandably, it left many British people of colour alarmed over the contingency of their status in the country.

A situation that sees one relatively secure minority express fears of having to pack their bags, while at exactly the same moment a structurally vulnerable minority really is forced to pack up and leave, feels almost impossible to address within one progressive camp. As we try and find ways to respond, I'm reminded of the words of the journalist Stephen Bush, who wrote that 'privilege' – since it is often so context-dependent – is not always a useful tool with which to analyse racism or power dynamics. 'What matters is not what privileges we may have in one situation or another, but the rights we are owed as human beings and the obligations we have to others', he wrote. This honest attention to the obligations we owe each other needs to run through the fabric of coalition-building, in all directions. It has to be imprinted in the way we treat each other, the way we acknowledge and share with each other. We have to find a way to hear everybody's distress, even when we do not agree that such fears are founded in reality. Not just because it is the right thing to do. But because if we don't, that pain will find comfort in the arms of bad-faith actors on the right, which has proved incredibly adept at speaking to people's unaddressed vulnerabilities and using these in service of its own, divisive agendas.

Trauma nation

In Israel, where seventy-five per cent of the population is Jewish, the 7 October Hamas attack tore open a gaping, collective wound – the grief and shock quickly spreading out to Jewish communities worldwide. Those who survived or were first responders to those Hamas atrocities witnessed people rounded up into rooms and machine-gunned, burned in their homes, pulled out of barricaded shelters and garages to be shot, or surviving only because they were hidden in cupboards or beneath dead bodies. It is not surprising that many Jewish people reached for the words 'Holocaust' or 'pogrom'. That is what they were reminded of on a day that saw the largest loss of Jewish life since the Second World War. But the trouble is that such language, as well as the trauma that informs it, can all too easily be commandeered and manipulated for political ends. Right after those Hamas attacks, it was obvious that the hard-right Israeli government would use this trauma to justify an incomprehensible assault on the people of Gaza – 'incomprehensible' in that we truly cannot take in the scale of its violence and destruction.

Israel was stuck in time on 7 October, frozen in a collective fear that reverberated across TV screens and in the repeated, retraumatising stories of the horrors, the public billboards pleading for the return of the hostages, the slogan #bringthemhomenow on everything from shop windows to bus stops, T-shirts and dog-tag necklaces. And Israeli government figures constantly invoked the language of the Jewish people's darkest period in history to describe the 7 October attack. Prime minister Benjamin Netanyahu immediately announced: 'Hamas are the new Nazis.' He declared: 'The savagery that we witnessed, perpetrated by the Hamas murderers coming out of Gaza, were the worst crimes committed against Jews since the Holocaust.' The Israeli ambassador to the United Nations, Gilad Erdan, and his team appeared at a UN Security Council meeting in late October wearing yellow stars bearing the words: 'Never Again.' Erdan gave a speech declaring that Hamas wanted a 'Final Solution – the annihilation of the Jewish people.' This terminology served both to dehumanise Palestinians and to justify the severity of Israel's response: if Israel was, as it was being claimed, fighting Nazis, then a massive and violent loss of Palestinian lives would be a price worth paying. Those attacks on 7 October were war crimes. But Jewish people living as a Western-backed majority in their own, heavily militarised and nuclear-armed state are not the same as Jewish people who historically lived as persecuted minorities across Europe. Indeed, the director of Israel's Holocaust remembrance centre Yad Vashem pointed this out when he rebuked Erdan for those yellow stars at the UN. 'The yellow patch symbolises the helplessness of the Jewish people and being at the mercy of others', Dani Dayan, who is also a hard-right former settler leader and a vociferous opponent of the two-state solution, posted to X. 'Today we have an independent country and a strong army. We are masters of our destiny.' The use of Holocaust language coming from Israeli leaders was a horrible manipulation of deep-seated Jewish fears.

And so here, writ large in the aftermath of an atrocity that was met with a vengeance-fuelled bombardment is that same question about the role of the left in these moments. How do we care for people experiencing shock and distress, even while those sentiments are being used in service of an apocalyptic, trauma-inducing war on another people? If we don't acknowledge Jewish anguish in this moment, speak to its fears and in its cadences, how can we hope to be heard as an inclusive and expansive movement? Why would those clinging to the idea of a fortressed, militarised, brutally aggressive Israel, believing it a guarantor of Jewish safety, be persuaded by anything we might have to say about that?

There has rarely been a more urgent need for us to stretch our compassion, to hold Jewish trauma even while a savagely catastrophic war is inflicted on Palestinians in its name. As the Israeli army pulverised the Strip, I read accounts from aid workers in Gaza, of small children left as the sole survivors of entire killed families, or teenagers wanting to die so as to stop their endless suffering. I watched the video clips of babies screaming in hunger and the reports of children blown apart or buried under the rubble of bombed-out buildings, or enduring amputations carried out with no anaesthetic, or witnessing their siblings ripped by searing shrapnel. I watched the images of toddlers shaking with terror and wondered how they would ever heal. How families would ever recover. How Palestinians around the world, witnessing the erasure of their people via phone screens in real time and for months on end, would ever not be paralysed with grief. How any of us could watch and not fall apart.

The Israel–Palestine conflict is steeped in suffering built into its genesis, with the horrors of the Holocaust leading to the creation of a state that would bring catastrophe upon another people. Acknowledging the fears of every person in that region is not going to be straightforward, at a time when there is a moral imperative to stand against the violence inflicted upon Palestinians by the state of Israel, to halt a genocidal war. It seriously challenges what can often seem like a leftist allergy to messy complexity. But it is key to building a movement that brings everyone together quite simply because it has to; because that's our only chance of fostering an alternative to endless loss, misery and pain.

Splitting the march

The challenge of creating bigger, better politics within an increasingly right-wing global landscape that thrives on fear and division is, unsurprisingly, one the left keeps stumbling over. Very often, and distressingly, antisemitism functions as the tripwire. One way or another, we keep slamming into that question of how we build antiracism movements that stretch to encompass all minorities. It happens far from the Middle East, in different contexts and at varying registers. With devastating consequences, it's a question that was written, almost as a blueprint for failure, into the story of the Women's March movement in America.

A day after the inauguration of Donald Trump in January 2017, the Women's March protest erupted onto the streets of America and worldwide, becoming the largest single-day protest in US history. There were more than 600 events in sixty countries. Trump's policy positions, alongside the misogyny that saturated his election campaign, were seen as direct threats to the rights of women.

But as the first Facebook call to protest quickly snow-balled into a giant movement, some of the thousands of messages pouring out on social media were pointing to the uniform whiteness of the women behind it, with some dubbing it the 'White Women's March'. As one of those organisers, Bob Bland, recounts in the documentary by Amy Berg about the Women's March, *This is Personal*: 'I thought, "Oh shit, we all are [white]." Because I had never thought of analysing it based on that, because of my privilege.' The lack of diversity within the feminist movement has long been an issue. Since fifty-three per cent of white women had voted for Donald Trump and since so much of the new president's policy platform seemed likely to imperil minorities, it was an issue that needed urgent attention.

That's when Tamika Mallory, a long-time civil rights campaigner, got a call from the march organisers. They had seen a photograph of Mallory at a protest with Linda Sarsour and Carmen Perez – both civil rights organisers with long track records – and had thought: that's the image we want. These three women of colour were made co-chairs of the Women's March, putting intersectionality front and centre of this movement, so much so that media outlets started publishing pieces on what that term actually meant.

It all seemed great; the women at the helm of this organi-sation were fêted on front pages, on red carpets and in *Vogue* magazine. They were included in *Time* magazine's '100 most influential people' list. 'This is the rebirth of the women's

movement', read the *Time* entry. 'These women are the suffra-
gists of our time. And our movement isn't going away – it's just
the beginning.' Only a year later, things started to crumble. An
article in the Jewish magazine *Tablet* claimed that, right back
at the very first meeting, some of the co-chairs were berating
Jewish co-founder Vanessa Wruble (who subsequently left
the organisation) over the special collective responsibility that
Jewish people held for the exploitation of Black people. After
the piece was published, Wruble confirmed that it happened:
'I personally witnessed statements that were inaccurate about
the role that Jews have played in the slave trade and in the
prison industrial complex', she told *Vox* magazine. 'I was pretty
devastated.' The Women's March chairs refuted this claim. But
the *Tablet* piece had also pointed out that the group's unity
principles did not include Jewish women among the many
groups listed. And one of the co-chairs, Tamika Mallory, was
in the spotlight over her attendance at the Nation of Islam's
annual Saviours' Day event in February that year, where the
organisation's leader Louis Farrakhan had made noxious
comments about Jewish people, namely stating that 'powerful
Jews are my enemy' and that he had 'pulled the cover off
the eyes of the satanic Jew'. Mallory also faced questions over
posting to Instagram a picture of herself with Farrakhan a year
earlier affectionately describing him as 'the GOAT' (greatest
of all time). Farrakhan is reported to have blamed Jewish
people for slavery and Black oppression. While Farrakhan has
denied accusations of antisemitism, arguing that he 'honors,
respects, and even admires many members of the Jewish
community,' he has also shared conspiracies about Jewish

global control and claimed: 'I'm not an anti-Semite. I'm anti-Termite.' He has also made transphobic, homophobic and patriarchal comments – all, needless to say, antithetical to the aims and spirit of the Women's March. Three of the four women heading the march had praised Farrakhan or the Nation of Islam.

This quickly turned into a media storm, snapped up by right-wing detractors looking for reasons to rubbish the march. Caught in its epicentre, the co-chairs responded slowly, badly and defensively. 'How can a Black woman be racist?' asked co-chair Bob Bland on Twitter/X. These leaders saw the criticisms over antisemitism as part of an expected, predictable and inevitable attack on women of colour in leadership positions. Initially Linda Sarsour, while distancing herself from Farrakhan, wrote: 'It's very clear to me what the underlying issue is – I am a bold, outspoken BDS-supporting Palestinian Muslim American woman and the opposition's worst nightmare', in an open letter responding to events, referring to the Palestinian-led campaign promoting boycott, divestment and sanctions against Israel. 'They have tried every tactic at their disposal to undermine me, discredit me, vilify me.'

The march chairs did eventually apologise for the sluggish and clunky response. 'We regret that', they said. 'We are deeply sorry for the harm we have caused, but we see you, we love you, and we are fighting with you.' They tried to explain that the initial defensiveness was in no small part down to the ferocity of the attacks they faced. But it came too late. Many of the organisation's partners and celebrity backers were pulling out over the furore, a separate organisation was set up and it got so bad that by January 2019 there were two Women's Marches in New York: the original and an offshoot. Mallory, Sarsour and Bland all stepped down later that year.

Looking at this mess now, is it possible that things could have turned out differently? Trump's rise unleashed waves of hateful bigotry across the nation, with an immediate and dramatic rise in incidents of racism. Just within the first week of his presidency, the Southern Poverty Law Center, a racial justice organisation with offices across southern America, reported over four hundred instances of intimidation against Black people, Muslims, immigrants, women and the LGBTQ community. A woman in Colorado reported that a young boy had told her pre-teen daughter: 'Now that Trump is president I'm going to shoot you and all the Blacks I can find.' And the hate was coming from the top. In early 2017, Trump signed an executive order dubbed the 'Muslim ban' because it denied entry to the US to people from seven Muslim-majority countries: Iraq, Iran, Libya, Somalia, Sudan, Syria and Yemen. Minorities felt betrayed by their fellow Americans, who had been willing to vote into the White House a man who had made his dangerous bigotries so clear. White women voted for Trump in droves and Jewish women were viewed as white. So again, there was the sense that complaints of antisemitism within the movement were only coming up with such force because of Jewish white women using their privilege, centring themselves, having a spat and derailing a movement. Several times, the Women's March co-chairs alluded to this dynamic to explain the volume of attention given to complaints of antisemitism, noting that they had sat through endless expressions of racism within progressive spaces, without the luxury of leaving the table.

But Jewish women were not part of the wider problem. They mostly didn't even vote for Trump. The majority of American Jews voted Democrat in 2016 and again in 2020. At the same time, much of the racial intolerance unleashed by the Trump presidency was targeting Jews. The number of antisemitic assaults doubled by 2018. It had turned deadly at a shooting at the Tree of Life synagogue in Pittsburgh. Like many others, Jewish progressives were frightened, anxious and having to make sense of the consequences of the far-right political shift at speed. And in that moment, when white nationalists had put Jews back into the firing line of race hate, they saw the Women's March, then the largest progressive movement in America, dismissing their fears over antisemitism. Inevitably, panic ensued.

But at the same time, the Women's March organisers felt that they could not denounce Farrakhan in the way that was being asked of them. Tamika Mallory, a gun control advocate, has long worked with the Nation of Islam as part of her anti-violence campaigning, and especially since her son's father was murdered in a fatal shooting in 2001. In a statement responding to her association with Farrakhan, published in March 2018 she had written: 'In that most difficult period of my life, it was the women of the Nation of Islam who supported me and I have always held them close to my heart for that reason.' The Nation has supported Black people across some of America's most deprived and forgotten neighbourhoods. It showed up when nobody else did, offering care and security and helping the formerly incarcerated – basically providing an informal social services system and safety net. Eric K. Ward, executive vice president of Race Forward, has pointed out that, if you are a Black community organiser working on these issues, the chances are you will have worked alongside the Nation of Islam. Clearly Black activists *have* spoken out against Farrakhan. But what Ward points to, above all, is the prolonged absence of other sources of support for the disenfranchised. 'An organisation like the Nation of Islam is prosperous because it has no competition', he says.

Mallory herself explained that condemnation is not a component of the work she does – and cannot be, since this work puts her into contact with many people she does not agree with, including police chiefs and violent criminals. In a 2019 radio interview she noted that she had not even condemned the men who killed her child's father. She asked to be judged not by the words of Farrakhan, whom she did not agree with, but on the merits of her own work, a twenty-year record of diligent, passionate campaigning with no sign of homophobia or antisemitism. In an essay for the *Atlantic* magazine, Adam Serwer wisely pointed out that the only real winner in this horrible mess was the Nation of Islam leader himself. 'Watching Farrakhan bask in the media attention, as yet another generation of black leadership faces public immolation on his behalf, it is impossible to see him as worthy of [Mallory's] loyalty', he wrote. And meanwhile, as this row burned through endless news cycles, it brought a rain of racist attacks and abuse, particularly on the heads of the three women of colour. The crisis was pitting Jewish and other minority groups against each other at a time when everyone was feeling vulnerable and endangered.

In *This is Personal*, the documentary film about the Women's March, Mallory goes to meet with progressive rabbi Rachel Timoner at Beth Elohim, the largest reform synagogue in Brooklyn. Timoner explains how she feels to Mallory: 'We thought we were in it together but maybe you don't care about me … maybe you think I am the enemy the way [Farrakhan] is saying that I'm the enemy, that I'm evil … And it seems like you would, as someone who cares about all human beings, directly, clearly, loudly, unequivocally denounce that language and say that is not who we are.'

Rabbi Timoner wanted Mallory to help her understand why this had not been the case. And Mallory responded that Black leaders are routinely subjected to a litmus test over Farrakhan and having to denounce him. She explains that this is not possible, because of the community work she does and that holding her accountable in this context is not a reasonable demand. 'That's not my responsibility', she says. 'My responsibility *is*, though, to say I don't agree with those things and I organise in a completely different way and that's very clear. There's nowhere that you can pull up in my life where I've said these things, where I'm living in these ways … That's not me. I'm being held responsible, literally, for the words of someone else.'

Mallory was talking about a reality in which women of colour are held to account on higher standards than anyone else and under the glare of a relentless scrutiny. But the woman in the room with her felt that she wasn't coming from that place or channelling this dynamic. 'I'm saying, I want to be in this with you', Timoner replies. 'I'm saying to you, can we be allies to each other? Can you – and not because I have power over you and I'm gonna make you do it … I want you to want to do it because you see something that you think is wrong.'

Watching this, it seems that both these women knew all too well that they needed each other in a joint struggle, that they had to work together and that there was incredible power in doing so. But the rupture over antisemitism, the inability to find a way through it, had put a seemingly insurmountable obstacle in their path. They were trapped in the contours of a simplifying, divisive, politically driven media narrative about different racisms and could not, amid the overwhelming pressures it exerted, navigate a way out. The sheer intensity of that screaming political narrative, with its ugly power plays, made it impossible to jointly compose a different story.

A wedge issue

What is so painfully clear in the story of the Women's March is that we are having to work out these dynamics within a wider political and media conversation that is actively forcing major rifts between us. That onion we've been peeling in that stupid, impractical way was all this time sitting in a pressure cooker. And it exploded. It exploded because antisemitism has become a wedge issue in our politics – an issue that can singlehandedly derail progressive camps. Political wedges such as policies around immigration or women's rights, or indeed Brexit, force divisions amid otherwise unified groups. The issues in themselves – how do we respond to immigration, or gender inequalities, or calls to leave the European Union? – are real enough. But they gain political salience because of our inability to mount a swift or adequate response, handle disagreements and come up with a unified policy. And these issues become prominent because our political opponents use them to divide us. We know that politics is grubby. So far so obvious, but one problem with the left's response to antisemitism – and you could see examples of this within Corbyn's Labour and within the Women's March – is that the analysis begins and ends there. Writing about the Labour party's antisemitism crisis, Ben Gidley, Brendan McGeever and David Feldman, at the Birkbeck Institute for the Study of Antisemitism, noted in 2020: 'The complaint that antisemitism is being used as a stick with which to beat the Labour party is unworldly'. They explained that such attacks from opponents have long been the grim reality of politics. 'From the ancient world to the contemporary scene, political adversaries have drawn attention to their opponents' ethical weaknesses. In the case of the Corbyn-led Labour party, it was politics as usual when its rivals, both outside the party and within, drew attention to what they perceived to be a grave and persistent failure of principle.'

This is what brings us back to our overarching theme of so-called 'privilege' in the context of Jewish people. Because whose privilege is it, really? When we look at antisemitism as a wedge, it allows us to ask where all the media and political noise is actually coming from. After all, Jewish individuals and community bodies might voice concerns over antisemitism within progressive spaces, or within political parties. They might at times voice it unreasonably and disproportionately – as I believe was sometimes the case during the Corbyn years. And it might well be that the Jewish groups raising the issues are prominent organisations – like the US Anti-Defamation League or the Board of Deputies of British Jews. But it is not those Jewish individuals and community bodies that are making the decision to centre parliamentary politics on such claims, or to plaster them on our front pages and jam our airwaves with the issue, day in day out. That is where the 'privilege' is. That is where the power in this equation truly lies.

The fever pitch media focus is not something that was ever wished for by most Jewish people trying to get on with their lives like everyone else. Mark, the Jewish fortysomething from the north of England, also told me that, at the height of Labour's antisemitism crisis in the summer of 2018, all he wanted was for the issue to fall off the news cycle. 'There really *were* other issues that were more important', he recalls. 'An ordinary person with no skin in the game, someone who is not a political person – which is most people – might get sick of seeing Jews in the news and that's not good for Jews. I'd wake up in the morning and think "Please, no Jews on the front page.'" One Jewish community organiser in London puts it this way: 'Jews don't want to be obsessed over, not in good or bad ways. We like obsessing over ourselves, between us, but not being the centre of attention.' That Labour campaigner in the kitchen of the summer party, Bob, rightly observed that anti-Black racism or Islamophobia were not generating the headlines warranted by the dangerous prevalence of such bigotries in politics. He wanted front pages on those stories, because that is how issues generate the sort of attention and understanding that might lead to positive change. And yet as we have seen, this is the exact opposite to how Jews generally respond to being in the news. As one British woman I spoke with put it, since antisemitism is premised on the idea of Jewish people being all-powerful, 'any attention like that is a double-edged sword at best'. A front-page story about antisemitism is the moment when Jewish people might feel the least safe.

But there is one more stumbling block in the path of our coalition-building here. Our work to make space for different struggles against various forms of racism is taking place while the dominant political narrative is producing hierarchies of priority or attention. The struggle to combat antisemitism is something that political leaders across the West champion, quite often while omitting to take seriously the forms of racism that target Black, Asian or Muslim communities. Indeed, the reality is much worse, in that our media and political spaces are often the source of racism targeting those communities in the first place.

So what is going on? If all of this is *not* down to so-called shadowy elite Jewish power after all, then why are Western politicians embracing this position? To understand a critical factor here, there is no better place to look than the current political debates over memorials for the Holocaust and for transatlantic slavery in Britain – and the stark differences between the two.

What to remember, what to forget

Britain, one of the world's most prominent slave-trading countries, has a slavery museum in each of the port cities that were key hubs during the 400-year period of this horrific transatlantic trade. Within the Museum of London Docklands, there is a floor dedicated to the subject; Bristol's Georgian House Museum has a small exhibition set in the former home of a sugar plantation owner; and Liverpool is home to the International Slavery Museum, where you could easily spend days learning about the scale of the terrible tragedies contained within its many illustrative displays across four floors.

Memorials are different, but just as important. They stand as testimony to lives lost and are powerful, often deeply emotional statements that those lives are not forgotten. The UK has erected statues only to influential British abolition-ists such as William Wilberforce or Thomas Clarkson, which speaks to a lack of reflection on the subject. And so the British charity Memorial 2007 was set up that year to erect a statue in memory of enslaved people. It was the bicentenary of the 1807 Slave Act, which abolished that unconscionable trade across the British Empire. There was a public competition for the memorial itself, won by sculptor Les Johnson, who designed a monument entitled *Remembering Enslaved Africans and Their Descendants*. It portrays six adults on a plinth in a setting that evokes both slavery and its abolition, intended to convey that, contrary to British mythology, enslaved people had fought for their own freedom. A plot in the Rose Garden at London's Hyde Park was secured as the location, but without government support, Memorial 2007 has not been able to raise the £4 million required to realise the project and planning permission expired in 2019.

Meanwhile, across the same timeline, successive Conservative governments have committed to founding a Holocaust memorial and learning centre at London's Victoria Tower Gardens, a small park nestled next to the Houses of Parliament. So far, the project has been promised some £75 million in state funding and the current government has provided support even in the face of objections (over practicalities and congestion issues) from the local authority responsible for that part of London.

So why exactly is the state so invested in a memorial to the Holocaust and not to slavery? Few put the case better than Oku Ekpenyon, the founder of Memorial 2007, when she spoke to the BBC Radio programme *Front Row* in an episode on memorialisation in the twenty-first century, which first aired in May 2021. Memorial 2007 of course has no objection to public funding for a Holocaust memorial, but Ekpenyon got to the heart of the discrepancies in state support. 'Although the government has funded and supported other memorials, I think the subject of the slave trade and slavery is particularly sensitive', she said. 'And it's easier to acknowledge the atrocities of someone else than it is to look at one's own history, which is brushed under the carpet.' In that short response about a slavery memorial, she got to the core of what the Holocaust memorial does – not for Jewish people, but for Britain's sense of self.

Memorialising the Holocaust is a way for Britain to showcase its 'saviour' role within that horrific period in history. There's the national story of rescuing children through the Kindertransport – which in reality, involved 10,000 unaccompanied kids and was organised entirely by individuals and charitable bodies, not the British state, which blocked hundreds of thousands of other applications. Over a million children went on to be murdered during the Holocaust. Then there's the matter of fighting Hitler, defeating evil and allowing good to prevail. The function of a Holocaust memorial in the UK is not just about remembering the atrocity in itself – although undoubtedly that is important. A memorial allows Britain to cast itself on the right side of history, projecting an image of freedom, tolerance and goodness. The need to remember the mass extermination of Jewish people in Nazi Germany goes beyond the respect owed to those Jewish lives and wanders into the realms of national myth-making.

And as Ekpenyon pointed out, there is no way a memorial to those millions of lives brutally lost or irreversibly scarred during the transatlantic slave trade could serve this purpose in Britain. Where in that is the nation's redemption story? That is why we only raise statues to the abolitionists. The rest is too terrible a reminder of the country's own deep involvement, far too damning to acknowledge out in the open, in an elegant and solemn statue in the middle of one of London's most visited parks.

Now in truth, the way the Holocaust is memorialised in the UK doesn't exactly serve Jewish people, either – as many Jewish voices (an assortment from the political right and left) have pointed out in objections to the proposed Holocaust memorial and learning centre in London's Victoria Tower Gardens. When I spoke with the historian Tony Kushner, who sat on the advisory board for this memorial, he recalled how he and other Holocaust experts had pointed out that Britain did not need another memorial (we already have one in Hyde Park). Rather, the government should invest in Holocaust education, in the study and the teaching of this subject – not least of Britain's not entirely squeaky-clean track record during this period. He suggested that the learning centre, were it to go ahead, should avoid triumphalism and try to be a little self-critical, and look at the British roots of racist thinking and the impact of colonialism in advancing the sort of racism that would inform Nazism. He also suggested that £4 million of the funds set aside for this Holocaust memorial project could be reallocated to the slavery memorial. But, he recalls, the response was akin to him 'suggesting a 5,000-ft statue of Boris Johnson dressed in a ballet outfit'.

In 2019, just as the Hyde Park permit for the proposed slavery memorial was set to expire, Madge Dresser, a history professor at the University of Bristol (and herself Jewish) told the *Guardian* newspaper that the government's approach to this issue was needlessly divisive. 'It is important to memorialise both the Holocaust and the enslavement of Africans and they should not be in competition', she said. 'In the interests of community cohesion the government needs to fund a proper memorial to the victims of the Atlantic slave trade.' I think we can apply those wise words more widely. Antiracism alliances could and should work to ensure that each of these heinous periods in history is remembered honestly and memorialised respectfully. But the spirit of this practice can equally be applied to the way we organise, the way we work together – ever mindful, as Stephen Bush wrote, of the obligations we have to each other. It seems to me that one of our responsibilities is to generate a language and analysis that are neither led by nor replicate the noxiously divisive, racial-hierarchy-producing contours of our mainstream political conversation on such issues. Only then might we gain a deeper understanding of how different kinds of racism operate, how each still impacts on society today. Only then might we forge a compassionate, powerful and unshakeable understanding of our joint struggle. As antiracists all in it together.

THREE

Which Side Are Jews On?

Which *side* are Jews on? What the hell kind of a question is that? Believe me, I know, but it's not so much a question as an appraisal of the world we're in. Everything's a battle. A simplified, amplified story of 'us' and 'them'. Heroes and villains. Good and evil. We, the left, talk a good talk in standing against the volkish, divisive invocations of in-groups and out-groups, the accepted and the othered. Ours is a politics of inclusion and diversity. We are all about rejecting polarisation, shattering the zero-sum binaries so often deployed in the noxious culture wars of the political right. We blow apart the very assumptions on which these are built, expanding the 'us' to include all humanity, standing with the groups that the populist right keeps targeting and vilifying as a hateful 'them': refugees and asylum seekers, Muslims, minorities, LGBTQ communities, the poor, the ailing, the less fortunate. Exposing the mythologies of us and them is part of our critique of a globalised exploitative economy, one that needs to racialise and vilify and segregate, first to justify the extraction of lands, resources and labour and then to keep the fortress closed and the wealth flowing upwards. Our baddies are systems: crony capitalism, surveillance capitalism, unregulated markets, exploitative multinationals, environment-wrecking industries, sweatshop manufacturers and wage-slave gig economies.

But while we campaign and advocate and urge for it to be otherwise, we still inhabit this shattered, adversarial world. And it inhabits us too, sometimes. We also have lists of baddies in our own camp. The terrible politicians wearing contempt for the disenfranchised on their sleeves and the billionaires exploiting the global workforce, of course. But also the lefties that aren't quite like us, perhaps the ones deemed to have strayed too close to the other side. Not 'real' lefties. When it comes to antiracism, we do a version of the whole 'sides' business in casting people as either oppressor or oppressed, powerful or persecuted. It's at this point that Jews, what with all their perceived whiteness and privilege, *can* end up cast on the other side: not as racialised and vulnerable but rather in a position of power and influence.

There are several factors at play here. As we have already seen, one is that, post-Second World War, Jews in the West were by and large absorbed into whiteness and its corresponding power structures. Another is that Jewish people – especially the ones who aren't visibly non-white and the mostly secular ones who aren't visibly Jewish – seem fairly well established and unlikely to be racialised. But there are other factors too. For one, the ubiquitous invocations, across Western nations and across the political spectrum, of a so-called 'Judeo-Christian heritage' whereby Jewish people are folded into the cultural and power dynamics of a domineering West. This hyphenated heritage is kind of iffy, to say the least. But this supposed tradition locates Jewish people inside the tent with the West's majority white culture, while other 'othered' minorities are cast outside. And then there is that major impasse, the one never far from our minds: the state of Israel. What you think about Israel immediately pigeonholes you. Years ago, a kindly Englishman who tirelessly campaigns for Palestinian rights told me that, on the subject of Israel, there were 'good' Jews and 'bad' Jews and that he had long given up talking with the latter. If we were honest, we would admit that this sentiment is not an isolated one.

Lest there be any doubt over what I'm getting at here, the first thing to say is that the state of Israel's position on the 'bad' side is hardly unwarranted. We can easily point to the country's very formation, its aggressive ethno-nationalism and its violent brutality towards Palestinians. It's discernible in our domestic politics: our governments support Israel at all costs and regardless of serious, serial violations of human rights and international law. If any of this was previously in doubt, it became crystal clear after 7 October 2023, when Israel invaded Gaza – effectively an open-air prison since 2007. The horrors inflicted on a tiny strip as densely populated as London, packed with children, were unprecedented in twenty-first-century warfare; they exceed our comprehension. In its first two months, Israel's aerial bombardment surpassed the destruction inflicted by the Allies upon

Dresden in the Second World War. The American military historian Robert Pape called the destruction in Gaza 'one of the most intense civilian punishment campaigns in history'. The scale of it made us lose our minds. In what world was any of this justifiable? Why did Western nations, including the US, Britain and Germany, provide Israel with military aid and the necessary diplomatic cover? The most obvious rationale fits a timeworn story, of white, Western nations either carrying out or turning a blind eye to the most sickening atrocities against Brown people, whose lives are considered worthless.

In those months when the war on Gaza dominated our news feeds, more and more people began to pay attention to what was going on and why. Around the world, people learned about the oppression that is a daily feature of Palestinian life. They found out about Gaza being completely blockaded since 2007, an act of collective punishment after Hamas drove its political rival Fatah – which rules the West Bank – out of the Strip and seized power. They learned that Israel has since controlled exactly who and what goes in and out of the Strip, including the availability of baby bottles, chocolate or coriander. The level of control is such that the Israeli military knows Gaza's daily calorie needs. Even before the events of 2023, Palestinians in Gaza already suffered several deadly bombardments, senselessly killing and injuring people in their hundreds while flattening homes, schools and hospitals. There was a terrible twenty-two-day assault in 2008, with the stated aim of stopping Hamas rockets firing out of the Strip into

Israel's southern towns, which left over 1,400 Palestinians and 13 Israelis dead. There was another eight-day onslaught in 2012, killing 167 Palestinians and six Israelis. Then there was a savage seven-week war in the summer of 2014 after Hamas kidnapped three Israeli teens, when some 2,200 Palestinians in Gaza, including over 500 children, were killed and thousands were injured, while sixty-seven Israeli soldiers and six civilians were killed and over eighty civilians wounded. Eleven days of war in 2021 left some 260 people dead in Gaza and thirteen in Israel. From March 2018 until the end of 2019, as tens of thousands of Palestinians took part in the grassroots March of Return protests near Gaza's border fence, demanding the return of Palestinian refugees and an end to the blockade, the Israeli army killed over 200 people and injured over 36,000. This unfathomable number of injuries sustained by unarmed protesters was, in thousands of cases, caused by live bullets, overwhelmingly to the legs and resulting in multiple disabilities and amputations.

And all of this only accounts for the most recent years. You could rewind further, to find that some seventy per cent of Palestinians in Gaza are refugees – they were among the 700,000 or their descendants who had to flee their homes in the 1948 war that created Israel. Or that Gaza, the West Bank and East Jerusalem were placed under military occupation after the Six-Day War with Syria, Egypt and Jordan during 1967. While Israel pulled Jewish settlers from Gaza in 2005, illegal settlements continue to sprawl across the West Bank and East Jerusalem, turning occupied Palestinian lands into a Swiss cheese.

Most nations and international bodies, including the UN, the EU, the International Committee of the Red Cross and parties to the Fourth Geneva Convention, have long recognised that these Jewish settlements are illegal under international law. And yet, the settlements remain and keep expanding. Keep winding back across the decades and you find that right from the start, Israel unleashed ethnic cleansing, displacement, mass arrests, home demolitions and military rule upon the Palestinian people. Israel, as it has been experienced by Palestinians, unambiguously rests on the oppressor side of the equation.

What makes this all the more obvious is the easy parallels made with the violence and subjugation experienced by Black and Brown people the world over. It should not be surprising that those who experience racism or who come from colonised parts of the world look at Israel's treatment of Palestinians – the crushing of non-violent resistance, the mass imprisonments, the midnight military raids, the confiscation of lands, the separation of families – and see the familiar contours of oppression. In 1997 the former South African president Nelson Mandela, a long-time advocate for the Palestinian right to self-determination, said: 'We know too well that our freedom is incomplete without the freedom of the Palestinians.' It is no wonder that South Africa, with its bitter history of apartheid, was the country that took Israel to the International Court of Justice in December 2023, with the court finding it 'plausible' that Israel's war in Gaza could amount to genocide and ruling that Israel should take recommended measures to prevent genocidal acts (it did not).

For anyone who lives with or has witnessed the realities on the ground, it is also no surprise that several human rights groups, including the Palestinian Al-Haq, the Israeli B'Tselem, Human Rights Watch and Amnesty International, have in recent years described Israel as exercising a system of apartheid. If that doesn't count as oppression, if the left isn't going to name it as such and stand against a present-day system of state-sponsored racism, then what are we even doing?

Our frames of understanding − about colonialism, oppression and subjugation − all hold up. But the trouble is that they are incomplete. What's even more frustrating is that they are incomplete from a left-wing, antiracist and anti-imperial perspective. It's like we are looking through a high-powered telescope, one offering an unparalleled view but also filtering out some parts of the picture. Not that any of this amounts to antisemitism, to be clear. I am not going to ambush you with a declaration that everyone who cares about the plight of Palestinians is harbouring unacknowledged antisemitism. Instead, what we are trying to do here is to take a look at the various factors that might explain why, especially after the 2023 outbreak of war in Gaza, it can be harder to see Jewish people as a racialised minority, as the oppressor 'side' in Israel who are nonetheless allies against oppression and also simultaneously vulnerable to race hatred and attack. And so, once again, our task is to re-examine some of the assumptions and frames of reference that got us here. We need to remove that occluding filter from our view of Israel and look again at the dynamics of racism and oppression in the region. That way, we can build a more inclusive and expansively antiracist 'us', one that brings in a left-wing critique of the full extent of harm caused by European colonialism in that blighted part of the Middle East.

The people on the 'land without a people'

For Palestinians, there are no two ways about it: the formation of Israel was achieved by colonisation. Up until the 1880s, what was then Palestine had been home to a Jewish community of around 20,000 to 25,000 people, some eight per cent of the total population. Palestinians of all faiths had been minding their own business when Jewish people from Europe started turning up from 1882. Among these early arrivals were the forerunners of Zionism, a movement conceived by European (Ashkenazi) Jews in pursuit of a Jewish state, as one response to endless antisemitic persecution across Europe. And the effects of this movement on Palestinians looked exactly like settler colonialism.

In fact, Zionist leaders of the time spoke about it in these terms. The Austro-Hungarian journalist Theodor Herzl, credited as being the founding father of Zionism, wrote in his diaries in 1895 of the process of creating a Jewish homeland, a few years before Palestine became the focus of that project: 'We must expropriate gently the private property on the estates assigned to us. We shall try to spirit the penniless population across the border by procuring employment for it in the transit countries, while denying it employment in our own country.' By 1923, Ze'ev Jabotinsky, leader of the revisionist Zionist movement which was about maximising land for the Jewish state, saw that Palestinians would naturally reject such advances. 'The native populations, civilised or uncivilised, have always stubbornly resisted the colonists', he wrote, adding that Palestinians felt towards their own land the same way the 'Sioux [felt] for their rolling prairies' – referring to the Native, Indigenous and First Nations peoples and communities who were violently displaced from their lands in the process of European settler colonialism in North America. The leading lights of Zionism understood that Palestinians would resist any outside attempts to take over, just as other peoples had and would. By the late 1980s, partly as a result of the declassification of state and miliary archives, a loosely termed group of Israeli 'New Historians', including Benny Morris, Ilan Pappe, Avi Shlaim and Tom Segev, began writing about those earlier decades, updating Israel's origin story to factor in its colonial treatment of native Palestinians.

After the First World War, Palestine passed from Ottoman rule into British hands, becoming one of its Mandates in the Middle East. According to treaties agreed between the war's victors, these were independent nations-in-waiting, deemed (not that anyone asked them) in need of Western supervision on the path to statehood. It was stealth-colonialism, a twist on the 'ruling-over-you-for-your-own-good' mode that was the European way. The Brits gave Jewish settlement in Palestine their blessing with the 1917 Balfour Declaration, which was in turn formally approved by the

League of Nations in 1922. Jewish settlement from Europe accelerated, as did the purchase of chunks of land, mostly from 'absentee' landowners, which led to evictions of tenants who lived there. Unsurprisingly, these developments alarmed Palestinians.

In April 1936, Palestinians launched a general strike that spiralled into an armed insurrection, with the revolt enduring until 1939. It was suppressed by the British army with the assistance of Zionist paramilitaries. For Palestinians, then, a European-Jewish colonialism was being aided and protected by a Western imperial force on the ground. And even with this imperial force long gone, the West's influence in terms of aiding and protecting Israel has continued to this day.

After the First World War, parts of the former Ottoman Empire were being carved up by European imperial powers – with lines drawn in the sand, for instance, to divide Syria and Iraq – to engineer nation states. After the Second World War and the Holocaust, and with Zionist groups engaged in guerrilla attacks against both the British and the Arab population in Palestine, the UN backed a partition plan to divide the region between its Arab and Jewish inhabitants. But the 1947 UN plan gave just over half of the land to the Jewish community, which by then constituted a third of the total population. Jerusalem was to be a *corpus separatum* – a zone under international governance, justified on the grounds of its importance to all Abrahamic faiths. Neither the Jewish nor the Palestinian leaderships at the time were happy with the proposed UN borders, but the Zionist groups accepted this internationally backed plan because it established a modern Israeli state. Rejected by the Palestinians and Arab nations, they went to war – with Iraq, Syria, Egypt and Transjordan joining the Palestinian side – and lost. Thus the state of Israel was founded, recognised as such by the UN a year later. Independence Day for Israel was the Palestinian *Nakba*, or catastrophe: some 15,000 (figures vary) were killed, while upwards of 700,000 were forced to become refugees and none were ever allowed to return. Around 150,000 – just twenty per cent of the entire non-Jewish population at the time – remained, becoming Palestinian citizens of Israel (who today, numbering some two million people, still make up just over twenty per cent of the population of Israel). Meanwhile Jerusalem did not become an international enclave of peace, but was split into two parts, with Transjordan controlling East Jerusalem, including the Old City, and Israel controlling West Jerusalem.

At the moment of Israel's founding, Palestinians were displaced, traumatised and scattered across refugee camps in Lebanon, Transjordan (which became the Hashemite Kingdom of Jordan in 1946), Syria, Egypt and Iraq. An organised political opposition to their dispossession, when it coalesced, was framed as a struggle against colonialism with the aim of restoring Palestinian ownership and control of the land. With everything that had happened, it would be impossible for Palestinians not to view this new Israel as a colonial undertaking. As the Palestinian historian Rashid Khalidi writes: 'Such radical social engineering at the expense of the indigenous populations is the way of all colonial settler movements. In Palestine, it was a necessary precondition for transforming most of an overwhelmingly Arab country into a predominantly Jewish state.'

But Israel's expansionist ambitions did not end after the state was established – and this ongoing quest for land is itself one of the defining features of settler colonialism. In June 1967, as tensions escalated between Israel and neighbouring Arab states, Israel launched a pre-emptive air strike on Egyptian troops mobilised on the border, almost instantly destroying ninety per cent of its air force. Within six days, Israel won an astounding ground victory against Egypt, Syria, Jordan and Iraq and swiftly moved to occupy the West Bank and Gaza, then held by Jordan and Egypt respectively, as well as the Syrian Golan Heights. Some 130,000 Syrians fled or were expelled, while the few thousand that remained refused to take Israeli citizenship when the Golan was unilaterally annexed in 1981. Meanwhile a new wave of around 300,000 Palestinian refugees were displaced following Israel's military occupation. Palestinian resistance turned to liberating these territories and making Israel retreat behind its pre-1967 borders. The PLO, set up in 1964, grew more prominent and took to launching guerrilla attacks from Jordan, where it was based, until it was expelled during the 1970s.

Geopolitics shifted too. America was the first to recognise the state of Israel in 1948, supported the nation through food aid and began to provide substantive military assistance with the presidency of Lyndon B. Johnson from 1963. But it was not in those early years the staunch ally it is today. That changed after the Six-Day War of 1967, when America clocked Israel's military might and wanted to muscle in. It was the Cold War period. Having battle-winning Israel as its client state in a region that was closely aligned with the Soviet Union held obvious appeal. That was the start of what is now, as the hackneyed phrase goes, an 'unshakeable alliance' of unqualified diplomatic cover and unparalleled military support for Israel. At around the same time the dynamics of Israel–Palestine post-1967 drew the attention of newly postcolonial Global South countries. They saw the occupying country, Israel, now backed by America and other Western powers, and they saw the occupied Palestinians, resisting oppression in what looked like familiar struggles against colonial rule.

This narrative took hold as Israel escalated its settlements project in the occupied West Bank, East Jerusalem and Gaza. The unstoppable impulse of settler colonialism – seize the land and settle it – went against international law and, as many Israeli liberals have consistently argued, against the interests of the nation itself. As Israeli authors Idith Zertal and Akiva Eldar set out in the book, *Lords of the Land: the War over Israel's Settlements in the Occupied Territories*, these settlements are Israel's largest enterprise, chewing up cash and siphoning resources away from citizens within the country's internationally recognised borders.

Jewish settlements, and their continuous expansion, also pose a formidable obstacle to creating any lasting peace in the region. Palestinian opposition to Israel's military occupation and to the settlements broke out spontaneously across the occupied territories in 1987, in what became known as the First Intifada, and lasted over five years. Also dubbed the Stone Intifada, this was a wave of protests, civil disobedience and clashes between heavily armed Israeli soldiers and Palestinian youth wielding stones, slingshots and Molotov cocktails. Images of these battles raced around the world, showing the Palestinian protesters as the David to Israel's Goliath. In 1988, the then defence minister Yitzhak Rabin told his forces to use 'force, might and beatings'. Tens of thousands of Palestinians sustained injuries including broken bones. Against the background of the uprising, Israel and the PLO, under the leadership of Yasser Arafat, secretly met in Oslo in 1993 to start a direct peace process. With the agreement of the Oslo Accords, there was hope a new milestone had been reached in Israeli–Palestinian relations. In reality, over the seven years before the peace talks broke down, Israeli settlement building accelerated so dramatically that the negotiations process itself came to be seen as a cover for Israeli expansionism. The Accords prohibited the establishment of new settlements or otherwise changing the status quo on the ground. But the settlements project steamed ahead anyway, largely through 'outposts' set up ostensibly without official government approval but which were later made legal. (In 2005 an Israeli government inquiry, the Sasson Report, found that government bodies had in fact secretly funnelled state funding and resources into those illegal outposts.) There are now over 750,000 Jewish Israelis living in 279 settlements across the occupied West Bank and East Jerusalem.

The Oslo negotiations ran aground following the assassination of Yitzhak Rabin, by then Israeli prime minister, in 1995 by a right wing Jewish extremist. Coming to power in 1996, Rabin's eventual successor, the hardliner Benjamin Netanyahu, had little interest in Oslo. With no clear goal, constantly missed deadlines and stalled negotiations on core issues such as borders, settlements and Jerusalem, Palestinians felt their path to statehood was being obstructed by the vicissitudes of internal Israeli politics and the whole effort ground to a halt. In 2000, Ariel Sharon, then the Israeli opposition leader, staged a provocative visit to the Temple Mount, home of the third holiest site in Islam, the Al-Aqsa Mosque compound. Riots broke out even as he was descending the Mount and the Second Intifada against Israeli occupation was launched. Peace talks were now off the table. This Palestinian Intifada saw a wave of suicide bomb attacks striking at Israeli civilians and killing over 1,000 from its outbreak in late 2000 until early February 2005. With no political settlement in sight, the situation on the ground kept getting worse. Israel's choking military occupation; the Israeli separation barrier erected from 2002 and cutting through Palestinian lands, neighbourhoods and streets; the fanatical and often violent Jewish settlers running riot across the West Bank and East Jerusalem; the Israeli army's endless midnight raids and arrests and house demolitions. And there was Gaza, blockaded since 2007 and then crushed in repeated wars. And all this before the catastrophe that began in October 2023. At the time of writing, bombs are still falling on the Strip, where over 30,000 people have been killed.

'A cop is a cop, anywhere'

As the Palestinian cause became a global movement, and increasingly articulate in its aims and tactics, a new academic field burgeoned – settler colonial studies. It gave solidarity movements a way to connect the dots between what was happening in Palestine and global structures of injustice. Of course, right from the start, Palestinians themselves, scholars, campaigners, lawyers and intellectuals recognised and documented the settler colonial characteristics in their own experiences of Israel and of Zionist settlement. But the new academic field gave their work wider reach and traction. Settler colonial studies was kick-started by the Australian historian Patrick Wolfe. His pivotal work came in the context of Australia's High Court decision in 1992 to nullify land laws that described the country as 'terra nullius' – in other words, land that belonged to no one prior to occupation. The Mabo decision, named after Eddie Mabo, the Indigenous Australian activist from the Torres Strait Islands who took the case to court, paved the way for the Native Title Act the following year, which created a framework for recognising the land rights of indigenous Aboriginal and Torres Strait Islander peoples. Wolfe sounded a note of caution over the difficulties in the path to restorative justice. The snags came down to the nature of settler colonialism, a twist on the regular variety. Colonialism was about extracting materials to take back to the mother country, the metropole, but settler colonialism sought to possess the land, oust the natives and create a new metropole. Settler colonialism is not primarily concerned with exploiting resources or labour, but with acquiring land while removing or neutralising indigenous populations. And it is ongoing, since the settlers come to stay: 'Invasion is a structure not an event', in Wolfe's words. Palestinians have been saying as much for decades.

This academic field gained traction precisely at the time that the Oslo negotiations collapsed. Their failure had exposed some fractures that the peace process itself had occluded. Oslo was premised on a two-sides narrative that located the primary source of conflict as Israel's 1967 occupation of Palestinian lands, to which the solution was Palestinian sovereignty over those lands in their own independent state alongside Israel. Yet the roots of the problem were not only in the Israeli occupation but went back to the very beginning of Zionist settlement. Whether living in the occupied territories, within Israel's borders or elsewhere as refugees, Palestinians were all impacted by Israel's creation and subsequent actions. Significantly, Wolfe saw Israel as a settler colony no different to the white European colonies of Australia, North America and New Zealand. He said Zionism was 'settler colonialism pure and simple'. As we shall see, it was *not* so simple. But all this has shaped the way Israel–Palestine is viewed beyond the pages of academic journals, bolstering solidarity with the Palestinian cause. It is a powerful framework, a way of seeing the world that lends itself to solidarity-building across different communities. The Palestinian cause has intersected with the movements of Native and First Nations peoples across settler colonial countries.

Global solidarity with Palestine has also grown through the Black Lives Matter (BLM) movement, with connections between the two struggles forged during the summer of 2014. In August that year, police in Ferguson, Missouri shot dead an unarmed Black teenager, Michael Brown, prompting protests that spread nationwide. Israel's assault on Gaza during that same summer led to joint rallies across US cities, where demonstrators chanted: 'From Ferguson to Palestine, occupation is a crime.' The affinities of experience gained international prominence following the murder in May 2020 in Minneapolis of African-American George Floyd when a white police officer knelt on his neck for over nine minutes, choking the life out of him as he lay in the street handcuffed and unarmed. At around the same time, our social media feeds were full of stories of Jewish settlers in occupied East Jerusalem, forcibly taking over Palestinian homes in the neighbourhood of Sheikh Jarrah, while Israeli politicians, police and the courts looked on. Mohammed el-Kurd, whose family was living in one of those homes and who became an icon of Palestinian resistance in the face of incremental, piece-by-piece displacement, said at the time: 'People who are able to watch what's going on in Sheikh Jarrah are able to see that a cop is a cop is a cop anywhere in the world.' BLM has built networks with Palestinian campaigners, foregrounding the parallels in state racism and asymmetric power. As the BLM account posted on Twitter/X in May 2021: 'Black Lives Matter stands in solidarity with Palestinians. We are a movement committed to ending settler colonialism in

all forms and will continue to advocate for Palestinian liberation. (always have. And always will be.) #freepalestine.'
A section of Israel's separation wall near Bethlehem now
features a graffiti mural of the late George Floyd on the
Palestinian side of the wall.

Over many years, there has been a continuum of
growing political understanding across global networks
and movements. It is exactly what a compassionate, values-
driven, internationalist left should look like. This same
left might say that tackling antisemitism has not been a
mobilising element within these solidarity networks quite
simply because there was no pressing need for it to be.
Many Jewish leftists would probably, until quite recently,
have said the same thing. But the truth about antisemitism
is that the antiracism of the left would never really be
complete so long as it didn't substantively include combatting anti-Jewish hatred. OK, you might say, but what
has this got to do with the growing global solidarity
around the Palestinian struggle? To reiterate: I am still not
leading you down a path that ends with the surprise declaration that Palestine solidarity equals antisemitism. No,
instead, the point of all this is to suggest that the rights-
and justice-driven support for Palestinian freedom has
not always reckoned with the full impact of European
colonialism and its ongoing reverberations in the Middle
East. This story so far has yet to take into account how
European powers saw Jewish people, first as not fitting
into Europe and then as 'fitting in' with their imperial
designs elsewhere.

Refugees of the refugees

Zionism would not exist and would certainly not have suc-
ceeded in its stated intent to establish a Jewish homeland were
it not for the rampant and deadly antisemitism across Europe
at the time of its conception and in the centuries before. It
was envisaged as a way out of the endless cycles of violence
in Europe which, by the late nineteenth century, had forced
Ashkenazi Jews to formulate an escape plan. This movement
was driven not by imperialism, but by desperation.

It wasn't an especially popular plan initially; many
European Jews had no interest in starting from scratch in
a distant land. One Jewish movement, the Bundists, advo-
cated a stay-and-fight approach to antisemitism: they saw
safety through a shared struggle with the working classes
and in establishing Jewish cultural autonomy. They did not,
in short, believe Jewish people required a separate nation
state. Among Jewish people living across Arab and Muslim
countries, there was little interest in Zionism, since there
was little of the virulent antisemitism that had propelled
the ideology into being. Jewish people had been an integral
part of the Middle East for centuries and, for the most part,
had no cause to worry about their status in those lands.
Indeed, Iraqi Jews were more drawn to Iraqi nationalism,
communism and socialism than they were to the Zionist
movement that struggled to gain traction among Jewish
communities of the Middle East.

The thing that eventually made Zionism appealing to
the masses wasn't that Ashkenazi Jews woke up one day

and fancied doing a bit of colonialism. It was that European antisemitism kept on escalating, while other escape routes were closing. The same Arthur Balfour, so keen to promise Jews a national home in 1917, had been an enthusiastic campaigner for the 1905 Aliens Act, designed to keep Jewish immigrants out of Britain. By the 1930s, Jews were escaping the Third Reich. Palestine was hardly the destination of choice for most Jews in dire straits. They looked to America or to Britain, but both countries had by then closed their doors to Jewish arrivals. And so, as a consequence of Zionist mobilising and borders closing around the globe, the Jewish population in Palestine swelled. After two-thirds of Europe's Jewish population was killed in the Holocaust, few countries were willing to welcome survivors in the numbers needed. As late as 1947, 250,000 Jews in Western Europe languished in Displaced Persons camps, with no home to return to. With almost every other alternative closed during that immediate postwar period, Palestine became the last safe haven.

We should be able to recognise this and still condemn the injustices perpetrated by the state of Israel. But all too often, as the British-Jewish philosopher Brian Klug writes, progressives put forward 'a discourse that folds Zionism completely – without remainder – into the history of European imperialism and colonialism, as if Zionism does not have its roots in the Jewish experience of centuries of exclusion and persecution in Europe.' In other words, it is as though Jewish communities running from the deadly violence of Europe into Mandate Palestine were doing so with the sole purpose of planting a flag and subjugating another people.

Palestinians are all too aware of the tragedies that propelled Jewish migration into the region. In 1999, the Palestinian intellectual Edward Said described Palestinians as 'victims of victims, the refugees of the refugees'. The Palestinian political philosopher Raef Zreik has elaborated on this duality: 'The Europeans see the back of the Jewish refugee fleeing for his life. The Palestinians see the face of the settler colonialist taking over his land.' The deadly violence perpetrated in Europe against Jews does not exonerate Israel for its violent treatment of Palestinians. It is no justification. It should not prompt a sort of what-can-you-do, shoulder-shrugging dismissal of the terrible and deadly injustices that Palestinians suffer to this day. But it does bring us into a wider understanding of the forces of racism and imperialism impacting this particular conflict. It allows us to see the Western considerations and influences at play. Writing about the hostilities in this region, professor of Hebrew and comparative literature and Middle East studies, Gil Hochberg, argues we should direct our attention to: 'the "third party" as I shall call it: the always absent-present Christian West, which intrudes, navigates, manipulates and manoeuvres the interactions between Jews and Muslims but itself remains a largely invisible force.' By this reading, it is not that we have been looking at the region through an occluding filter. It is that we weren't panning the telescope wide enough to take in that third party, the Christian West, which, as Hochberg writes, is often too big to be seen.

Britain's most fateful intrusion, the Balfour Declaration, was just the beginning in helping to create a 'side' of Jewish people with claims to this particular land. Herzl and others pitched a Jewish homeland in Palestine as 'a portion of a rampart of Europe against Asia, an outpost of civilisation, as opposed to barbarism.' Undoubtedly, he and other Zionists were imbued with the European colonial thinking of the time. That way of thinking about native populations, as 'backward' and irrelevant to imperial ambitions, is part of the reason why Zionism appealed historically – and to this day – to a European audience. For the architects of Zionism, the solution to Jews being 'othered' in Europe was not to reject this racialising process in its entirety. Instead, their solution was to project the 'othering' onto Palestinians while corralling Jews from Arab lands into the process of creating a Europe-oriented country in the Middle East. Yet the Balfour Declaration was premised on the idea that Jews, regardless of where they lived, really belonged 'over there'. Yair Wallach, senior reader in Israeli studies at the School of Oriental and African Studies, University of London, summarises how Western states approached the question of Zionism from the Declaration onwards as a 'national conflict between two non-European communities, one of them native to the land, and one of them re-established there'. In other words, the rationale for accepting Jews as indigenous to the Holy Land was, by default, acknowledgement by British political figures that they did not see Jews as European at all. Wallach argues that the Zionist movement, after the Balfour Declaration, was able to gain international support 'not because it was seen as a straight-forward European settler enterprise, but precisely because it was *not* seen as such.'

The Brits viewed Jewish communities as superior to the indigenous population in Palestine, but just as Semitic and Oriental as those Arab populations. The term 'Semitic', which started as a linguistic category for a family of languages including Arabic, Hebrew, Aramaic and Amharic, had by then evolved into an orientalist term to describe peoples of the Middle East. British political leaders at the time saw those Jews as European in outlook, but not European, exactly. They were uncategorisable, somewhere in between. (They were off-white.) But, as Wallach argues, their presumed likeness to the other Semites of the region explains why Palestinians and Jews were framed as comparable national groups. This was not, in other words, Britain viewing the Jewish population in Palestine purely as colonial. Rather, it was Britain putting Jewish people through its racial sorting and categorising system, which directly informed its approach to the region (and variations of which were applied in other parts of its empire). By panning out to take in that third party too big to be seen, the Christian West, we can see that the 'sides' in this conflict did not always exist. They were manufactured by the broader dynamics of racism and colonialism.

And such dynamics were not limited to appraisals of European Jews and their claims to Palestine. During the 1940s, parts of the Middle East and North Africa were trying to shake off the yoke of British and French colonialism, including the puppet regimes thoroughly managed by European states. In countries like Iraq, Egypt, Algeria, Tunisia and Morocco, all boasting thriving historical Jewish communities, Jewish people ended up caught in the middle. Colonial powers struggling to keep hold of their influence tried to extend patronage to Jews, as they were seen as European allies. Jewish communities in these countries became a useful foil, elevated by the European colonisers and placed in a different category precisely because they were seen as in-between – because this is how divide-and-rule is done. But at a time of nascent nationalisms this put Jewish communities in a tricky spot. We can see how this unfolded in Iraq, where right-wing forces tried to foment tensions by suggesting Jewish loyalties to colonial powers. This was one factor which, alongside a pro-Nazi coup attempted by intermittent Iraqi prime minister Rashid Ali al-Gaylani, set off the 1941 *Farhud* – a deadly riot in which violent mobs attacked Baghdadi Jews, killing over 100 people. It was a shocking interruption to an otherwise long and peaceful existence in Iraq.

Despite the *Farhud*, even in the 1940s, Iraqi Jews were largely supportive of the country's nationalist movement and did not see Zionism as relevant to them. But both Zionism and Iraqi nationalism were putting Jewish communities under the strain of having to prove their loyalties, constantly suspected of being potential fifth columnists. After 1948, the government imposed restrictions on travel overseas and halted the foreign trading licenses issued to Jewish banks, while also reducing the number of Jews employed within the army, the police and public services. These laws were intended to curb the activities of Zionism, which was declared illegal. But in practice, Jewish life in Iraq became more difficult. A fragile Iraqi government, threatened by the constant calls for democracy – and given a green light by the British – drew up a law that allowed Jewish people to leave for Israel. A subsequent law meant those Jews left as refugees, stripped of possessions and their Iraqi citizenship (this last revocation pained my Basra-born father for as long as he lived). Between 1950 and 1951, some ninety per cent of the Jewish community left. Initially there was not much enthusiasm to board the planes bound for Israel. But this changed dramatically after synagogues and other Jewish community buildings were bombed. Many Iraqi Jews – even some of those I have interviewed who now live in Israel – still wonder whether the bombings were actually carried out by the underground Zionist movement to hasten the emigration to Israel.

By 1951 the Jewish presence in Israel had almost doubled, and half of all new arrivals were from the Middle East. Once Zionism became a serious factor in Palestine, and especially after the 1948 war in which Arab nations fought alongside Palestinians, Jewish populations across the Middle East were caught in a pincer movement of competing nationalisms, Jewish and Arab, often while elevated in status by imperial powers in the region – variations on what had played out in Iraq. What had been unselfconscious hyphenated identities as Arab-Jews rapidly unravelled, uprooting Jewish communities that had lived as part of the

Arab world for millennia. Arriving in Israel, those Jews were labelled 'Mizrahi' or 'Eastern' (and also, pejoratively, 'Black') and were deemed inferior in a country that so desperately wanted to be European, despite being in the Middle East. No doubt Israel's Ashkenazi founders were reacting to being told in Europe, for centuries, that they were not and could never be European; that they were 'Oriental' and 'Asiatic' and immutably 'other'. Perhaps this racism turned towards Arab-Jews was itself an internalising of European racial thinking at that time. Or perhaps those Jews from the Middle East were too close, culturally, linguistically and in appearance, to the Palestinians and surrounding Arab nations, who now had to be cast as the 'enemy'. In any case, the consequences for Mizrahi Jews were derision and discrimination from the ruling Ashkenazi elite, while their Arabic culture and heritage, celebrated in their countries of origin and integral to Jewish history in the region, were mocked or diminished in Israel. In a self-fulfilling prophecy of the low expectations projected onto them, they became Israel's lower class, a disadvantaged majority. Regardless of origin or heritage, they also learned through this whitewashing and de-Arabising process to fit in with Israel's self-projection as European.

A single catastrophic history

What happens when we put all these different strands of history together? We start to see a tangle of communities in

Israel–Palestine, all caught in some way by European colonialism and its attendant prejudices. Writing in *The Arab and Jewish Questions*, Hakem Al-Rustom views the displacements of different peoples – Palestinians, European Jews and Arab-Jews – as products of 'European interests in the region and race politics in the colonies during the nineteenth century.' He urges us to consider 'the Holocaust, the Nakba and the question of the Arab-Jew as part of a single catastrophic European history' and to 'narrate against identity-based insular histories that promote hierarchical segregations of populations'. This is exactly the sort of approach that gets us to the joined-up antiracism that I want to believe in. Or, as Al-Rustom puts it, rather more eloquently: 'Accounting for their historical interconnectedness, where the history of one cannot possibly be narrated without the others, is a methodological intervention that rids us of the binary between populations and their histories.' Narrating these oppressions and displacements in tandem means we can see these histories as strands of the same rope, tightly braided together.

It is the sort of thinking that reconnects us to the intellectual left of the postwar period, the thinkers who urged against separating the Jewish experience of persecution from European racial colonialism. As Aimé Césaire, the Martinican politician and intellectual, wrote, Hitler 'applied to Europe colonialist procedures which, until then, had been reserved exclusively for the Arabs of Algeria, the "coolies" of India, the [n-word] of Africa.' Prior to their mass industrial extermination of six million Jews, Germany had already committed a genocide against modern-day Namibia's indigenous population, the Herero and Nama, between 1904 and 1907. They wanted control of the land, in South-West Africa, and those tribes refused to be colonised. Germany killed and tortured and used starvation, sexual violence and incarceration in concentration camps. By the end, tens of thousands of people were killed: some eighty per cent of the 100,000-strong Herero population and around 10,000 Nama people, half of the total tribe numbers at that time. It has been termed the first genocide of the twentieth century. It also gave Germany a template for the Holocaust, in which up to half a million Roma and Sinti people, long persecuted in Europe, were also murdered alongside six million Jews. If we allow ourselves to see the settlers of Israel as victims of the European racial hierarchies that subjugated and killed millions across Africa, Asia and the Middle East, we can see that the modern conflict between 'Jews and Arabs' is in no small part constructed by the same forces that perpetuated those catastrophes. In other words, we start to see that the 'baddie' here is not a 'side', but the overarching system that produced the 'sides'.

I think this is what Columbia professor Gil Hochberg was getting at in urging us to pan back and see the invisible third party in the Israel–Palestine conflict. In authoring this 'tragic drama', she writes, the Western intervention has helped create the impression of a historic enmity between two peoples, Muslims and Jews, rather than see the conflict as a product of 'the long European legacy of colonialism, racism, Islamophobia and antisemitism.' Of course, none of this is to remove the agency or motivations of the actual parties involved, historically or in the present day: the Zionist movement, the state of Israel and the Palestinian people. But as Hochberg puts it, the conflict was 'Europe's way to cleanse itself from its two modern historical crimes – antisemitism on the one hand and colonialism on the other – by transferring their weight onto its primary historical victims.' With this onus duly transferred onto Jewish people, a new role is activated for Europe, which gets simultaneously to turn Muslims into the new antisemites and to offer Jews protection from it.

Panning back to view a single catastrophic European history, as Hakem Al-Rustom suggests, allows us to imagine a decolonisation process that recognises the different displacements and persecutions that brought about the Israel–Palestine conflict in the first place. This is not to suggest we suddenly drop all those decades-long rigorous studies of the oppressor–oppressed asymmetries of settler colonialism here. It does not change the reality of violent dispossession experienced by Palestinians historically and into the present day. It does not alter the recognisably colonial mechanisms of this displacement. Nor should it allow unqualified support for a Jewish ethnonationalism that can only survive as a fortressed, heavily militarised state that constantly perpetuates crimes against another people. None of that is justifiable, sustainable or beneficial, not even to Jewish Israelis. But reckoning with Zionism as a national project of a persecuted people takes us to a different place in terms of thinking about what a just future for all the irreversibly bound peoples of the region might look like. As Zreik writes: 'For Europe, these two trends unfold on different geopolitical domains: nationalism in Europe and colonialism beyond the sea, in India, America, Australia and Africa. But for Zionism the site of the nation is the site of the colony itself. This makes the national intertwined with the colonial in such inseparability that it is almost impossible to disentangle them from each other.' We can strive to take what is colonial out of Israel–Palestine, for instance in pursuing equal rights, dismantling structures of Jewish privilege and building a framework of restorative justice. And yet whatever form of solution you support – whether two-state, one-state, binational or federation – one cannot take the Jewish national project, now a thriving country that gives meaning and identity to millions of people, out of the equation.

In a February 2024 piece entitled 'Restoring the Past Won't Liberate Palestine', the *New York Times* columnist Lydia Polgreen wrote about a tendency amid strands of the pro-Palestine left to take complex academic theories about decolonisation and turn them into crude and reductive slogans concerned with who is a native and who is a settler in the land between the Jordan River and the Mediterranean Sea. Polgreen explores how antipathy towards Israeli Jews might be facilitated by a frame of reference that sounds progressive – that colonised lands should return to their original indigenous inhabitants – but which, with the hark back to the past, can become a 'left-wing echo to the ancestral fantasies of the far right', as she puts it. The sort of originalism she describes can end up resembling the nativist, far-right fantasies of blood and soil, over who is entitled to live where.

In her piece, Polgreen interviews the Palestinian writer and activist Iyad el-Baghdadi, who tells her: 'I don't care if they're settlers or not. The solution is not to constantly try to moralise. The solution is to fix the power imbalance. The future needs to be rooted in the truth that all human beings are equal and that Jewish life is equivalent to Palestinian life and that we can together work on a future in which nobody is oppressed and we can address the inequities of the past.' In this region, decolonisation cannot involve drawing up rigid lists of the indigenous and the colonisers. It cannot mean that when hundreds of Israelis are mutilated and slaughtered in a gruesome Hamas attack, the response from some on the left is to intone that actually, *this* is what decolonisation looks like (as far too many did). Or to say, as some did, that 'settlers are not civilians', with the implication that those tragically killed within Israel's internationally recognised borders should not be there or are fair game. No self-professed leftist should feel comfortable in taking a break from universal values or a commitment to human rights when it comes to Israeli Jews. Nor should decolonisation demand the collapse of any people's nationhood. Left movements could be a lot clearer about that. Because if the left does not paint a just and inclusive vision for the future, we can be sure that the right wing will jump in with bad-faith, trauma-fuelling interpretations of intent, from the expulsion of generations of Israeli Jews to an open season for pogroms. As we know all too well, this fearmongering has already happened.

Our so-called shared heritage

In 2017, then US president Donald Trump pronounced: 'We are stopping cold the attacks on Judeo–Christian values … We're saying "Merry Christmas" again.' Trump's invocation of this shared heritage is something that has been happening across the right. In 2014 Britain's Nigel Farage, who has led various Eurosceptic, nativist right parties including the Brexit party and the UK Independence Party (UKIP), said: 'My country is a Judeo–Christian country. So we've got to actually start standing up for our values.' Steve Bannon, Trump's former chief strategist in the White House, and now a political strategist rallying the former president's MAGA faithful through his popular daily podcast, *The War Room*, frequently talks about how the 'Judeo–Christian West' is in crisis. Marine Le Pen is fond of the term too. But while this phrase has been picked up by the far right as a way of demonising Islam, politicians of all stripes regularly use 'Judeo–Christian' as a signifier of a united cultural front premised on shared, faith-based values and world-view. The former Labour prime minister Tony Blair talked about Judeo–Christian values. The former president of the European Union, Romano Prodi, spoke of 'Europe's Judeo–Christian roots and common cultural heritage.' The current French president Emmanuel Macron has described Europe as a civilisation with 'Judeo–Christian roots'. Even former German chancellors Helmut Kohl and Angela Merkel, both from the centre-right Christian Democratic Union party, have referred to the Judeo–Christian tradition as the foundational values system guiding the German state. Which is an extraordinary claim, when you think about it.

The Judeo-Christian heritage spoken about politically from the postwar period onwards is not actually a thing. It isn't real, religiously or philosophically or even culturally. In religious terms, it makes no sense at all. Go back to the start of the relationship between these faiths and the 'heritage' here was that Christians got super-uppity that Jews would not recognise Christ as the Saviour and so proceeded to demonise and persecute them for it. Perhaps the religious context for that hyphen is that Christians embrace the Old Testament (the Jewish Tanakh), but for Jews their scriptures are not a religious stepping stone. They are the final destination. If anything, the actual shared heritage, historically, is Judeo-Islamic. Judaism is not only about the Hebrew bible but about all the teachings, commentary and interpretation around it – and much of that took place in the Middle East, including the development of the Babylonian Talmud, a core text penned in what is now Iraq. And then there was the Judeo-Islamic heritage forged during Muslim rule across the Iberian Peninsula, then known as Al-Andalus. That period of interfaith advancement began at around 711, although its duration is contested, not least because the full seven hundred or so years of Islamic rule in Al-Andalus, before the Spanish Reconquista of 1492, were marred by episodic anti-Jewish violence. One such incident came in 1066, when a Muslim mob stormed the royal palace at Granada, killing a high-ranking Jewish political adviser and thousands of Jewish inhabitants of the city. But it does not minimise events to note that, relative to the experience under Christian rule at the same time, the Islamic era was one of tolerance and stability for Jews. They were able to thrive, both economically and culturally, and rise to positions of prominence. This period, most notably between the tenth and eleventh centuries, was one of such rich cultural collaboration that it is considered a Golden Age. Working together in Arabic, Jews and Muslims forged incredible advancements in science, literature, architecture, mathematics and music. The period produced still-lauded Jewish luminaries such as the philosopher and poet Solomon ibn Gabirol and the rabbi, poet and philosopher Yehudah Halevi. The celebrated philosopher Moses Maimonides is also a product of this age, although he was forced to flee Al-Andalus and eventually settled in Egypt after the religiously intolerant Almohad dynasty took power in 1147. However, the cultural and religious autonomy during this Golden Age of coexistence did mean that Al-Andalus became a centre of Talmudic thought and a region of key Jewish scholarship, which developed not least because of the symbiosis between Hebrew and Arabic. During this same time frame, European Christianity was circulating hate-filled conspiracies about Jewish people, while murdering Jews and Muslims alike in the Crusades.

The idea of a Judeo-Christian heritage really took hold in a secular, political context during the mid-twentieth century as US president Dwight Eisenhower announced in 1952 that the American form of government was based on Judeo-Christian moral values. Coming immediately after the Holocaust, this was a way of bringing Jewish immigrants into the American fold with a shared, inclusive identity. For Jewish communities who longed to be absorbed into American society, it held obvious appeal. As Gil Hochberg writes: 'Within this new fabricated Judeo-Christian alliance, Jews who had quite recently been considered loathed Semitic parasites could finally become *almost* Christian and *almost* white.' But while this label spread into Europe it also became an exercise in Western rebranding. The same supposedly 'civilised' countries that had either carried out or turned a blind eye to the Holocaust, while not providing refuge to Jews trying to flee the Nazis, were giving themselves a makeover – while also throwing Jews a bone. It really wasn't the Jewish side of the so-called Judeo-Christian heritage that needed the label, so much as the Christian Western side looking for a redemption story. Reflecting on this rebrand more generally, and its effect on Jewish people, Brian Klug explains: 'In the new Europe, the one that emerged from the Second World War, our role has been inverted: we have gone from being despised foil to admired model. What has not changed, however, is that collectively we – or a constructed identity that is called "Jewish" – perform a function for how Europe defines itself. *Plus ça change.* Old habits die hard.' As Klug also notes, this evolving dynamic has been terrible for Palestinians: hit once by the European racism that sent Jews to Palestine in pursuit of a homeland and then hit again by the postwar European revamp that made of Israel a staunch ally to be given impunity over its crimes against Palestinians.

The hyphenated heritage was, decades after the postwar period, drafted into an attack on those excluded minorities in a 'clash of civilizations' narrative that defined Islam as the biggest threat to Western development and values. The chief storytellers of this bigotry-infused theory were the American political scientist Samuel P. Huntington, who wrote a book on the subject, as well as US historians Daniel Pipes and Bernard Lewis. These figures hold Judeo-Christian values as a protective shield against a supposedly alien and violent Islam. And of course the story of a civilisational clash has been embraced by the far right because it offers up, on a plate with a cherry on top, a means of attacking and scapegoating Muslim communities. At this point, it is impossible to refrain from reminding these Islam-bashing authors, commentators and politicians which religion, historically, persecuted Jewish people across Europe. As Jill Jacobs, an American rabbi and director of T'ruah, a rabbinic human rights organisation, posted on Twitter/X years ago: '1) Much of "Judeo-Christian" tradition involves centuries of Christians trying to kill us. 2) If you mean "not Muslim" say it.' That second point, about excluding and then demonising Muslims, seems the main purpose of this hyphenated values system as it is used by the far right today.

Speaking in June 2014, before her far-right party revamped as Rassemblement (National Rally), Marine Le Pen said: 'I do not stop repeating it to French Jews … Not only is the National Front not your enemy, but it is without a doubt the best shield to protect you. It stands at your side for the defence of our freedoms of thought and of religion against the only real enemy, Islamist fundamentalism.' It is an extraordinary statement to make of a party with deep fascistic and antisemitic roots. Perhaps more surprising is that some Jewish group leaders have taken up their appointed role in the hyphenated heritage and sometimes in the Islamophobic manner in which it is used today. That this would hold any appeal at all speaks in part to the increase in antisemitic attacks across Europe and most particularly in France from the early 2000s.

The country, home to the world's third-largest Jewish community, was rocked in 2006 by the gruesome anti-semitic murder of Ilan Halimi, a twenty-three-year-old Parisian Jew who was kidnapped, tortured for three weeks and then finally doused in acid and dumped. The gang that abducted Halimi thought that Jews were 'loaded' and would pay a ransom. But the French police initially did not believe the attack was motivated by antisemitism. Meanwhile, protests against the Gaza war in 2014 turned violent, targeting a Jewish-owned business and synagogue and looting shops amid chants of 'Death to Jews' in the Parisian suburb of Sarcelles, home to a large Jewish community. That came two years after a French-born armed Islamist extremist attacked a Jewish day school in Toulouse, killing a young Jewish studies teacher as well as three children, including an eight-year-old girl. Then in 2015, a gunman pledging allegiance to Islamic State stormed a kosher supermarket in Paris, killing four people and taking several as hostages. The perpetrator told a journalist that he had shot dead those four men 'because they were Jews'. And in 2017, 65-year-old

Sarah Halimi, a retired doctor and teacher, was viciously beaten and thrown out of her Parisian balcony window, in a deadly attack, which French authorities initially did not recognise as antisemitic. Once again it is important to note that Jewish communal bodies have their own agency. In the midst of a trajectory of horrifying antisemitic hate crimes and murders, no group is being forced to take up positions hostile to Islam or to reproduce anti-Muslim stereotypes. Yet in 2015, Roger Cukierman, then president of the Representative Council of French Jewish Institutions (CRFI), said that, when it came to attacks against French Jews, then National Front leader Marine Le Pen was irreproachable, explaining: 'The National Front is a party for which I would never vote but it's a party which today doesn't commit violent acts. Let's be clear: all the violence is now committed by young Muslims.' In an interview with the Israeli *Haaretz* newspaper in 2018, the French progressive rabbi Delphine Horvilleur observed: 'Unfortunately, within the Jewish community, a minority has become so anti-Muslim that it considers creating alliances with French right-wing parties, including those that are classically antisemitic.' Mainstream French Jewish officials do, largely, rebuff the rebrand advances of far-right politicians. Nonetheless, we can once again see the far right strategically filling a political vacuum here. Because if left and antiracist movements do not talk about antisemitism when it appears in the form of violent attacks, if we do not offer a coherent analysis of it and stand as a place of refuge from it, then we can be sure that the far right will come along and fill the gap. We have seen one example in recent months when the chant heard at demonstrations, 'From the river to the sea, Palestine will be free', is picked up by right-wing politicians and interpreted in the worst faith, despite what protesters themselves say, as a call for the ethnic cleansing of Jews.

The 'villa in the jungle'

This bogus Judeo-Christian heritage really comes into its own in the context of Israel. It fits so neatly into the founding and continuing mythologies of the state. After all, from the start, the nation's founding fathers were keen on branding Israel as a European construct. And the idea throughout Israel's history has been to project it as a country of supposedly European values such as liberalism, freedom and democracy. Theodor Herzl, the Austro-Hungarian father of Zionism, thought the Jewish state in Palestine would be a European rampart against the uncivilised Middle East. Decades later, Ehud Barak, a former Israeli prime minister, would describe the country as a 'villa in the jungle'. And in 2017, speaking in Paris, then Israeli prime minister Benjamin Netanyahu said: 'We are part of the European culture. Europe ends in Israel. East of Israel, there is no more Europe.'

The war on terror, instigated by 9/11, turbo-charged the whole story about Israel being the West's first line of defence in the region. Asked in its immediate aftermath about the impact of 9/11 on US-Israel relations, the current Israeli prime minister Benjamin Netanyahu responded: 'It's very good', before adding: 'Well, not very good, but it will generate immediate sympathy.' It was, for Israel's hawkish leaders, a timely narrative match with the country's own experience of suicide bombs during the Palestinian Second Intifada erupting in late 2000. Those suicide attacks, striking randomly at cafés or clubs and killing schoolchildren on buses, were terrifying for Israelis and substantively changed the mood of the country, generating a besieged fearfulness and anger. But after 9/11, Israeli leaders exploited this public terror in drawing parallels. They claimed that, instead of dealing with Palestinian resistance to violent occupation and dispossession, Israel was battling a local franchise of the global war on terror. In other words, this conflict was not a political one over land, rights or freedom; it was the same clash of civilizations again, the same presumed attack on our way of life that we saw as those planes hijacked by al-Qaeda ripped through the Twin Towers. On the one-year anniversary of 9/11, the Israeli prime minister Ariel Sharon said: 'Israel, an embattled democracy, has been fighting terrorism for over 100 years. On this day, we stand together with the American people: we remember, grieve and will never forget.' Israeli leaders located their country as a frontline fighter in the war on terror while in the same moment, that war conflated Muslims with terror and stoked waves of anti-Muslim hatred across the West. Small wonder that the Islam-bashing far right began to champion Israel.

During the gruesome months following 7 October, when the Israeli state pounded, flattened and starved Gaza, those same justifications came to the fore. In November

2023, Israel's Diaspora Affairs minister Amichai Chikli declared that his country was on the 'front line in the battle for western civilisation'. This, he explained, was why Israel had to win the war. 'I think that it is absolutely crucial', he said, 'not just for the state of Israel, but also for western civilisation and European countries specifically that Hamas is totally defeated, morally, politically, territorially.' Around the same time, the Israeli prime minister affirmed this position in an interview with the American *Fox News* network. 'If we don't win now, then Europe is next, and you're next', he said. 'We have to win.'

There is a clear geopolitical strategy behind all this, a recognised advantage in binding the state of Israel, in its identity, outlook and values, to Europe and to the West. But in purely technical terms, the claim is plain weird considering the country's actual geographic location, not to mention that its majority population – factoring in both Mizrahi Jews and its Palestinian citizens – are Middle Eastern. This invention requires not just the erasure of Palestinians but also a whitewashing of Israel's population of Jews from Arab and Muslim lands. And yes, the myth itself does reflect a colonial mindset. But it's a mythology that has taken hold. While based in the region, I saw many a Western reporter or aid worker flummoxed by the reality that most of Israel's population do not look like the offspring of Paul Newman in the narrative-warping 1960s Hollywood epic *Exodus* and Barbara Streisand in, well, anything at all. Meanwhile, critics of Israel have also found it convenient to adopt the construct, leaning into it to make some pretty dumb comments about its Jewish population. As Lydia Polgreen observed in her *New York Times* column on left appraisals of Israel–Palestine, at one point during the war on Gaza there were claims going viral on social media about Israelis getting higher rates of skin cancer (not true), what with being pale-skinned and not indigenous to the region.

Now to be clear: Israel is an independent state in control of its own destiny. The nation's leaders are obviously not occupying and subjugating Palestinians because Western allies are asking them to. In fact the reverse is true: Israeli leaders know that Western buy-in and impunity is available in part through this constructed shared-heritage narrative; that's why they keep banging on about it. So why, then, is any of this important to a left-wing analysis of the region and to antiracism more widely? Why spend so much time on this Judeo-Christian heritage? If Israel sees itself as part of a Judeo-Christian alliance, if Western allies support and endorse that, if Jewish diasporic communal bodies embrace it, if predominantly European Jews living in the West have been willingly absorbed into a definition of whiteness that is premised on and upholds such values, why get so bothered by it? Why does it even matter? Coming from an Iraqi-Jewish family I admit I do feel personally affronted by the mythology of the Judeo-Christian heritage, precisely because it papers over a long, creative and meaningful Judeo-Islamic relationship. It is as though none of that ever happened. It is another erasure. It is also abhorrent to see this conjured-up shared heritage used to bash and scapegoat Muslim communities. And all this *does* matter when it comes to building universal antiracist movements. First off, to tackle conspiracy theories about Jewish people and the state of Israel, we must pan out wider to see the Western influence and the fictions that maintain it. Israel is certainly a core issue in US domestic politics, because of those perceived shared values and because of the impact of both Christian Zionist and Jewish pro-Israel lobbies. But if Israel were no longer considered (however misguidedly) a strategic asset in the region by Western governments, an appraisal based on a confluence of military, security and geopolitical goals, it would no longer be shielded as a client state. Seeing the Judeo-Christian invention for what it is offers our multi-layered, multiracial left a means of understanding how it has prised our minoritised experiences and our affinities apart. It could set the foundation for imagining a joint political framework. It is yet another way for us to shatter the 'sides' narrative imposed by European colonialism and racial thinking. In disputing and disrupting the so-called Judeo-Christian heritage, we can get past a sides-based narrative that was not of our making. We can build a collective narrative more rooted in the historical and geographic reality of all the people who live in the region.

In the second of the *Hunger Games* film series, there's a pivotal moment when the young female protagonist Katniss Everdeen is told by her mentor Haymitch to 'remember who the real enemy is'. If you have somehow skated past this series of young adult dystopian novels-turned-blockbuster-films, Everdeen inspires a revolution against totalitarian rule in a sort of futuristic America called Panem. Everdeen, played by Jennifer Lawrence in the films, has to fight-to-the-death two young adults plucked from each of the eleven other similarly impoverished districts of Panem in a macabre reality-TV show, used by the regime to impose its rule through fear. But at a crucial juncture, the words of her mentor echo in her mind and she turns her fire not on one of her reality show adversaries but on the regime itself. Her actions give a growing revolutionary movement the chance to stage a vital intervention, disrupt the games and boost the revolt. The blaring stereophonic message is, of course, that oppressive powers use divide-and-rule to keep us down and so we need to keep our shared goals in mind.

Do I watch too many mass-market films? Absolutely, yes. But consequently, this is what I think about when I try to imagine getting rid of all the fake divisions and invented labels plaguing the Israel–Palestine conflict, or about trying to fuse together our currently siloed understandings of oppression, Islamophobia, racism and antisemitism. We all need a Haymitch whispering in our ear, telling us to remember who the real enemy is – in this case, the origin stories behind all those intersecting racisms, the power too big to see, the force of European racial thinking and colonialism. Not so we can turn and shoot an arrow in its direction. But so that we can join together in a deep, powerful and liberating understanding of exactly what keeps us fearfully torn apart.

FOUR

The 'New' Antisemitism

On 10 November 1975, the United Nations General Assembly (UNGA) passed a vote in favour of a resolution that stated: 'Zionism is a form of racism and racial discrimination.' UNGA resolution 3379 was a declaration to eliminate all forms of racism, including apartheid and neo-colonialism. It passed overwhelmingly, with seventy-two votes in favour, thirty-five against and thirty-two abstaining. It would be revoked by a larger majority sixteen years later. The 1975 racism resolution, mobilised by the Soviet Union and backed by nations across the Middle East, Africa and Asia, came in part as a rebuttal to the US and the Western nations in its orbit. At this time the Soviet Union was pulling non-aligned countries onto its side of the Cold War and the vote was part of its efforts to shore up support across Arab nations, while inflicting a loss on the United States on the diplomatic stage. But it was also a clear response to Israel's military occupation of Palestinian territories in 1967, immediately dispossessing and crushing the inhabitants of Gaza, the West Bank and East Jerusalem.

It came at a time when many nations in the Global South had decolonised and gained a seat at the international table. On top of this, Palestinian intellectuals and scholars had been analysing the impact of Israel as settler colonialism premised on racism, a decades-old methodology demonstrating that the Palestinian experience paralleled that of other peoples under colonial rule. So when formerly colonised nations showed up at the UN General Assembly, many with friendly relations with Israel, they felt both minded and able to articulate a solidarity with the Palestinian people. The UNGA vote was a statement, a principle, a line in the sand against the subjugation of a people, a subjugation now assessed as a reprehensible anachronism.

But at the same time, the line wasn't without its problems. In the shadow of the Second World War, Israel's creation was still broadly viewed in the West as an appropriate and progressive response to European antisemitism, even if unjust to Palestinian people. To this day, many Jewish people, even those who would describe themselves as avowed anti-Zionists, appraise the ideology as both racist *and* a response to racism. As Brian Klug has argued: 'Like the Roman god Janus, [Zionism] has two faces that look in opposing directions at once; that is to say, it belongs to two opposite histories at one and the same time.' You could also argue that, while non-aligned nations at the UN were taking a principled stand against colonialism, Soviet anti-Zionism *was* a cover for antisemitism unambiguously directed at Jews living within the Soviet Union. Under Stalin, the religious and cultural practices of Judaism had been violently repressed and this atmosphere persisted during subsequent decades. The 1967 Six-Day War revived Soviet Jewish identity and prompted desires to emigrate to Israel, but Russia was refusing visa requests, claiming it a matter of national security. Jews who did ask to leave faced imprisonment, harassment and job losses. That spawned the Refusenik movement of Soviet Jews who generated a global campaign over the issue (although given the choice, many Soviet Jews favoured moving to the States). America was publicly pressuring Russia to back down and the whole debate was folded into the dynamics of the Cold War. But in any case, that statement at the UNGA, that overwhelming vote in favour of the declaration that 'Zionism is racism', set off a chain reaction, the consequences of which profoundly impact our discussions over antisemitism to this day.

For Israel it came as a shock to discover it was no longer viewed as a just cause on the international stage. The country was morphing in the world's eyes, from the plucky little homeland for long-persecuted, but now heroic and idealistic, Jewish people, as depicted in the Hollywood film *Exodus*, into a regional bully and oppressor. That was a gut-punch for the leaders of a nation not yet three decades into its existence and still trying to establish itself in the shadow of the postwar period. Israel was still reeling from the national disaster of the Yom Kippur War of 1973, in which the country suffered a surprise attack from a coalition of Arab armies led by Syria and Egypt, hoping to free the Palestinian land captured and occupied during the 1967 Six-Day War. The shock of the UNGA resolution precipitated a new way of thinking about the very nature of the Israel project and how to reconcile it with unexpectedly hostile global reactions. Up until that point, the state of Israel had held itself up as the solution to the problem of antisemitism in the European diaspora. The idea was that Israel, by virtue of its very existence, would eradicate antisemitism, turning Jews into regular people with a regular state. Theodor Herzl had said of the Zionist project for a Jewish state that 'if we only begin to carry out the plan, antisemitism would stop at once and for ever'. But this idea of Israel representing the end of antisemitism was about to change.

When condemnations of the occupation of Palestinian territories burst onto the international stage through that UNGA resolution, the official Israeli response was not to take a good hard look at the occupation itself, to understand why it had provoked anger. Although many prominent Israelis urged this sort of national self-reflection, imploring the government to immediately relinquish the Palestinian territories and foretelling disaster if Israel continued to occupy them, few of the decision-makers were willing to listen. Instead, officials, academics and think-tanks began to develop a new theory: that criticism of Israel was happening because antisemitism itself had changed. It had morphed from its diasporic state, from an attack on the individual Jew, into an attack on the collective Jew embodied in the state of Israel. As Dov Waxman, professor of Israel studies at the University of California, Los Angeles, explains: 'It shifted, so that rather than see Israel as a break from Jewish history, it became subject to Jewish history and subject to the antisemitism that Zionism holds is a constant theme of Jewish history.' This is the spark that set off the firestorms we've been seeing over antisemitism ever since: a narrative turn where criticisms of Israeli policy are reframed to constitute antisemitism. And it gave rise to a sort of mirroring of slogans. With condemnation of Israel recast as attacks on the collective Jew, responses to such attacks would adopt an opposite but equal position. If people were going to say that Zionism was racism, well then the response would be that anti-Zionism was racism. That it was antisemitism.

In his book *Whatever Happened to Antisemitism?*, Antony Lerman, former head of the Institute of Jewish Affairs at the World Jewish Congress, charts the evolution of this line of thought, from an organic development into an organised strategy. According to Lerman, the new definition was pioneered by Abba Eban, Israel's foreign minister for seven years from 1966, in an article for an American Jewish Congress magazine in 1973: 'Let there be no mistake', Eban wrote. 'The new left is the author and the progenitor of the new antisemitism. One of the chief tasks of any dialogue with the gentile world is to prove that the distinction between antisemitism and anti-Zionism is not a distinction at all. Anti-Zionism is merely the new antisemitism.' That UNGA resolution prompted a flurry of discussion over Eban's appraisal. 'Clearly by the mid-1980s', writes Lerman, 'much opinion among Jewish academics – historians, political scientists, philosophers, theologians and so on – as well as politicians, legal experts, Zionist officials and communal leaders, was moving firmly in the direction of equating anti-Zionism with antisemitism.'

A critical factor in shaping and promoting this 'new anti-semitism' narrative was the evolving relationship between the state of Israel and diasporic Jewish organisations. Prior to 1948, you could find plenty of disagreement over Zionism within Jewish groups globally. In both America and Britain, communal bodies worried that Israel would adversely affect Jewish communities, hindering efforts to integrate. But after the Holocaust and Israel's foundation, and after the 1967 Six-Day War, which many Jews across the West viewed as existential, communal organisations began to view the new state as a core part of Jewish identity. Organisations sprung up across the West with the purpose of cementing this relationship. Perhaps the best known, the American Israel Public Affairs Committee (AIPAC), was set up in 1963 (though it was originally established as the American Zionist Committee for Public Affairs a decade earlier) with the idea of creating bi-partisan support for the Jewish state. Emily Tamkin, author of *Bad Jews: A History of American Jewish Politics and Identities*, writes that the Six-Day War had a significant impact on American Jewry. She explains that it 'united and galvanized many of America's Jews', who worried that an Israeli defeat would mean the end of the Jewish state, whereby 'Jews would once again be crushed or killed or uprooted or some combination thereof'. Tamkin explains that the experience created for American Jews 'a new narrative about themselves', while the perception of Israeli heroism moved the country 'to the center of their Jewishness'. But the occupation of Palestinian lands post-1967 drove Israel rightwards. A more openly expansionist, nationalistic and Jewish-settlement-driven period set in, advanced by Menachem Begin, prime minister from 1977 to 1983 and founder of the right-wing Likud party. It meant that Jewish diaspora communities, who typically skew liberal and left on domestic issues, were now yoked to defending an Israel that was careering rightwards and turning increasingly illiberal.

The right wing in Israel duly put the 'new antisemitism' narrative to work. In 1982, Israel invaded neighbouring Lebanon with the stated aim of pushing the PLO, exiled to that country, back from the border. This military incursion inflicted mass destruction and loss of life: nearly 50,000 Lebanese and Palestinian civilians were killed or wounded, while the capital Beirut was bombarded. Up to 3,500 Palestinian refugees were killed in the Sabra and Shatila massacre by a right-wing Lebanese militia in coordination with the Israeli army, a horrific slaughter described by the UN as an act of genocide. Begin, the Israeli prime minister, responded to global outrage over the carnage in Lebanon by declaring it a 'blood libel' – invoking the Christian European conspiracies of Jewish people using the blood of children for ritual practices. So there it was: the claim of new antisemitism used to deflect justified criticism of Israeli aggressions in the region. But conversely, during periods of relative quiet, we were less likely to hear Israeli officials issue such proclamations. During the Oslo peace process years of 1993 to 2000, the country was not engaged in disproportionate military rampages of the sort that make the headlines and draw international criticism. On the global stage, at least, there was less condemnation of Israel while it was viewed as trying to make peace. So there was, correspondingly, little of the 'new' antisemitism to object to.

But with the collapse of the peace talks in 2000, the world's eyes were on Israel again. Everything deteriorated, with the outbreak of the Second Palestinian Intifada, including deadly suicide bombings in Israeli civilian areas and a crushing, disproportionate Israeli military response. There was the construction of the Israeli separation barrier that began in 2002 and put swaths of Palestinian land on the Israeli side – deemed illegal by the International Court of Justice in 2004, though Israel ignored that and carried on anyway. Israel went to war with Lebanon again in 2006. The illegal blockade of Gaza that began when Hamas won the Palestinian legislative election in 2006 became a complete siege by 2007, and was followed by wars on Gaza in 2008 and 2014. And all the while, the expansion of illegal Jewish settlements on Palestinian land and the demolitions of Palestinian homes continued apace.

The 3 Ds

In his 2012 essay, 'Interrogating "New Antisemitism"', Brian Klug writes that work developing the 'new antisemitism' definition flourished during the post-Oslo period and the Second Intifada. He cites a series of what he describes as 'books in this idiom', such as Phyllis Chesler's 2003 book, *The New Antisemitism: The Current Crisis and What We Must Do About It*, and Gabriel Schoenfeld's *The Return of Antisemitism*

(2004). The focus on a 'new' definition was also spurred by antisemitic attacks in European countries, which had spiked during the hostilities of the Second Intifada, especially with Israel's harsh military reoccupation of Palestinian cities across the West Bank in 2002. At a UN conference against racism in Durban in 2001, attempts had been made again to equate Zionism with racism. Jewish delegations to a parallel NGO conference in Durban were shocked to find distinctly 'old' antisemitism, in the form of leaflets about Jewish power, Holocaust minimisation and, according to several reports, one stand selling copies of *The Protocols of the Elders of Zion*.

Academics, think-tanks and specialist conferences, some of them Israeli-sponsored, began to focus on the new anti-semitism. In 2003, Natan Sharansky, then a minister without portfolio within right-wing hawk Ariel Sharon's govern-ment, founded a Global Forum against Antisemitism. A Ukraine-born Soviet dissident who was imprisoned by the KGB during the 1970s, Sharansky, along with his wife Avital, was one of the prominent figures of the Soviet Refusenik movement and had spent time gathering evidence of Russian antisemitism masquerading as anti-Zionism. The minister set out a '3D test' of the new antisemitism, first published in 2004. The Ds – delegitimisation, demonisation and double standards – are laid down as a guide to discern valid criticism of Israel from what could be considered antisemitism. The stated intention here – separating out justifiable criticism from anti-Jewish hatred – is not in itself a bad idea. More than that, it should ideally be an ingrained practice among the left. It would be strange if criticism of

Israel, the state with the largest population of Jewish people globally, was not occasionally a cover for individuals who harbour antisemitic feeling – especially considering that antisemitism is a conspiracy about power. It is also naive to think that anyone, however well-intentioned, is somehow immune from the antisemitism that, like other racism, is stitched into Western societies. But far from providing a useful tool, Sharansky's 3D test confused and blurred the distinctions. His tests are near-impossible not to fail.

The first D, for 'delegitimisation', is the idea that Israel's right to exist is denied in a way that does not apply to other nations. We have an immediate problem here because the 'right to exist' discussion is an odd one to be having of a country that does, in fact, exist and was internationally recognised as existing from 1948 onwards. But regardless, this first test still does not hold. After all, if Jewish people are theoretically denied the right to self-determination, what of the many other peoples – Basques, Catalans and Kurds among them – who are currently and practically refused this right? This test would only work if Jewish people were solely and exclusively considered somehow unsuited to or undeserving of nationhood. Meanwhile Jewish people themselves, from the early days of Zionism into the present day, have rejected the idea of Jewish self-determination. More than that, some early Zionists did not even believe in the idea of a Jewish nation state. For instance, the Ukraine-born intellectual Asher Hirsch Ginsberg, known by his Hebrew pen name Ahad Ha'am, is credited as the founder of Cultural Zionism, envisaging Jewish nationalism as a project for a spiritual home in Palestine. We cannot credibly be saying that all these Jewish people, historically and into the present day, are antisemitic, too.

The next D is for 'demonisation', which is what happens when Israel's actions are blown out of all reasonable proportion and grossly vilified. To me, this is the one that is worth being reflective about. Sometimes when I see pronouncements that Israel is uniquely evil, or singularly monstrous, or for example referred to as a plague or a cancer or Satan on earth (all on social media during the war on Gaza), I wonder what that is about, in a world where many nations, from Russia to the US, from China to Syria, behave intolerably. We *should* be asking why – leaving aside for a moment the Iranian state's labelling of the US and Israel as Great Satan and Little Satan, respectively – those particular words denoting disease or greatest evil are chosen to describe the state of Jewish people. And so we come to the third and final D, which is for 'double standards'. This is the idea that Israel is singled out and criticised over human rights abuses and war crimes in a way that does not happen to other nation states. But for a start, this isn't even true: many leftists, in the tradition of international socialism, do in fact also focus on Yemen, Syria, Sudan, Afghanistan, Iraq and other conflict zones or sites of injustice or persecution around the world. And meanwhile there are perfectly good reasons why Western leftists might focus on Israel, if that actually is the case.

It could be that the decades-long occupation and dispossession of Palestinian people is seen as an especially pressing, modern-day injustice. The colossal scale of death and destruction now wrought by Israel in Gaza certainly makes that clear. Or perhaps it is that the critics live in countries whose governments are supporting and enabling Israel, a Western ally, while there are no such alliances between the West and other rogue actors, such as Russia, or Syria, or Iran. It could also be the affinities of experience: that people living in the aftermath of colonialism and slavery recognise the contours of the injustices inflicted upon Palestinians. In January 2024, Reverend Cynthia Hale, the founder and senior pastor of the Ray of Hope Christian church in Decatur, Georgia, told the *New York Times*: 'We see them [Palestinians] as a part of us. They are oppressed people. We are oppressed people.' Or it could truly be a double standard, but a valid one. In an interview with the *London Review of Books* in March 2010, the British-Jewish historian Tony Judt, discussing the need to end the exceptionalism that Israel seemed to enjoy, made this observation: 'People will say… "What about Libya? Yemen? Burma? China? All of which are much worse." Fine. But… Israel describes itself as a democracy and so it should be compared with democracies, not dictatorships.' Now, it is true that when the democracies of America and Britain launched illegal invasions, in Iraq and Afghanistan in 2003 and 2001 respectively, it opened a crack in this argument which meant expansionist-Israel-defenders could ask: 'Why aren't those Western warmongers in the Hague?' But the left response to that is: 'They should be!' So again, no double standard from where I'm sitting. None of this is to say that criticism of Israel is *never* antisemitic – there are certainly times when it is manifested in a way that constitutes antisemitism. You will probably find occasional examples at mass demonstrations and copious instances on social media: claims that Israel or Zionists control the world or the media, or images of the Israeli prime minister eating a baby or depicted as a devil or bearing a Hitler moustache (again, all recent examples in the context of the Israeli war on Gaza). Still, it is not possible or even plausible to assert that a focus on Israel is *always* or even *mostly* antisemitism. Never mind any Ds, this does not pass the one big 'R' for 'rationality' test.

Sharansky's Ds were contested at the time, perhaps more widely and confidently than would be the case today. Writing for *The Guardian* in March 2004, Max Hastings, a former editor of the right-leaning *Telegraph* newspaper, noted that antisemitism was indeed rising in Europe – there had been attacks on Jewish property and synagogues across the continent. But he wrote: 'Attempts to equate anti-Zionism, or even criticism of Israeli policy, with antisemitism reflect a pitiful intellectual sloth.' Rather than defend this false equivalence, Hastings argued: 'The most important service the world's Jews can render to Israel today is to persuade its people that the only plausible result of their government's behaviour is a terrible loneliness in the world.' Yet throughout that decade, although there were still plenty of critics and challengers, this new definition had practically become an orthodoxy among Jewish bodies and representative groups and research institutes, both in Israel itself and globally. All the while, American Jewish groups such as AIPAC were becoming increasingly effective lobbyists for Israel, setting a muscular example for Jewish bodies around the Western world and, indeed, in Israel itself.

In early 2010, the Reut Institute, an Israeli think-tank, put out a paper entitled: *Building a Political Firewall Against Israel's Delegitimization*. The document was launched that year at the Herzliya conference, an influential annual policy and ideas exchange in Israel, attended by politicians, policy makers, academics and journalists. As you might guess, the document expanded on one of Sharansky's three Ds, setting out the problem of delegitimisation: 'Israel has been successfully branded by its adversaries as a violent country that violates international law and human rights.' This came after a decade characterised by Israel's harsh crackdown on the second Palestinian uprising, the separation wall deemed unlawful by the International Court of Justice, the siege of Gaza, the deadly and aggressive war in Lebanon and a deadly and aggressive war on Palestinians in Gaza, killing over a thousand people who, because of the Israeli blockade, could not escape the onslaught. It was a decade of settlements expansion and settler violence across occupied East Jerusalem and throughout the West Bank.

A description of Israel in this period as 'a violent country that violates international law and human rights' would hardly be wildly inaccurate. Yet rather than consider that Israel might have a reality-based problem, the Reut Institute packaged the whole thing as an adversarial branding problem. It could be fixed with better PR.

Among this institute's recommendations was that defending Israel's reputation should be a bottom-up, network-based approach rooted in the Jewish diaspora, to match the pro-Palestinian solidarity that was mobilising around the world across progressive coalitions and grass-roots groups. 'Because Israel's delegitimization is often a modern form of antisemitism', its report read, 'Jewish communities can and should be mobilised toward this cause as well.' What if diasporic Jewish communities or individuals did not see it as a form of antisemitism, or wish to be corralled to the cause in this way? It is not a question that the institute seems to have considered.

The Reut Institute did, albeit within the parameters of its own definitions of antisemitism, make some distinction between 'legitimate' criticism and outright delegitimisation. Its paper noted that too often, Israeli officials had blurred the two, thereby sending the legitimate critics into the arms of the outright haters (to paraphrase). But in the decade after its publication and as successive Israeli coalition governments under Benjamin Netanyahu lurched ever-rightwards, even those qualified caveats faded out of view. Several government departments were tasked with tackling the new antisemitism, but the most overt in this endeavour was the Ministry for Strategic Affairs. Set up in 2006 to tackle strategic threats, including Iran's nuclear programme, this ministry has periodically closed and reopened, but in 2015 it was given a funding boost and a remit to deal with the 'strategic threat' of delegitimisation. From then on, much of this ministry's efforts went into fighting the Palestinian boycott, divestment and sanctions (BDS) campaign.

Launched in 2005 by a coalition of some 170 Palestinian civil society groups, BDS draws inspiration from the international boycotts of South Africa during the apartheid era.

It targets organisations that through financial, academic or cultural relationships are seen as funding – even inadvertently – violations of Palestinian human rights. The Israeli government quickly moved to shut down this campaign, which was denounced as antisemitic. And supportive politicians and organisations followed suit, whether due to their own domestic strategies and calculations or simply toeing the same line. Speaking at the AIPAC annual conference in March 2018, the American Democrat Chuck Schumer, who since 2021 has been serving as the Senate Majority Leader, said of BDS: 'There's only one word for it: antisemitism!' He added, in a clunky tongue-twister: 'Let us delegitimise the delegitimisers by letting the world know when there is a double standard. Whether they know it or not, they are actively participating in an antisemitic movement.' Attempts to implement a US federal ban on the boycott movement have so far failed, although fresh efforts are ongoing and especially since 7 October. But thirty-five American states have so far passed anti-boycott legislation. What that means is that any person or business contracted by the state has to sign a pledge not to boycott Israel. If you wanted to boycott Israeli products, or if your company decided to divest from Jewish settlements, this could end up in cancelled jobs and contracts.

A 2021 documentary film on the subject, *Boycott*, follows several opponents of this legislation who argue that it goes against the US Constitution's first amendment on free speech. One of the film's protagonists, Alan Leveritt, publisher of the *Arkansas Times*, took the anti-boycott bill to court over this principle. In the film, he says: 'I have the right to boycott whoever I want to and the state has no business getting involved with that. Period. It is none of their business.' *Boycott* also interviews Rabbi Barry Block of Temple B'nai Israel, the largest synagogue in the state of Arkansas. He says that, while he could not be stronger in his opposition to boycotts of Israel, he was not consulted about the bill and was 'appalled that a newspaper would have to sign an oath that it would not participate in any kind of political action'. You don't have to agree with the BDS campaign to see that shutting it down is not something that any self-respecting democracy would do. And there is a further worry here: once you start silencing critics of Israel, you can copy-paste anti-boycott legislation onto other issues that you don't want people talking about. Several American states are using anti-BDS templates to try to shut down boycotts of energy companies and gun trade associations. Anti-BDS bills are gaining ground internationally. One version, banning any public institution in Britain such as universities or local councils from boycotting Israeli goods, is currently winding its way through Parliament. It has already been voted through several readings in the House of Commons and is set to be scrutinised in the House of Lords. Another similar law already passed in Germany in 2019. The German motion to outlaw BDS noted that the campaign was reminiscent of the Nazi-era boycott of Jewish businesses, which used slogans such as: 'Don't buy from Jews.' The country that invented those repulsive anti-Jewish laws now projected its past sins onto Palestinian campaigners simply trying to get Israel to conform to international law.

The chill factor

In 2016, the International Holocaust Remembrance Alliance (IHRA), an intergovernmental body of thirty-one states, adopted a working definition of antisemitism. This new code initially came about because Jewish people in European countries were victims of race-related violence, in which the attackers' declared motive was often opposition to Israel's policies. Increasingly, Israel's aggressions towards Palestinians, such as the bombardment of the Gaza Strip in 2014, would precipitate attacks on Jewish people in Paris, or London, or elsewhere in Europe. So the IHRA code was conceived in a context of monitoring antisemitic hate crime. It was 'written primarily to help data collectors, and was intended to take a temperature of antisemitism over time and across borders', says Kenneth Stern, one of the code's lead drafters and the director of the Bard Center for the Study of Hate at New York State's Bard College. IHRA's actual definition is just thirty-eight words: 'Antisemitism is a certain perception of Jews, which may be expressed as hatred toward Jews. Rhetorical and physical manifestations of antisemitism are directed toward Jewish or non-Jewish individuals and/or their property, toward Jewish community institutions and religious facilities.' That definition, though, is accompanied by eleven examples, some of which are practical, but many of which could be misused to prevent criticism of Israel. So, for instance, among the reasonable examples is this one: 'Making mendacious, dehumanising, demonising, or stereotypical allegations about Jews as such or the power of Jews as collective – such as, especially but not exclusively, the myth about a world Jewish conspiracy or of Jews controlling the media, economy, government or other societal institutions.' This fits a classic understanding of antisemitism. Another example is about denying the 'fact, scope, mechanisms ... or intentionality' of the Holocaust. Another points to criticism of Israel as antisemitic when it holds Jews collectively responsible for the actions of Israel. So far, so helpful. The trouble starts with the examples relating to Israel. One of these refers to 'Denying the Jewish people their right to self-determination, e.g. by claiming that the existence of a State of Israel is a racist endeavor.' Another example is 'Applying double standards by requiring of [Israel] a behaviour not expected or demanded of any other democratic nation.' As we already saw with Sharansky's three Ds, these are not necessarily or immediately examples of antisemitism. Concerned over freedom of speech in the context of discussions of Israel and Palestine, Britain's cross-party Home Affairs Committee sought clarification of the code and recommended adding some caveats to allow for criticism of the Israeli government. But the Conservative government ignored it and adopted the code in 2016.

Quickly termed 'IHRA', this definition was widely adopted by governments across Western countries. Its eventual adoption by the Labour party in 2018 came after a protracted media storm as part of the endless rows over its failures to tackle antisemitism under then leader Jeremy Corbyn. IHRA has since spread into British universities which, regardless of any concerns around free speech, were cornered by the government in 2020. As David Feldman, a professor of history and director of the Birkbeck Institute for the Study of Antisemitism, wrote on the subject: 'The vast majority of [university] vice-chancellors resisted until Gavin Williamson, when secretary of state for education, threatened punitive sanctions. With their arms twisted most have now fallen into line.' In 2019 the then US president Donald Trump signed an executive order to adopt the IHRA definition. The Biden administration continued to use it, although stopped short of endorsing this definition in its national strategy paper on antisemitism issued in 2023. Over forty countries have now adopted the IHRA definition.

But the code was not designed as a legal definition, much less a guide to hate speech. As Kenneth Stern has explained, IHRA 'was not drafted, and was never intended, as a tool to target or chill speech on a college campus'. But that is exactly how some groups have tried to apply it. In Feldman's view, various advocacy groups and individuals now abuse the IHRA working definition by 'frequently casting aside the important caveat that we must assess cases *taking into account the overall context"*. Once this happens the dangers inherent in the IHRA working definition are heightened: its examples are no longer invoked as guidelines which require careful assessment, but as so many boxes to be ticked.' This exact danger was predicted by Geoffrey Robertson KC in 2018, when he wrote of the IHRA code: 'It is likely in practice to chill free speech, by raising expectations of pro-Israeli groups that they can successfully object to legitimate criticism of Israel and correspondingly arouse fears in NGOs and student bodies that they will have events banned, or else will have to incur considerable expense to protect them by taking legal action.' The misuse of this definition has generated court cases, controversy and paperwork and so that in itself acted as a deterrent to free speech about Palestinian rights and Israeli violations. Soon after it was implemented in Britain, universities were urged to cancel Israeli Apartheid Week – a lecture series that raises awareness of Zionism and Palestinian liberation – on the basis of IHRA. Similarly, in 2019 the local authority for the London borough of Tower Hamlets cancelled a Ride for Palestine event, a cycling fundraiser to send sports equipment to children in the Gaza Strip.

In the UK, IHRA has impacted free speech at universities in a way that, by its very nature, is impossible to quantify. A 2023 report from the British Society for Middle Eastern Studies (BRISMES) and the European Legal Support Centre, which provides legal support for Palestinian rights activists, looked at forty cases that had been lodged across UK universities between 2017 and 2022 using the IHRA definition. It found that all but two ongoing cases had been rejected. In one of nine cases made against students, a university in June 2021 received an anonymous complaint of alleged antisemitism posted online. The student had shared an infographic about Israeli apartheid in the occupied West Bank, referring to it as 'ethnic cleansing' and as 'reminiscent of South African apartheid'. It took two months for the university to decide this did not in fact breach IHRA and to drop the investigation. The BRISMES report also refers to the case of an academic who teaches on the Middle East being investigated for six months in 2020 over social media posts. The complaints were made by a graduate who had not been taught by the academic in question and referred to over twenty posts or 'likes', criticising the ideology of Zionism, linking to pieces about the *Nakba* and commenting about allegations of antisemitism within the Labour party. Such investigations, even when the individuals concerned are cleared, exert an emotional toll and the frightening burden of seeking legal advice and dealing with what is effectively a trial. Most of these incidents in universities involved Palestinians and people of colour. The BRISMES report quotes a university staff member against whom one of the cases was made. 'When you are in the process, you don't understand how stressed you are', they said. 'My nerves made me hyper vigilant for two years. The impact of the cases, continual media coverage and constant communication to deal with the case resulted in chronic stress.' A student who had been caught up in a case described it: 'They make you waste time, sap your energy and make you exhausted. They make you not perform to your ability because you have other things to think about ...' Fearing the considerable time, expense and adverse publicity of potential cases, universities are pre-emptively cancelling Palestine-related events, not wanting to risk getting snared by the very broad IHRA criteria.

The effect of this has been devastating for Palestinians, now unable to describe their own experiences of the Israeli occupation without risking accusations of antisemitism. In the collection of essays *On Antisemitism: Solidarity and the Struggle for Justice in Palestine*, Dima Khalidi, the director of Palestine Legal, an American advocacy group, wrote that attempts to conflate criticism of Israel with antisemitism and support for terrorism was 'contributing to the atmosphere of fear, intimidation, and public condemnation that activists face, and sometimes resulting in serious consequences for activists who are exercising their First Amendment rights.' In late 2015 Palestine Legal published a report entitled *The Palestine Exception to Free Speech*. It showed that most of the cancellations or alterations of Palestinian-advocacy-related events in 2014 were due to spurious accusations of antisemitism. Most of the cases the organisation received in six months of 2015 and categorised as either threats to academic freedom, lawsuits, legal threats or criminal investigations were over false claims of antisemitism.

This Palestine exception grew so much worse during the months of Israeli bombardment and decimation of Gaza. In the UK, a Palestinian journalist told me that he writes every piece about the issue as though it is his last. 'You have to be careful, because it is of course justified not to want to offend people', he explains. 'But the lines are blurred, deliberately blurred and some of the accusations are baseless, so it ends up as a form of self-censorship because the parameters of what you can and can't say are so vague.' This journalist has family in Palestine and wants to accurately describe what they are dealing with. 'Each time I press "Send" I worry. I feel like it's only a matter of time that I'm going to get accused of antisemitism. It messes with my head.'

Julia Bacha, who made the film *Boycott* and is the creative director of Just Vision, a non-profit media and storytelling organisation that describes itself as filling a media gap in Israel–Palestine, says that during the endless months of the catastrophic war upon Gaza, she heard versions of that story every day, from Palestinians and others critical of Israel's actions, who either faced consequences for speaking out or worried that it could happen at any time. 'It was bad before this, but it is now at a level I have never experienced before', she says. 'People feel they will risk losing their jobs, their livelihoods. I've had so many conversations with doctors, filmmakers, school teachers, lawyers, journalists, all different professions, who think that because of something that they have already said, or because they participated in a protest or posted something on social media, that they are going to lose their jobs and not be able to get another one.'

Necessary and factual criticisms of Israel have resulted in dropped work contracts, cancelled speaking engagements and trashed reputations. Examples stretch across universities, book festivals, cultural events and even Hollywood. In November, the *Scream* actor Melissa Barrera was fired from the latest instalment of the franchise over social media posts about Israel committing a 'genocide' in Gaza and 'brutally killing innocent Palestinians, mothers and children, under the pretence of destroying Hamas.' The film production company confirmed the decision was due to interpretations of her posts as being antisemitic. That same month a resident doctor at the University of Ottawa was suspended for social media posts with the phrase 'From the river to the sea, Palestine will be free.' By early December 2023, the *Financial Times* was reporting that 'The backlash in the arts world has been particularly fierce for those advocating for the Palestinians – including Jewish artists critical of Israel's bombardment of Gaza – with exhibitions, awards ceremonies and talks cancelled.' It also cited the European Legal Support Center, which defends advocates of Palestinian rights in Europe and describes an 'explosion' of repressive incidents since 7 October, including cancellations, threats of legal action and loss of public funding. Palestine Legal described getting dozens of reports of firings, in 'an exponential increase like nothing we've seen before'. And in November, a group of UN special rapporteurs issued a statement about the silencing of expressions of solidarity with Palestinians amid claims of antisemitism and support for terrorism. 'This stifles free expression, including artistic expression, and creates an atmosphere of fear to participate in public life', it read.

Nowhere has this stifling of speech been more apparent than in Germany, which has a long history of shutting down the faintest hint of criticism of Israel. This is done, ostensibly, in the name of the country's Holocaust remembrance culture, Germany's *Staatsräson*, the 'reason of the state', which has been construed as blanket support for Israel. In October 2023, the Frankfurt Book Fair postponed an award ceremony for the Palestinian writer Adania Shibli, amid fears of how this would land in the context of the war on Gaza. That same month, the professional footballer Anwar El Ghazi was suspended from his German league club after posting 'From the river to the sea' on Instagram. Two public broadcasters terminated contracts with TV host Malcolm Ohanwe after he posted to X about the context of the violence of the 7 October attacks on Israel. The global media giant Axel Springer, which has support for Israel as company policy, fired a twenty-year-old apprentice who challenged this position and posted a YouTube video on his private channel questioning the viral and since disproven claim that forty babies were beheaded in the 7 October Hamas attacks. In November, the Jewish artist Candice Breitz's exhibition in Saarland, Germany was axed, after she had posted to social media condemning both the 'grotesque bombardment' of Gaza and the 'horrific carnage' of 7 October. Shortly after in Berlin, a DJ wearing a T-shirt with the word 'Palestine' in Arabic had his set cut. The list runs on and on.

When the effects are so punishing and destabilising, many feel they have no choice but to stay silent over Israel's war on Gaza. That's the chill factor. Whatever your view, whichever 'side' you fall on, such devastating censorship of free speech cannot possibly be justified. With exactly this in mind, back in 2021, hundreds of leading Jewish scholars and experts produced the Jerusalem Declaration on Antisemitism (JDA), a guide in part responding to the speech-curbing implementations of IHRA. As such, the JDA separates out the intentionally blurred lines between antisemitism and anti-Zionism, treating each as a separate category, giving instances of when criticism of Israel slips into antisemitism and when it clearly does not. This JDA definition sits alongside another issued in 2021 from the Nexus Task Force, a group of academic and policy experts, also intended to allow for debate on issues relating to Israel and Palestine without being subjected to reflexive accusations of antisemitism.

'When antisemitism is everywhere, it is nowhere'

In early 2022, the actor Emma Watson, best known for playing Hermione in the Harry Potter movies, posted a photograph of a pro-Palestinian protest on Instagram with the words: 'Solidarity is a Verb.' Soon after, the former Israeli ambassador to the UN, Danny Danon, posted on X, declaring that Watson was 'an antisemite'. His comments were ridiculous and widely condemned. As many pointed out at the time, it was exactly the type of baseless accusation that is routinely used to bludgeon criticism of Israel. But this sort of claim is driving a wedge between antiracism campaigners, who are pushed to pick a side. Does Emma Watson want to use her vast platform to speak out against antisemitism, or instead to express solidarity with Palestinians? That's the false binary imposed by those sledgehammer claims of antisemitism: that it is impossible to do both. And so, at a moment when antisemitism is intensifying, one of the effects of the groundless claims about it is to sever antisemitism from other racisms. If fighting antisemitism is seen as congruent with supporting an illiberal and racist state, how could it be viewed as part of an antiracist struggle? If anything, this partisan conflation of antisemitism with criticism of Israel pushes the perception that the opposite is true: that both of them are in fact attempts to silence condemnation of anti-Palestinian racism. This sets up a hierarchy, in the suggestion that the free speech rights of Palestinians are not significant or equally valid. And divisions deepen when claims of antisemitism become the focus of Western politicians who, all too often, do not seem overly concerned with, for instance, a sharp spike in Islamophobia in recent months. It can seem nigh impossible, in this context, to battle all racisms collectively.

During the months of Israel's war on Gaza, the claims of antisemitism were made so often and in so many directions, that it ended up dulling the capacity to take the issue seriously. Palestinian slogans such as 'Free Palestine' and 'From the river to the sea', which have for decades been chanted at marches, were deemed antisemitic. Entire marches in protest against the war were defined as hateful and antisemitic and in some countries shut down altogether. There were claims that calling for a ceasefire was antisemitic. Newspapers and broadcasters were tarred as antisemitic. The United Nations and aid agencies were antisemitic. A hearing in January 2024 about the Gaza war at the International Court of Justice, which found plausible grounds that Israel was perpetuating a genocide, was dismissed by an Israeli government spokesperson as 'an absurd blood libel', while senior Israeli ministers accused the court of antisemitic bias. The Swedish environmental campaigner Greta Thunberg and the Welsh singer Charlotte Church were decried as antisemitic. The accusation was even directed at the British-Jewish film-maker Jonathan Glazer. During an Oscar acceptance speech for the Holocaust film *The Zone of Interest*, Glazer said that his film's examination of where dehumanisation could lead was a message for the here and now. 'All our choices were made to reflect and confront us in the present. Not to say "Look what they did then" – rather, "Look what we do now"', he pointed out. 'Our film shows where dehumanisation leads at its worst. It shaped all of our past and present.' Glazer then added: 'Right now, we stand here as men who refute their Jewishness and the Holocaust being hijacked by an occupation which has led to conflict for so many innocent people. Whether the victims of 7 October in Israel or the ongoing attack on Gaza – all the victims of this dehumanisation, how do we resist?' A month earlier in February 2024 an Israeli filmmaker, Yuval Abraham, was pulled into a similar row when the documentary *No Other Land*, which he co-directed with the Palestinian Basel Adra, won a Berlin International Film Festival award and German officials described the prize ceremony as 'antisemitic'. Weaving the need to unconditionally defend Israel into its own redemption story over the Holocaust, Germany had completely gagged Palestinians and was now lecturing a Jewish-Israeli about antisemitism. Abraham told the *Guardian*: 'To stand on German soil as the son of Holocaust survivors and call for a ceasefire – and to then be labelled as antisemitic is not only outrageous, it is also literally putting Jewish lives in danger.' When the German officials had made their pronouncements over antisemitism, Abraham had received a storm of death threats, while a right-wing mob turned up at his Israeli family's home and forced them to leave. Where to even begin with the grotesque irony of all this?

Many supporters of the Palestinian cause are so accustomed to being unreasonably, viciously and sometimes career-endingly accused of antisemitism, that there is now the tendency to reflexively treat such claims with suspicion or derision. If you and your fellow campaigners are constantly being hit by the same hammer, then everyone looks like a nail. Julia Bacha at Just Vision tells me that this is one of her biggest fears. 'I worry that at some point people are going to be like, "Whatever, it doesn't matter"', she says. 'I find that really scary and it preoccupies me a lot, because the accusations over antisemitism are so pervasive right now and it has gone to such an extreme that I do think activists are beginning to say, "Well there is nothing you can do, they will call you antisemitic no matter what."' Appearing on *France 24* news channel in March 2024, the Egyptian-American comedian Bassem Youssef was asked how he felt about being accused of antisemitism and responded: 'It became an empty accusation. It doesn't mean anything anymore. There [was] a time when the accusation of antisemitism would freeze the blood in people's veins. Not anymore. Because now it has been overused.' Youssef mentioned that Jewish people had also been accused of antisemitism, including Jonathan Glazer, before adding: 'I think this accusation of "antisemite" has now become a comical accusation, it doesn't mean anything.' Which is exactly what Brian Klug warned about in January 2004 when he wrote: 'When antisemitism is everywhere, it is nowhere.' Prolific misuse of the term is stripping it of any meaning. And the current, authoritarian policing of free speech carried out in the name of Jewish minorities is a grim exploitation of Jewish fears in the name of right-wing politics. In telling people who are speaking out against the horrifying killing and maiming of Palestinians in Gaza that this constitutes antisemitism, politicians in the UK and elsewhere are setting up dangerous divides. And this is not just about the gulf between support for Israel at state level and the public outrage at street level. As the American philosopher Susan Neiman wrote in November 2023, on Germany's unconditional support for Israel and crackdown on criticism: 'The repetition of vapid formulas increases my growing fears of backlash. Germany's reflexive defences of Israel while refraining from criticism of its government or its occupation of Palestine can only lead to resentment.'

This terrible degradation of the term 'antisemitism' has come at exactly the moment when awareness of it is most needed. When antisemitism globally is surging. When Jewish people are frightened of publicly wearing a yarmulke or a Star of David necklace. When anger over Israel's war in Gaza is being viciously turned against Jewish people outside of Israel, who do not live or vote there and cannot be held responsible for its actions. In 2023 in the UK alone, of the 4,103 incidents recorded by the Community Security Trust (CST), a charity that monitors antisemitism, two-thirds took place after 7 October. Antisemitic abuse was yelled at random people on the streets, mostly from cars. For that time frame during 2023, the CST cites 151 incidents of assault, 151 instances of damage or vandalism and 228 threats. In some cases, bricks and bottles were thrown at people, while schools and synagogues received threats. In one instance in November, a man getting a haircut in a London barbershop overheard a conversation in which one customer said: 'Maybe Hitler was right, he knew what he knew', to which another replied: 'Definitely, that's why he left some of them, so we could see.' A spokesperson for the CST told me that the recorded incidents of verbal abuse could not be confused with straightforward criticism of Israel, even on the occasions when the slogans might match. So, for instance, chanting 'Free Palestine' at a demonstration is clearly about Israel. It is not the same as phoning a synagogue to deliver the message (as one London rabbi described to me) or shouting it arbitrarily at passers-by presumed to be Jewish.

Bad education

When I was based in Israel as a reporter in the mid-2000s, my parents would fly in to visit our extended family and we would not infrequently get into combustible rows about current affairs over Friday night dinners with our large and loud clan. During one of these, a relative turned to my father and told him that my views on Palestine were his fault, since he had taken his children out of Israel and taught us supposedly to 'hate' it. Without pause, my dad replied that when it came to the realities on the ground: 'I'm not teaching her, she is teaching me!' I still think of that evening and of my late father's supportive, generous spirit in that moment. But he was right about the first part: until I asked him about Israel–Palestine, we really didn't talk about it. And then we did, a lot, sharing articles and books and documentaries and, in his case, recollections and lived experiences.

But looking back, I think what the aggrieved relative at the Friday night dinner table was getting at was that I did not have what other Jewish people might describe as a Zionist education. Arriving in Britain at nursery school age, I had bypassed its delivery mechanisms in Israel and then dodged them again in the UK. Growing up in Britain, we were not raised within a Jewish community, which I later understood to be because both culturally and politically our Iraqi-heritage family was out of place. It had seemed odd to my parents that British Jews talked so much about Israel, supporting it and defending it, weaving it into their lives and prayers. We, the actual Israelis, were not doing that. What would be the point? There was no need to affirm our Jewish identities through Israel, because they were self-evident, like the sky being blue. Our Jewishness had already been set by way of Israel and Iraq. While my parents had lived in Iraq and subsequently during our time in Israel, Jewish communities were not fearful minorities but rather, albeit in different ways, confident and established.

When we could, we'd spend summer holidays in Israel, surrounded by a smiling, sprawling family, immersed in the country's landscapes, languages, smells and rhythms. In adulthood I understood, viscerally and emotionally, the incredible good fortune of having the freedom to visit a land that felt like home, to spend time amid loved ones and places that grounded and affirmed a sense of self. I began to imagine the deep and unshakeable pain for Palestinians, exiled, banished and denied the right to do so. But back then, back in Britain there was no Jewish school, no Jewish youth group or summer camp or even synagogue. We were secular but faithful observers of the High Holidays, during which my father relished reading Jewish religious texts in Iraqi Arabic. And so, in a quirk of timing and upbringing and heritage, I ended up with an identity that is unquestionably in part Israeli, but did not pass through Zionism.

This is not how it goes for many diaspora Jews. Yair Wallach from the University of London says: 'After the second world war, Jewish communities worldwide built Israel as a primary locus of identity, a supplement to congregational religious practices. And so Jews learned to think of Israel as a part of their identity. And it has been like that for over seventy-five years now.' Wallach points out that this is one of the success stories of Zionism, that for diaspora Jewry it morphed from ideology to identity. 'It becomes a form of diaspora nationalism with a sense of identity that is meaningful to those who don't live in Israel or have any plans to, whose support for Israel can mean very different things, but they have a sense of Jewish national identity and for them that is called "Zionism".'

All of which sounds familiar to a forty-something British-Jewish progressive I speak with, who attended a Jewish primary school and grew up within an observant, solidly pro-Israel family. 'As school we would celebrate Israel's independence day and there were Israeli flags everywhere', he says. 'The connection to Israel was inextricable and central to our identity. The narrative I was given about Israel was absolutely that there was nothing there before we came and we took over this land that was empty, that was ours anyway.'

It took university and encounters with other people with different experiences and viewpoints for this person to start questioning the story he grew up with.

Simone Zimmerman is one of the protagonists of the documentary film *Israelism*. Directed by Erin Axelman and Sam Eilertsen and released in early 2023, the film narrates the experiences of Jewish-Americans who grew up in proudly Zionist households only to discover that the stories they had been raised on had giant holes in them. Zimmerman is co-founder of IfNotNow, an American Jewish group campaigning, according to its website, to 'end US support for Israel's apartheid system and demand equality, justice and a thriving future for all Palestinians and Israelis.' But she grew up attending Jewish kindergarten and school and youth group and summer camp. She spent a week in Poland through a Jewish youth programme, visiting former concentration camps and reciting the Kaddish, the Jewish mourners' prayer, atop the ruins of a crematorium where Jews were killed, while wrapped in Israeli flags. 'The narrative of "From the ashes of the Holocaust to Israel" was the narrative of my upbringing', says Zimmerman, adding that anyone who grew up in a traditional mainstream American Jewish community would have these experiences. 'I was not exposed to a super, extra-nationalist Zionism', she explains. 'It was the normal amount, the same as what everyone was getting.'

Her wake-up call came in the aftermath of Israel's war in Gaza in 2008, while she was attending the University of California, Berkeley and there was a major debate on campus over passing a motion that the institution divest from companies profiting from Israel's war. 'I remember listening to hours and hours of Palestinian testimonies and thinking that there was no way these students could be lying about everything they were talking about', she recalls. 'They were students, just like me, at a campus.' At that time, Zimmerman was involved in campaigning against BDS motions such as the one her university's student senate had just passed and didn't understand why her own camp did not have better arguments to counter what she'd heard from the pro-Palestinian side on campus. 'I couldn't get anyone to engage with me in a real way', she says. 'The whole strategy was deflection and victimisation.' Zimmerman describes a realisation that all that time, she had been asked to check her liberalism at the door of her pro-Israelism, which itself set off the process of finding out more about what those pro-Palestinian students on campus had been talking about. She spent a summer meeting with one of the Palestinian families that had been evicted from their home in Sheikh Jarrah in occupied East Jerusalem. 'It flipped my world upside down and completely broke my heart', she says.

This trajectory is something that Kenneth Stern, at the Bard Center for the Study of Hate, has also spoken about, in relation to the debates around free speech at American universities. In an interview with the *New Yorker* in March 2024, he points out that some of the pro-Palestine protests taking place on campus are organised by and attended by Jewish students, young people who had been raised to care about Judaism and Israel, but who then turned up to university and 'heard about this thing called the occupation', he tells the magazine. 'And what do they feel? Betrayed. They feel they've been lied to. "Why was I not told about this?"' Young American Jews are now considerably less supportive of Israel than older cohorts, with record numbers joining the swelling ranks of anti-occupation movements such as IfNotNow and Jewish Voice for Peace and rallying to oppose Israel's war in Gaza. It is one of the reasons that Stern did not want the IHRA definition to become a bigot-detection code. As he says regarding Jewish students: 'Who am I to say that their view of what being Jewish means is something that I can define as antisemitic?' Jewish people voicing criticism of Israel are all too often attacked and disparaged and sometimes told that they are not even Jews. In mid-October 2023, the former American ambassador to Israel, David Friedman, posted a comment to X about a ceasefire protest organised by IfNotNow: 'Any American Jew attending this rally is not a Jew – yes I said it!' We are witnessing a willingness to cancel a person's Jewishness as a means of preserving a definition of antisemitism that simply refuses to fit reality.

It seems obvious to say, but Jewish identity is different for everyone. There is no one script or singular form (or secret global meeting where we all decide). Some Jews straightforwardly do not feel a relationship to Israel. The comedian and author of the bestseller book about antisemitism *Jews Don't Count*, David Baddiel, was one of them, having often spoken about not regarding Israel as a homeland and having an intellectual detachment from the country, albeit this appears to have changed for him after 7 October. For many Jewish people, the country does not factor in their lives in any way. Some, whether or not they choose to use this particular label, are essentially 'diasporists', focusing on a Jewish identity that exists independently of Israel, outside of and not defined by it. Others are anti-Zionists, rejecting both the state's foundational premises and its ongoing violence against the Palestinian people. Increasingly, young Jewish progressives point out that Zionism, in the way it operates against Palestinians in practice, demands an impossible abandonment of core values, an opting out of the belief that humans are equally deserving of freedom and justice and security. But meanwhile, writing in the *New Statesman* magazine, Yair Wallach observed that 7 October forced an unexpected reckoning for many Jewish leftists: 'Even if they reject Zionism as an ideology, they are still tied to Israeli society in a variety of ways – through familial and friendship ties, solidarity with activists there, or by the crisis in Palestine/Israel inevitably impacting their lives and dragging them into its orbit.' In other words, for some leftists who instinctively recoil at the idea of nationalisms and who will decry the horrors of Israel's horrendous onslaught in Gaza and apartheid rule over Palestinians, Jewish nationhood may nonetheless mean something. It may be an emotional connection to the idea of a Jewish collective or the cultural revival enabled by a Jewish nation. It may be to do with preservation: for instance, Israel is now home to the world's largest community of Iraqi Jews, who have against the odds held on to a distinct heritage. And meanwhile, one of the complications here is that Zionism as an ideology bound itself up with Jewish religious or spiritual attachment to the biblical land of Israel, to the extent that it has become impossible to separate one from the other. Across many conversations I have had with Jewish leftists firmly within Western Palestine solidarity camps, what keeps coming up, in one way or another, is that this movement has not really figured out a way to accommodate these attachments to Jewish nationhood. Instead, it is all interpreted as support for a violent, racist and expansionist ethno-state. Which *still* isn't antisemitism. But it does speak to the need to consider more inclusive strategies for wider coalition-building – because otherwise, the left, including the pro-Palestinian movement, is going to lose people who would otherwise be inside the tent.

Building the left's ethos

In his book, *Win Every Argument*, the journalist and broadcaster Mehdi Hasan spends a lot of time looking at the Greek philosopher Aristotle's three modes of persuasion, also known as the rhetorical triangle. Hasan has won plaudits and generated viral social media clips for his capacity to, well, win many arguments, whether that is on the BBC's flagship political programme *Question Time*, or interviewing politicians as the host of popular current affairs shows on Al Jazeera English or the American *MSNBC News*. Aristotle's idea, still relevant today, is that persuasiveness has three components: ethos, logos and pathos. The first is to do with credibility and expertise: it's the reason people find a speaker trustworthy. Logos is about presenting a rational argument, while pathos is the appeal to human emotion, because relatable feelings are persuasive and win people over.

But what stood out for me in Hasan's appraisal of this rhetorical device was his suggestion that winning arguments is in part about attacking the ethos, or credibility, of your opponent. 'Play the ball *and* the man', he writes, subverting the conventional wisdom that one should tackle the substance of an argument rather than the person making it. Hasan makes this point because credibility is such a key part of persuasion. You see people assert their own cred all the time: in debates, media interviews, presentations, work meetings, even at the staff coffee machine or at the pub. They might cite expertise, experience, research; they might tell a pithy story or anecdote that essentially functions as a delivery mechanism for displaying their own skills and accomplishments. Even the humblebrag is a way of showcasing some ethos. And so, if your professional arch nemesis in a televised debate is making unsubstantiated claims, Hasan suggests you might want to undermine their credibility: 'Calling your opponent's ethos into question is sometimes warranted.'

This is habitually the tactic used when it comes to dealing with bad-faith claims of antisemitism. Often, the progressive response is to do exactly what Hasan suggests: attack the credibility of the person making the accusation, by pointing to that person's hypocrisies, zeroing in on anything they've said or done that casts doubt on their current claims. It might be that the accuser has made antisemitic comments in the past, or that they overlook other forms of racism, such as Islamophobia, which punctures their antiracism credibility.

But while such attacks might be effective, what is all too often forgotten within the left is the need to also establish its own ethos upfront: its own credibility and trustworthiness when it comes to speaking about antisemitism. Emily Hilton, the UK director of Diaspora Alliance, which works to tackle antisemitism and deal with instrumentalised accusations of it, says: 'The first time you are speaking about antisemitism shouldn't be when you have been accused of antisemitism. We have to care about the issue and be speaking about the issue before that happens.' She is not suggesting that every person randomly accused of antisemitism for, say, turning up at a march to stop the slaughter in Gaza, should produce receipts to demonstrate their longstanding work to combat anti-Jewish hatred. Instead, the idea is to be considering it at a movement-building level. As Hilton points out, the right wing has its strategies for tackling antisemitism, whether that is more policing of speech, or support for Israel or implementing codes such as IHRA. And it is not enough for us to simply reject such strategies. 'What is the progressive answer?' she asks. 'This is a moment for us to really think about how we address anti-semitism, by thinking of it as a progressive cause and part of the progressive political platform.'

In the book *On Antisemitism: Solidarity and the Struggle for Justice in Palestine*, Rabbi Alissa Wise discusses building rela-tionships with interfaith partners, who countless times have asked: 'How do I deflect accusations that I am antisemitic?' To which she replies: 'Well, are you?' As she writes: 'While there is nothing inherently antisemitic in critiquing Israel, that does not mean one isn't also harbouring antisemitic sentiments toward Jews or isn't behaving in antisemitic ways.' Operating in a political climate where antisemitism is so often instrumentalised should not mean the left skips past these antiracism audits or ducks out of asking these questions. These should be a part of the left's ongoing anti-racism work – not just, as Hilton says, something that only comes up when deflecting accusations.

One of the episodes that has lodged in my mind from the Corbyn years is the image of the bulging-tentacled alien creature suffocating the face of the Statue of Liberty. In 2018, *The Times* newspaper ran the story of how a Corbyn supporter had posted to social media this image – the gro-tesque alien creature bearing a purple Star of David on its back. The post carried the comment: 'The most accurate photo I've seen all year.' The alien creature looks like it was lifted from, or inspired by, the film *Alien*, which is about, well, parasitical alien creatures that attack and kill humans and then take over their bodies. The person who posted this particular image, with the purple Star of David, had copied it from a far-right US website, where it was unequivocally captioned: 'Bloodsucking alien parasites killing America.' As *The Times* reported, a complaint about this post wound its way to Labour's Governance and Legal Unit, which is responsible for dealing with such matters, but the director of the unit did not initially take action. They thought the post might be 'anti-Israel, not anti-Jewish'. Although the bloodsucking alien poster was subsequently suspended, it seemed that the person in charge of deciding whether this repulsive image lifted from a hate-spewing far-right website was antisemitic initially wondered if, perhaps, it was just a reasonable comment on the Israeli occupation. That's the reason I remember this story: not because I think this post to social media has more salience than other instances of antisemitism, or other instances of racism for that matter. What I recall is how this case cemented my realisation that leftists who think they understand antisemitism may not, in fact, understand it at all.

That's the danger of not running that antisemitism audit. That is the risk in assuming, because of the frequency and ferocity of those unreasonable accusations, that all antisemitism claims are smears. Antisemitism has survived for nearly two thousand years by being a covert operator, a sneaky shapeshifter, slipping into social and political circles like a deadly clear gas. And at some point, a particular criticism of Israel may well crash into a manifestation of antisemitism so noxious that it should carry a health warning (I think about readers of *The Times* coming across that hideous alien image over their morning toast). What the bloodsucking alien and other Israel-related instances of antisemitism make clear to me is that, yet again, we ought to be approaching this subject in spite of – and not just in reaction to – the way it has been mobilised politically by the right. Antisemitism is not surfacing because of ever-growing and justified criticisms of Israel. It is coming up because those critical voices are operating within societies embedded in centuries-old patterns and structures of antisemitism. The moment we properly and meaningfully engage with this reality, we can work to grow an understanding of those antisemitic structures, making that an essential plank of our antiracism. At this precise moment when vigilance over antisemitism is needed, when it is spiralling globally and may well get worse, leftist movements of all stripes should be much better equipped to truly understand this form of racism – and to counter it.

FIVE

With Friends Like These

In mid-November 2023, tens of thousands of Americans took part in the March for Israel in Washington DC. In the midst of the onslaught on Gaza, demonstrators rallied to support Israel, to demand the release of its hostages captured by Hamas on 7 October and to stand against anti-semitism. Among those attending were the actors Debra Messing and Michael Rapaport and representatives from both sides of the US Congress. But there was one man, issued a last-minute invitation to speak at the event, whose presence set off alarm bells: John Hagee. He's a televangelist pastor from Texas and head of the powerful lobby group Christians United for Israel (CUFI), which has over ten million members. Hagee, CUFI and other evangelists end-lessly claim to love Israel. But the kind of love they talk about does not bode well for Jews.

Although he has since claimed these comments to have been misrepresented, Hagee, a megachurch evangelist, said in a sermon in 1999 that was unearthed in the mid-2000s that God 'allowed' the Holocaust to happen, with Hitler as a 'hunter' sent because the Lord's own priority 'for the Jewish people is to get them to come back to the land of Israel.' He has also said that Jewish people brought persecution upon themselves because of their 'disobedience and rebellion' from God. This pastor has made odious comments about Muslims, the LGBTQ community and Catholics – although he apologised for the latter in 2008. He also claimed that women exist only to be mothers. Matthew Duss, the executive vice-president for American foreign policy think-tank, the Center for International Policy (CIP), told me that such extreme views, as espoused by some evangelist leaders, represent a 'dangerous force in the world'.

Some American Jewish organisations pushed back at the pastor's Washington rally invitation. Hadar Susskind, president of Americans for Peace Now, which endorsed the march, said: 'I am horrified that he was given this platform. His history of hateful comments should disqualify him from decent company, much less from speaking on stage. He is not welcome and should not speak.' Another liberal pro-Israel advocacy group, J Street, concurred, with its X statement that: 'A dangerous bigot like Hagee should not be welcomed anywhere in our community. Period.' But welcomed he was. And speak he did – though no rabbi was invited to do so. As Emily Tamkin, author of *Bad Jews*, wrote in a piece for the American news channel *MSNBC*, the presence of John Hagee at the Washington rally demonstrated the problem: 'One can support Israel and also spread antisemitism.' One can indeed. And worse, in doing so, one is less likely to be called out for antisemitism. The whole sorry incident demonstrates a dismal aspect of our current politics: whether or not antisemitism is challenged depends on who is doing the antisemitism and to which political camp they belong.

The truth about antisemitism is that there is a double standard in the way that accusations of it are made. If spurious claims of antisemitism are undermining the fight against it, as we saw in the last chapter, then so, too, is the grim fact that this fight is steeped in hypocrisy. Screaming examples of anti-Jewish hatred get waved along, as long as the bigotry is coming from die-hard, right-or-wrong supporters of Israel. What this means is that a sanitising transference is taking place. Shifting the spotlight onto the left, creating the impression that it is the most significant source of antisemitism, has the effect of giving a hall pass to the dangerous antisemitism of the right. And with the focus on the political left, the Israeli government and its most hardline supporters can freely form alliances with far-right groups that might otherwise be deemed beyond the pale. Backing for a right-wing, expansionist Israel seems to be given primacy over everything else. Including antisemitism.

The effect of this is devastating and not just for free speech and the right to criticise Israel, although that is bad enough. When our political conversation is mostly about the supposed antisemitism of pro-Palestine marches and college students, we are not talking about the dangerous and violent forms of antisemitism in our societies. Meanwhile, this whole dynamic – fixate on the left, absolve the right – cements the idea that complaints of antisemitism are politically motivated and thereby not real. The double standard makes it harder to tackle antisemitism wherever it shows up, including within the left. It also chews up energy and bandwidth in the business of refuting those spurious claims made against the pro-Palestine left, claims that can have serious material consequences. So the dynamic turns into a godawful political spat, with claim and counterclaim, accusation and denial. It's an ugly bunfight. The antisemitism itself, whatever its source, remains unaddressed, causing chaos and spreading fear. It exists only to be instrumentalised. It falls between the cracks of the fight. And Jewish people who are targeted by it, far away from the political wrangling and the social media fights, are the ones whose physical safety is on the line.

It was the best of times, it was the End of Times

'I know you all think I'm crazy', says Yali Hashash, an Israeli academic in Jewish studies at the University of Michigan, in an online webinar organised by an American rabbinical organisation for human rights. 'Just Google it', she says. 'You will be amazed by what you find.' She is right, the whole thing does sound crazy. Hashash is talking about Christian Zionism, a global movement with a giant impact on both Israeli and American politics. Speaking about her own country, Hashash tells the online seminar: 'We've been evangelised. We've been conquered by Christ. We need help.'

What on earth is she talking about? OK. Christian Zionists span several denominations but, in the main, they are socially conservative evangelicals who claim a biblical duty to defend Israel, no matter what. They've been around for a while – some say Christian Zionism predates Jewish Zionism – but have gained considerable political influence in recent decades. The biblical duty bit is based on two beliefs. The first is a literal interpretation of an Old Testament passage from Genesis, one you'll hear adherents constantly quoting as a sort of prophetic support for Israel. In 2002, Christian evangelical Mike Pence, who years later became vice-president of America under Donald Trump, gave a version of it: 'God promises Abraham, "Those who bless you, I will bless, and those who curse you, I will curse."' According to the Hebrew bible, the promise made to the prophet Abraham is that he would father a great nation who would be assured the biblical land of Canaan. For evangelicals, there's a double bonus to their interpretation of the blessing: back Israel and you get divine credit; attack those who you think are attacking Israel and you also get the godly gold stars. This is how Christian Zionism brings anti-Arab bigotries and Islamophobia into the mix. They are viewed as the so-called 'enemies' of Israel who must be 'cursed' if one is to adhere to the biblical-blessings-upon-Israel belief. John Hagee is typical of the firebrand leaders of Christian Zionism, in declaring: 'Islam not only condones violence, it commands it.' Naked anti-Muslim hatred is recruited into a self-declared, biblically ordained so-called love for Israel. Or perhaps it is the other way around. Or both, in a grim feedback loop.

The second belief at the heart of Christian Zionism is related to the evangelical 'End Times' prophecy. This is the conviction that, for the longed-for second coming of Christ to happen, all Jewish people need to be in Israel. As Tristan Sturm, who researches this movement at Queen's University Belfast, puts it, what this means is that Jewish people must be 'unwaveringly supported as God's army, soldiering towards the apocalypse'. And let's say that Christ does in fact turn up, as prophesied, what then? Hallelujah, we're in the End Times! This means that everything kicks off in the battle of Armageddon, slated to happen at a real place, Har Megiddo in central Israel. Cue seven years of terrible war and bloodshed, after which Christ wins and everyone lives in peace for a thousand years. Sorry, not actually everyone though. All that winning and peace is for Christians only. Of the Muslims and the Jews who survive Armageddon, the ones who don't convert will die. So, like I said, not exactly a movement born out of love for Jewish people. Also, the idea of gathering Jews into Israel so that they can all be converted in an evangelical Christian fantasy-prophecy-whatever does not fit any understanding of the meaning of Zionism. No definition of 'homeland for Jews' has that as its end goal.

'It is straightforwardly an instrumentalization of Jews. They are a tool. Supporting Israel is a tool to bring about the End Times and the rapture into paradise', says Matthew Duss. He was raised attending an American evangelical church, just not the fire-breathing kind. Every religion has its unrepresentative fanatics and Duss considers Christian

Zionism to be 'a distortion' of his faith. Since the assumption that all Jews should live in Israel and support it is essentially antisemitic and since evangelism delivers this belief in a creepily philosemitic wrapping, Ben Lorber and Aiden Orly, analysts at the American social justice think-tank Political Research Associates, have described Christian Zionism as 'one of the largest antisemitic movements in the world today'. The significance of this cannot be overstated. It throws some recently dominant media narratives about allegations of antisemitism among, say, Harvard University students, into sharp relief. And the question has to be, why isn't *this* dominating the news instead?

Surveys place the number of evangelicals in the US at between 80 and 100 million, while globally that figure is around 600 million, with large populations across Africa, Latin America and Asia, in countries including Nigeria, Kenya, Brazil, Guatemala, Indonesia and the Philippines. There are more progressive forms of evangelism, of course, especially among younger generations. But the American-led conservative strain, which among other things is opposed to abortion and LGBTQ rights, is currently a majority and a considerable voting bloc in US politics. Most evangelicals are also Christian Zionists, although again, things are shifting away from this among younger believers. But a 2017 poll by the Christian research firm Lifeway shows that eighty per cent of US evangelicals think that the creation of Israel in 1948 was the fulfilment of a biblical prophecy, signifying that the second coming was actually approaching.

Since End Times evangelism can be – how to put it? – screamingly off-putting to Jewish people, pastor Hagee has claimed that support for Israel has nothing to do with all the Armageddon stuff. However, a sermon delivered one week after the Hamas attack of 7 October seemingly made the connection clear. He gave a timeline of the apocalypse, the resurrection of Jesus and the great wars that would restore the earth (there is a schedule of events; God does not skimp on the details). 'Israel is God's prophetic clock', Hagee said during his sermon, televised from Cornerstone Church which he founded in San Antonio. 'When the Jewish people are in Israel, the clock is running. When the Jewish people are out of Israel, the clock stops.' Christian Zionists are weirdly energised by the 2023 Israel–Gaza war. To them, it's one big pre-game to the End Times, cause for jubilation that the apocalypse must be drawing ever closer.

And yet despite these stomach-turning views about Jewish people as collateral for messianic prophecy, many Israeli organisations and officials, including prime minister Benjamin Netanyahu, consider Christian Zionists to be the country's best defenders. In fact, Netanyahu cannot stop gushing about them. In 2017 he sent a recorded address to CUFI's annual conference in Washington: 'The supporters of Israel, the many thousands who are in that hall and the millions, the many millions in the United States and elsewhere, Christian friends of Israel, you are always there for us. We have no better friends on earth than you.'

In 2019 Netanyahu was on a state visit to Brazil, where he praised the authoritarian then president Jair Bolsonaro and said: 'We have no better friends in the world than the evangelical community.' A lot of best friends, it seems. And no wonder. For the Israeli right, Christian Zionists are both considerably larger in number and politically more important than the Jewish diaspora, even in America. Listen to former Israeli ambassador to the US and current minster for strategic affairs, Ron Dermer, who in 2021 told an Israeli journalist that evangelicals were 'the backbone of Israel's support in the United States', adding: 'Look at the numbers. About twenty-five per cent, some people think more, of Americans are evangelical Christians. Less than two per cent of Americans are Jews.' At a time when growing numbers of Jewish-Americans are critical of Israel's occupation and military aggressions, the Christian Zionists are clearly more valuable.

Many Jewish pro-Israel organisations have played along with all this. Christian Zionist movements are minimised at best and embraced at worst. That's how you end up with John Hagee speaking at a pro-Israel rally. It's also why he was keynote speaker at the AIPAC annual conference in Washington back in 2007. It is why the Zionist Organization of America's president Morton Klein put out a statement in 2008 praising Hagee. Plus, Hagee is in the 2022 top ten Christian allies list compiled by political lobbyists, the Israel Allies Foundation. You get the picture.

Trying to explain why Jewish Israelis don't seem alarmed by the evangelicals, Yali Hashash tells the online webinar: 'They are able to numb us, because they use the idea of the love of Israel.' When I speak with journalist Sarah Posner, who has authored two books on the American Christian right, she says pretty much the same thing. 'You have a swell of Jewish leaders and organisations that say Israel needs all the friends it can get and who cares about this fantasy [the prophecy]? This thing is never going to happen.' Posner covered the AIPAC conference the year Hagee spoke and recalls interviewing a Jewish attendee about the pastor's theology. 'She just said, "I don't care. Israel needs all the help it can get."'

The rationale seems to be that since Jewish people don't believe in the second coming, they may as well just go along with these supportive evangelicals. There's an Israeli joke about the whole thing, that when Jesus does arrive, we can ask him directly whether this is his first or second visit to planet earth.

It's hard to fully grasp the scale of Christian Zionism's impact politically, but one of its most visible successes came in 2018, when former president Donald Trump, in a gesture to his evangelical base, moved the American embassy in Israel from Tel Aviv to Jerusalem. The first and most significant country to do so was swiftly followed by Guatemala, Honduras, Kosovo and Papua New Guinea. For Palestinians, East Jerusalem is the intended capital of their own future state. Trump flew in the face of a longstanding international consensus over Jerusalem to avoid anything that might prejudice negotiations over the city's final status. America's incendiary move set off protests across Jerusalem and the Palestinian territories and anger across the Middle East. In Gaza alone, at least fifty-eight died and 2,700 were wounded in protests on the day the American embassy opened.

For the leading figures of Christian Zionism, however, many of whom were present, it was a day of religious glory and praises-be. American televangelist Robert Jeffress gave a sermon at the opening, saying: 'We're seeing prophecy unfold. I don't know when the Lord is coming back but I know today, it got a little bit closer.' The *New York Times* reported this in an article with the headline: 'Robert Jeffress, Pastor Who Said Jews Are Going to Hell, Led Prayer at Jerusalem Assembly'. The article references a sermon he delivered in 2010, in which he denounced both Islam and Mormonism as 'wrong' and 'a heresy from the pit of hell' and then moved to Judaism, proclaiming: 'You can't be saved by being a Jew.' John Hagee also attended the embassy opening, of course. He delivered the closing sermon, in which he said: 'Jerusalem is where the Messiah will come and establish a kingdom that will never end. We thank you O Lord for President Donald Trump's courage in acknowledging to the world a truth established 3,000 years ago, that Jerusalem is and always shall be the eternal capital of the Jewish people.' You might wonder about the political specificity of a prophecy concerning a global superpower and its embassy, but don't. There is no point applying reason to any of this. You might also wonder how Palestinian Christians, such as the ones who live in the cities where Jesus was born and lived, Bethlehem and Nazareth, factor into this evangelical vision of things. But again, this is not a concept steeped in any kind of coherence. Or to put it another way, it throws the Palestinian Christian minority under the second coming bus.

Christian Zionism as a theology has been around since at least the seventeenth century, though the 1909 *Scofield Reference Bible*, which set out this messianic evangelism and was bought by millions, is credited with being an influential recruitment agent. But Israel's creation in 1948 really sent Christian Zionists into a frenzy. It served as confirmation of their prophecy about Jews returning to the Holy Land. The 1967 war, in which Israel defeated its Arab neighbours, was interpreted as further proof of divine intervention and gave Christian Zionism added momentum. This movement grew with the advent of televangelism. And with the parallel rise of a messianic Jewish settler movement that saw the occupied West Bank as biblical land to be reclaimed, End Times fervour took on a twist: if Christ was coming back, Christian Zionists could accelerate it. They could put rocket-boosters on the prophecy by encouraging settlements expansion, supporting conflict with Palestinians and opposing any peace initiatives. As Sarah Posner tells me, Christian Zionists 'believe they have a role to play in the fulfilment of biblical prophecy and what they believe to be God's commandments to them regarding Israel.' It's all on God's timing, as they see it, but they can take steps to obey him. In a 2023 documentary film about evangelicals, *Praying for Armageddon*, by Tonje Hessen Schei, a former evangelical preacher explains what all this means for American politics. An ex-fundamentalist from a Christian right family, Frank Schaeffer, says: 'The bedrock of support for the state of Israel is there because American evangelicals think it will bring Jesus back quicker.' And he adds: 'Without the Republican bedrock evangelical voter, no Republican anywhere in America, for any office, gets elected.'

Why is this relevant to our understanding of anti-semitism? Because Christian Zionists have scrambled the picture, tipping the scales with their blanket support for Israel, even as it violates Palestinian rights and international law. This politically influential group is pro-Israel but not Jewish. It is bad for all Jewish people while claiming to be good for Israel. So to add complexity to an already knotty subject, if we're going to challenge antisemitism, we need to separate all this out, rejecting the view of Jewish people as bit-players in the prophecy drama. And we must do this while some Jewish and Israeli organisations are insisting that everything is just fine as it is.

'They are Christians who love Israel!'

The Israel-supporting alliance between religious Jews and Christian evangelists is captured in the 2020 documentary *'Til Kingdom Come*, by the Israeli filmmaker Maya Zinshtein, which follows a Christian-Jewish non-profit organisation and an American church that fundraises for it. That church, Binghamtown Baptist church, is in Kentucky – sitting comfortably in America's Bible Belt – and it is led by a multigenerational family of evangelical preachers. Inside it stands a large wooden cross atop which is hung a Star of David, creating the unfortunate impression that the Jewish symbol has been crucified. Pastor Boyd Bingham IV tells the filmmakers: 'We expect God to bless our church because we help the nation of Israel.' Then we see him at the local Baptist church school, where he informs the children: 'Every good thing we know, all the things we love about the Bible, they were given to us of the Jewish nation, Israel. Their people, the Jews are better than all of us, they're better than all of us and you need to accept that.' It is unequivocally creepy. It is hard to imagine a Jewish person watching this and not having their antisemitism spidey sense immediately activated. And it gets *so* much worse. Later in the film Boyd's father, pastor William Bingham III, delivers a sermon about the End Times: 'And then Jews around the world, all the wealthy owners of the NBA basketball teams, and the movie moguls ... they're going to know there is a God in Israel.' But the trouble is that, rather than run a mile from this bigotry-in-neon-lights, some Jewish organisations are embracing it.

'Til Kingdom Come follows the American-Israeli rabbi Yechiel Eckstein and his daughter Yael (who was smilingly in attendance at the Bingham 'wealthy Jews' sermon) and their relationship with this Kentucky family of pastors. In 1983, Eckstein senior founded the International Federation of Christians and Jews (IFCJ), an organisation that now describes itself as 'the largest and most effective ministry providing Christians with opportunities to fulfill biblical prophecy by supporting Israel and the Jewish people with lifesaving aid.' The rabbi struggled to gain support at first but was discovered by the TV evangelist Pat Robertson and a phonathon on his show reportedly raised $4 million in

thirty minutes flat. *'Til Kingdom Come* shows Yael Eckstein delivering a box of food aid to an elderly Jewish woman in Jerusalem. As she hands over the food parcel, Eckstein tells the seventy-seven-year-old Edna about the donors: 'They are Christians who love Israel!' And Edna breaks down crying, saying that she feels forgotten, swept under the table and her hardships ignored. She is clearly in financial strife and says that the Eckstein outfit, the IFCJ, are the only ones helping her.

This fellowship runs over 100 programmes to support Israelis below the poverty line, including Holocaust survivors, as well as backing what are described as 'security projects around the country'. When her father died in 2019, Yael Eckstein took over as director of the organisation, which sees some $130 million donated by Christian evangelicals annually. According to a piece in *The Times of Israel* that year, the IFCJ runs around 450 programmes in total across Israel, with over 5,000 volunteers. And that's just one organisation.

Countless evangelical groups are raising funds and funnelling them into projects across illegal Jewish settlements in the occupied West Bank and East Jerusalem. Just like the national-religious Jewish settler movement, Christian Zionists have zero interest in Palestinian self-determination or in Israel relinquishing the occupied territories. For them, that would be like putting God's prophecy in reverse gear. And so the settler movement and the Christian Zionists have ended up on the same page. It's impossible to track funding, partly because American churches aren't legally required to say where their money is going, partly because many organisations operating across Jewish settlements are opaque. In 2018, the Israeli newspaper *Haaretz* estimated that in the previous decade, up to $65 million was going from American Christian evangelical organisations into West Bank settlements. According to Tristan Sturm at Queen's University Belfast, John Hagee and CUFI alone are channelling millions of dollars to the Jewish settler movement. One of the largest of these settlements, Ariel in the central West Bank, has a John Hagee Building as part of its sports centre, to which he donated $1.5 million, a dedication which must delight the pastor as he imagines Jewish Israelis, bench-pressing towards the End Times. Meanwhile, the International Christian Embassy Jerusalem, which has offices in eighty-six countries globally, has as its purpose the mission to affirm Israel's 'right' to the West Bank.

In *Praying for Armageddon*, Lee Fang, a reporter for the online American news organisation *The Intercept*, tries to make sense of this relationship between Christian evangelism and support for Israel, and its impact on US foreign policy. The film shows Fang following the trail of influence as he visits the City of David, or *Ir David* in Hebrew. Located just outside Jerusalem's Old City, this national park is promoted as an archaeological tourist site, a chance to discover the biblical remains and ancient history of the holy capital. But it's an illegal settlement run by a private settler organisation within the Palestinian village of Silwan, in East Jerusalem, which Israel annexed as part of its occupation in 1967. The City of David is seeking to 'Judaise' East Jerusalem – meaning to populate it with Jewish Israelis – and in so doing is forcing Palestinians out of their homes. The Palestinian human rights organisation Al-Haq described this venture as 'settlement tourism' in a 2022 report, which also charts how the City of David is ignoring and sometimes actually damaging the Byzantine and Islamic archaeology of the area. So the whole venture is not just evicting Palestinians, but also erasing a long Arab history and connection to the land. The Al-Haq report points to private funders, such as the Russian-Jewish oligarch Roman Abramovich, who is claimed to be the City of David's largest donor. He is not the only one, though. As Fang notes, the City of David 'looks like an effort simply to engage in archaeology, to find these biblical artifacts. But underneath the surface there is a lot of Christian right money and resources and support for this foundation that's leading the effort to evict Palestinian families.'

In recent years we have witnessed escalating violence in East Jerusalem as settler organisations have taken over Palestinian land and homes, with cooperation from Israeli authorities – from the government, to the courts and the border police. What has been less apparent is the extent to which these actions may be aided and abetted by Christian evangelism. According to the authors of *The Israel Lobby*, John Mearsheimer and Stephen Walt, in financially supporting the settlement movement and lobbying against territorial concessions 'the Christian Zionists have reinforced hard-line attitudes in Israel and the United States and have made it more difficult for American leaders to put pressure on Israel. Absent their support, settlers would be less numerous in Israel, and the US and Israeli governments would be less constrained by their pressure in the occupied Territories as well as their political activities.' Christian Zionists fervently back the building of a Third Temple, an idea pushed by fanatical messianic Jewish groups who now have allies in the Israeli coalition government. They want to build the Third Temple (the first and second having been destroyed by the Babylonians and Romans, respectively) on the Temple Mount, or in Hebrew, *Har Ha-Bayit*. This is where the Dome of the Rock and Al-Aqsa Mosque currently stand, on what Muslims call *al-Haram al-Sharif*, Arabic for the Noble Sanctuary. If this disastrous building plan were ever to be realised, all hell would break loose. But those fire-and-brimstone evangelist pastors would doubt-less see that as support for the prophecy.

While backing settler movements on the ground, American evangelists also play an outsized role when it comes to silencing critics of Israel. As we've seen, Israel began decades ago to dismiss criticism of its policies as antisemitic attacks on the collective Jew, with various think-tanks, universities and Jewish communal organisations coming on board with this definition of a 'new' antisemitism. But if Christian Zionists are biblically compelled to defend Israel and oppose its opponents, it follows that such groups would also join efforts to conflate criticism of Israel with antisem-itism, thereby, in their own terms, mounting a guard against opponents. Which is exactly what happened. One glaring example is in the efforts to shut down the Palestinian BDS campaign. Israeli ministries tasked with tackling what they view as the BDS threat have typically filtered their objectives through to American pro-Israel groups such as AIPAC and the Israel Allies Foundation and also to the various Christian Zionist groups. Attempts in America to ban BDS, resulting in thirty-five states already passing anti-boycott legislation, reflect the considerable impact of those Christian Zionist groups, at least in Republican states. Julia Bacha, who directed the 2021 documentary film *Boycott*, which examined these BDS-banning laws and attempts to overturn them, tells me: 'Christian Zionists were behind the majority of the bills.' She explains: 'In terms of the players they were the main ones doing that at state level in red states and showing up at legislatures arguing for these bills and organising constituencies in churches to show up and push for the bill.' If the seed was planted by the Israeli government and germinated by Jewish pro-Israel groups, it bore the fruit of anti-boycott bills at a vast scale largely because of Christian Zionists.

Despite the disproportionately large role Christian Zionism plays in American politics, we rarely look at it too closely. Of course, some journalists and researchers, including Palestinians and Israelis, *do* extensively cover this area. But the way it all plays out in domestic politics can skew our vision. Christian evangelicals reserve most of their political lobbying for the Republican party, where they dominate the Israel conversation lock, stock and barrel. But it's the Jewish pro-Israel lobbyists that operate on the Democratic side of the House. So, for instance, AIPAC is trying to shape the composition and policies of the Democratic party by targeting what it considers to be insufficiently pro-Israel candidates in the party's primaries. This has been going on for a while, but recently accelerated in intensity. In 2022, it was revealed that AIPAC was working to block Democratic candidates supportive of Palestinians by pouring in money from Republican billionaires, itself a terrible indictment of the distorting effects of all outsized, uncapped lobby groups within a democracy. This point was made by J Street, the smaller, liberal group which describes itself as pro-Israel, pro-peace, pro-democracy and committed to a negotiated resolution to the Israel–Palestine conflict, a position it considers to be the majority view of American Jews. J Street denounced AIPAC's moves as 'fundamentally antidemocratic' and 'dangerous'. AIPAC has constantly attacked 'the Squad' – a group of progressive congresspeople, mostly women of colour who are critical of Israeli policy, including Alexandria Ocasio-Cortez, Ilhan Omar, Rashida Tlaib and Ayanna Pressley. But this has all gone stratospheric since the 2023 Gaza war, with AIPAC pledging upwards of $100 million to unseat Squad members during the 2024 primaries by backing pro-Israel candidates to oppose them.

The left is necessarily focused on Jewish pro-Israel organisations, since those are the ones targeting progressive politicians. This is a vital and live confrontation, one that has immediate consequences for the political composition of the Democratic party and for the future of American democracy itself. But in the interests of building consistently antiracist movements, it would make sense to also foreground the impact of Christian pro-Israel lobbies.

As Yali Hashash says: 'It is difficult to make the shift that Zionism itself is strong, but evangelism is stronger. There are hundreds of millions of them.' In other words, there is a tendency to see those *Jewish* pro-Israel groups as exerting an outsize influence on American politics, but they are vastly outnumbered and outpowered by the impact of *Christian* Zionism. The largest pro-Israel lobby group, after all, is John Hagee's outfit, CUFI. To put this in perspective, I ask Matthew Duss if there would still be a significant pro-Israel lobby without American Jewish organisations. 'Absolutely. I have no doubt', he replies. Should those hawkish pro-Israel Jewish groups suddenly wake up one morning on the side of progressive politics, Duss says: 'It is very easy to see that antisemitism accusations will be extended to them.' I do see what he means, because that trajectory is already happening. In a 2021 interview, Donald Trump told the Israeli journalist Barak Ravid: 'The Jewish people in the United States either don't like Israel or don't care about Israel.' He added: 'I'll tell you, the evangelical Christians love Israel more than the Jews in this country.' If those right-leaning Jewish groups suddenly decided to be less belligerent on the subject of Israel, they might easily be told the same thing.

But again, we should avoid getting so caught up in the tussle between left and right that we side-line the actual antisemitism. Let's go back to the documentary *'Til Kingdom Come*. One of the most bone-chilling moments comes at the end, as filmmaker Maya Zinshtein poses a question to pastor William Bingham III at Binghamtown Baptist church. 'Some would argue', she says, 'that this cooperation between Jews and evangelical Christians has a certain level of hypocrisy. Don't you think so?' Here is his reply, in full:

'You don't want to hear me come across as, you blind, stupid Jewish people, can't you see this evidently set forth before you, the historical biblical evidence is here, how could you be so blind, because you're just a little bit arrogant? Now you're going to go through the tribulation and get your tail busted and get humbled down there, that you will say, "You know that little crazy whacky preacher, we went over there to Kentucky and he sat there and told us? He's right. And now we're going through all this big mess over here in Israel, it's unbelievable, why didn't we see this before? Now we've been humbled. We're not so arrogant, now. Now we see it."' [He laughs.] 'You don't want me to come across like that now, Maya, huh?'

Like I said. Bone-chilling.

Birds of a feather

Israel's prime minister Benjamin Netanyahu first clocked the perks of best-friending central European leaders back in 2004, when ten new countries, including Hungary, Poland, Slovakia and the Czech Republic (collectively the Visegrád Group) and the Baltic states of Estonia, Latvia and Lithuania, joined the European Union. With the EU increasingly critical of Israel's ongoing illegal occupation and settlements expansion, Netanyahu saw a counter-balancing force in those new member states. A year later, Viktor Orbán of the far-right Hungarian party Fidesz visited Israel and met Netanyahu in an attempt to neutralise – both domestically and internationally – the accusations of antisemitism that clung to him during the 2002 Hungarian elections (which he lost). It worked, too. According to Direkt36, an independent Hungarian media outlet, the nation's diplomats have been able to name-drop Netanyahu to bat off claims of anti-Jewish hatred. The Direkt36 website reports that a staffer to a US member of Congress told them that the Hungarian ambassador had raised this exact argument at a private event, with the staffer recounting it as a version of: 'We're not antisemites, just look at this nice little photo of Orbán and Netanyahu.' This friendship really is a win–win for both leaders.

It is less of a win for Hungary's 100,000-strong Jewish community, though. When Netanyahu took a three-day trip to the country in July 2017, this community made its feelings clear. Orbán's government had been running an antisemitic anti-immigration TV and billboard campaign using the image of the Hungarian-Jewish George Soros. The founder of the Open Society Foundations, Soros is a billionaire financier, philanthropist and Holocaust survivor who champions various causes from the rights of refugees to promoting education and the rule of law. But during his visit, Netanyahu said nothing about the anti-Soros campaign, focusing only on the bilateral ties between the two nations. Worse, when the Israeli ambassador to Hungary did call it out, weeks ahead of Netanyahu's visit, he was subsequently forced to retract and say that campaigning against Soros was in fact OK.

András Heisler, the leader of the Federation of Hungarian Jewish Communities, gave a speech lambasting both Orbán and the Israeli prime minister. 'It was possible to launch in Hungary a total propaganda campaign, whose language and visual tools revived in our minds the bad memories of the past', Heisler said, of the anti-Soros offensive. 'One can argue about the intent of the campaign but it became unacceptable for me for one thing: the Jews of Hungary started to live in fear. And a responsible Jewish leader cannot keep silent about that. Neither can a responsible head of government.' A few years earlier in 2014, a memorial dedicated to 'all the victims' of German occupation was erected in Budapest and immediately criticised for distorting the nation's role in the Holocaust. Some 450,000 Jews were deported to death camps – on the orders of the Third Reich, organised by Hungarians and rounded up by Hungarian gendarmes. This Jewish community was also worried by Orbán's praise in 2017 for the nation's wartime leader and Nazi ally, Miklós Horthy – under whose stewardship those deportations took place. A year later in February 2018, Poland passed a law that banned blaming that country for having any part in the Holocaust – another piece of Holocaust revisionism that the Israeli government found a way to accommo-date. Half of the six million Jews killed in the Holocaust were Polish, while the country itself was where much of the mass extermination took place. Writing for the Israeli

Haaretz newspaper in 2019, the Holocaust studies professor Yehuda Bauer described the Israeli government's approach as ignorant, amoral and a 'simple betrayal'. And the effect of the Polish Holocaust Law was to unleash a wave of antisemitic hate, including threatening phone calls, emails and other harassment, upon Polish Jews numbering some 20,000 and now viewed by the right as disloyal for daring to challenge the country's Holocaust revisionism.

In Hungary, Jews are rarely physically attacked by antisemitism. That said, responding to a survey by the European Union Agency for Fundamental Rights in 2018, a third of Jewish Hungarians reported experiencing some form of harassment. Meanwhile, Jews in this country are instrumentalised by the government as a way of attacking Muslims and refugees. And the dog-whistle invoked by Orbán's government has left many fearful of the deep undercurrents of antisemitism in this country. Hungary's liberal Jewish community has little to gain from an authoritarian nationalist government cementing an 'us' and 'them' ideology where the 'us' is a Christian Hungary. Zsofia Kata Vincze, professor of ethnology at Eötvös Loránd University in Budapest, has written on the emergence in Hungary of an antisemitic public conversation 'that has penetrated every level of society'. In 2018 she told the Israeli-Palestinian *+972 Magazine*: 'The antisemitic language, the antisemitic narrative, is brought into the nationalistic narrative.' This is done, she adds, so as to push a chauvinistic agenda whereby anyone loyal to the nation should defend its borders and keep Hungary Christian. Which leaves no room for any minority and certainly not the Jewish community at a time when George Soros, its most prominent figure, has been cast as disloyalist-in-chief.

In return for all that image-laundering, Hungary is one of Israel's most reliable allies within international bodies like the UN and the EU. In 2019 researchers looked at the positions taken by EU member states and found that Hungary worked hardest to derail decisions critical of Israel. Since EU foreign policy can be torpedoed by just one dissenting country, Hungary can significantly disrupt the bloc's foreign policy. Along with the Czech Republic and Romania, Hungary voted to stymie the EU's condemnation of the American embassy move to Jerusalem, while both Hungary and the Czech Republic voted to prevent special labelling for Israeli goods originating from illegal Jewish settlements. Those countries have also embraced definitions of antisemitism that consider criticism of the state of Israel antisemitic. Which means that Orbán and others can claim to be fighting antisemitism, rather than spreading it with anti-Soros campaigns or Holocaust revisionism. Once again, we see the dual impact of the 'new antisemitism' strategy. On the one hand, it shuts down pro-Palestinian voices and, on the other, condones pro-Israel ones, even when they propagate antisemitic narratives.

A few decades ago, affiliations with parties of central and eastern Europe with fascist roots might have been considered off-limits. Now they are prized partnerships in Israel's foreign affairs portfolio. And as Israel has taken a right-wing turn, its governments have been palling up with authoritarian and often antisemitism-spouting figures beyond Europe, from Donald Trump to Brazil's Jair Bolsonaro. All of this has happened because antisemitism, as long as it comes with stalwart support for Israel, is given a pass. The double standard we saw in Israel's accommodation with Christian Zionism has facilitated these friendships with some of the most virulently racist and antisemitic politicians in the world.

The effect of this is itself layered, convoluted and contradictory. One complication is that Israel and its far-right allies are unreliable narrators on antisemitism who nonetheless signal-jam our conversation on the subject. Another is that Israel's alliances with the antisemitic far right across the world are fuelling a perception that complaints of antisemitism only go in one direction: to the left. Meanwhile those attacks on the left are an all-consuming avalanche of accusations, that anything from the Palestine solidarity movements to Black Lives Matter, 'wokeism' and critical race theory to diversity equity and inclusion programmes are antisemitic, with these claims readily spouted by the right as a means of bashing the left. And then, as we saw with Christian Zionism, the attacks on the left help to absolve right-wing antisemitism and facilitate the forging of Israel-friendly alliances. This piece of the puzzle, which relocates the primary source of antisemitism from the far right to the progressive left, is a key mechanism by which the cordon sanitaire that previously prevented affiliations with antisemitic politicians is dissolved.

Populist glue

Not that long ago, there was an assumption that antisemitism had mostly been expunged from the far right, which
instead had tied itself to politically expedient Islamophobia
and hostility towards immigration. As we saw with the
strategic recalibrations of Marine Le Pen's National
Rally, populist right parties across Europe appeared to be
dumping all the traditional antisemitism, sensing that it
was the thing keeping them locked out of polite political
company. This tells us something about our socio-political
landscape: it speaks to the idea that people might at least be
aware that it is bad to be antisemitic, while Islamophobia
is not viewed in the same way. The Conservative baroness
Sayeeda Warsi explained back in 2011 that Islamophobia
has passed 'the dinner table test', meaning that it is considered socially acceptable. Bleakly, the far right found that
Islamophobia has traction – its appeal runs deep across the
political spectrum.

But as Ruth Wodak, author of *The Politics of Fear: The
Shameless Normalisation of Far-Right Discourse*, has noted, this
performative rebranding, a sort of racist sleight of hand, did
have an effect. She writes, 'Many scholars in the area of
right-wing populism believe that antisemitism has practically vanished from the political arena and become a "dead
prejudice" or that anti-Muslim beliefs and Islamophobia
have more or less completely replaced it.'

Aurelien Mondon, a senior lecturer who researches
far-right politics at the University of Bath, confirms that

the idea that antisemitism had effectively been buried by Islamophobia was 'a pretty common view in some circles until recently'. But more critical scholars continue to study the interplay between antisemitism and Islamophobia and how the two hatreds can feed off each other. And of course antisemitism never goes away – it just spends chunks of time in hibernation. Professor of political science at Atlanta's Georgia State University, Jelena Subotić, has examined how antisemitism within the contemporary far right works. She describes it as 'vital to the construction and maintenance of a counter-cosmopolitan transnational mobilisation'. It acts as a sort of 'populist glue', a cohering global force to undergird, pull together and organise this rising political force across disparate countries. Antisemitism is up to the job of being a sort of mobilising chief sergeant because the ancient hatred is so malleable. It can be anything its believer wants it to be. 'It is plastic, it is adaptable', notes Subotić. And it works so well for the far right precisely because it is contradictory, meaning that it can be put to use in multiple contexts. 'There are no wrong answers', explains Subotić. 'Jews are weak and pathetic, but they are also super powerful; they are inferior, but they also control the world. It is the perfect baseline for far-right populism because it means everything and nothing and it is about constructing the perfect enemy, the perfect elite, and the perfect antidote to the people, to the *volk*.' Recently, she says, we've seen the populist right switch this up even more, carving out fresh turf in which they can use antisemitism to gird a worldview while also 'performatively and declaratively positioning themselves as staunchly pro-Israel'. This is what she calls 'pro-Israel antisemitism'. It is a way of taking a pro-expansionist-Israel view with, at its heart, a belief system that is hostile to Jewish people. All of which has eerie parallels with Christian Zionism.

For the far right, there are many strategic advantages to being loudly pro-Israel. First off, it's a convenient bit of image rehabilitation. How can the far right be deemed nasty and fascism-adjacent when it Cares-A-Lot™ about the Jews of the Jewish state? As the American philosopher Susan Nieman has noted, figures on the far right strongly embrace Israel as cover, presenting the impression that 'as long as we support the state of Israel, we can't be Nazis but we can be as racist as we want to anybody else.' We can also factor in the straightforward appeal of like recognising like. Supporting the Jewish ethno-state of Israel makes ideological sense to a far right that believes nations should be mono-ethnic and that multiculturalism is a terrible, weakening force. In 2018, Israel passed the Jewish Nation State Law, which formally legalised the denial of democratic rights to its Palestinian citizens. You can see why Israel has become, as Subotić puts it, 'a natural friend to contemporary far-right populists'. Because this is exactly the sort of thing the far right believes in: a state in which ethnicity determines access to rights, belonging, equity and even citizenship.

Perhaps the biggest boon here for the far right is that it facilitates the mainlining of its current ideological obsession: agitating against Muslims. The far right sees Israel in the same way that Zionist and Israeli leaders over the years – notably Benjamin Netanyahu himself during the post-9/11 period – have worked hard to be seen: as a European bastion in an uncivilised Middle East. This is why Geert Wilders, leader of the far-right Dutch Party for Freedom, claims that Israel is 'the West's first line of defence' against Islam. It's why the English Defence League describes Israel as on the 'frontline of Islamic extremism and jihad'. In this imagining, Israel is a Western nation that must be defended as part of the supposed battle between the West and the Muslim world. It is the mythology of a Judeo-Christian heritage corralled into the business of isolating and demonising Islam. Wilders talks about the need to 'preserve our own Judeo-Christian civilisation', while Nigel Farage, former leader of UKIP, described the 2015 Paris terror attacks as an assault on 'our Judeo-Christian culture'. What is striking is that Israeli leaders, the far right and sections of the left all cast the country as 'European', but for entirely different reasons. For the right it is to attack Islam, while for the left it is to depict Israelis as European colonisers. None of it has much to do with Israel as it actually is.

For the Israeli state, there are plenty of benefits in its relationships with far-right global leaders. You could argue that such alliances, while morally bankrupt and damaging, are just plain old realpolitik in action. Right-wing Israeli governments have looked at the global political map, with its resurgent far right and increasingly critical left, and wondered how to protect what they consider to be the country's interests. In common with other nations, Israel is pursuing statesmanship and alliances in a changing political reality. Bluntly, Israel's right-wing leaders care about Israel first and would not see anything wrong in that. It is the logic of a nation state. But Israel's leaders are also following the logic of Zionism, the purpose of which is to bring Jews into their own nation state. We saw this sort of thinking in Benjamin Netanyahu's response to the extremist Islamist terror attack on a kosher supermarket in Paris in January 2015, in which four Jewish people were killed. In a televised address Netanyahu said: 'To all the Jews of France, all the Jews of Europe, I would like to say that Israel is not just the place in whose direction you pray, the state of Israel is your home.' French officials, in the country that is home to the largest Jewish population in Europe, did not take too kindly to such comments, with then French prime minister Manuel Valls telling the *Atlantic*: 'If 100,000 Jews leave, France will no longer be France. The French Republic will be judged a failure.'

The upshot of all this is that, with its rightwards realpolitik, Israel has pursued geopolitical alliances that run contrary to the fight against antisemitism, making it much harder to tackle. The country has made new friends in the Visegrád countries of Hungary, Poland, the Czech Republic and Slovakia in a bid to rebalance a European Union that has grown increasingly critical of the Israeli occupation. If those allies in Eastern Europe also happen to be promoting antisemitism, that is a price worth paying for the greater goal of protecting Israel on the global stage. If the far right uses a staunchly pro-Israel stance to image-launder and rehabilitate itself, well, as least Israel's interests are being protected. It is all of a piece with the sentiments we heard around the accommodations made with Christian Zionists: that Israel needs all the friends it can get. You could point out that Israel would gain more friends on the international stage by ending its occupation and subjugation of Palestinian people. But that is not a conversation that Israel, shifting ever-rightwards, seems willing to have.

The confusion is by design

When it comes to antisemitism, the far end of the political right is all over the place. There is the more populist variety of the radical right that pretends to care about Jews. *A lot.* For this grouping, a super-performative 'anti-antisemitism' is advanced in pursuit of political rehabilitation. The idea is to ditch all that socially unacceptable Jew-hatred, but also double down on the central brand theme, which is hating Islam. As we have seen, far-right claims to protect Jews from supposedly endemic Muslim antisemitism are a way of signalling both the rehabilitation and the core hatred. Then there's the white supremacists and ethno-nationalists for whom overt Jew-hatred is still a central organising tenet. This lot aren't trying to hide it. It is the logical core of the Great Replacement Theory espoused by the far right, the idea that Jewish people are conspiring to weaken Western democracies by 'flooding' countries with mainly Muslim migrants. This conspiracy, which we examine in more detail in the next chapter, is a tidy synthesis of different types of racism, whereby Jews are seen as crafty and Muslims as dangerous but lacking the organisational smarts required to do the flooding all on their own.

Sometimes it is hard to keep track across the extreme right spectrum of who is doing antisemitism and who is doing anti-antisemitism. We got a glimpse of this scrambled map during the Israel–Gaza war in 2023, when far-right social media influencers gained millions of followers by sharing pro-Palestine content, while in other corners of the internet the far-right was super-pro-Israel. Several notorious ultranationalists gained huge online audiences through the months of war, but none so much as Jackson Hinkle, a Trump fanatic and pro-Russian supporter who grabbed the opportunity to praise Hamas, slamming 'Zionists' and pumping out bile and disinformation. Within weeks, his X account went from 500,000 to 2.3 million followers. As a verified X content creator, Hinkle is able to turn a profit through his reach. Meanwhile, Tommy Robinson of the far-right English Defence League turned up, against the wishes of Jewish communal groups, at a London rally against antisemitism in late November 2023. What is clear is that none of this is about Palestinians or Israelis or Jews, so much as the instrumentalising of entire groups of people to fit fixed political agendas, or just for the sheer grift.

But holding contradictory views on Jews does not prevent far-right groups from teaming up in coalitions. The more extreme elements of Donald Trump's base are a prime example of that. As Julia Ebner, a specialist in the far right at the Institute for Strategic Dialogue, wrote in her book about extremism, *Going Dark*: 'The obvious question is: how the hell did pro-Zionist counter-jihadists and antisemitic white supremacists end up joining forces?' The answer, she explains, is simple: leverage. These groups have united to face down a common enemy: liberals and the 'woke' left. And yet the far-right tactical shift to Caring-A-Lot about Jews and being staunchly pro-Israel has completely befuddled the political picture and confounded our understanding of what it means to oppose antisemitism. Hannah Rose, a hate and extremism analyst, authored a report on the new philosemitism and the far right, writing: 'Supported by the co-existence of antisemitism, anti-antisemitism and pro-Israel sentiments within the same parties, far-right leaders in formerly Nazi-occupied countries simultaneously claim to combat antisemitism, oppose an Islam that is supposedly comparable to Nazism, and fail to acknowledge fully the crimes of the Holocaust.' This is such a weird and chaotic mess of beliefs. And the far right, which holds significant state power in several countries, pushes all this into our air supply with such volume that it obfuscates and confuses. It is hardly any wonder that people then struggle to comprehend, much less actually to tackle, the antisemitism that keeps showing up in our politics. Even those sincere about wanting to address antisemitism are unlikely to have either the time or the bandwidth to wade through this quagmire.

When Palestine advocacy is shut down with claims of antisemitism while the far right simultaneously proclaims to Care-A-Lot about antisemitism, it can feel like the right has effectively colonised this terrain. Which makes it harder for the left to feel inclined or able to stake a claim in it. Haggai Mattar, executive director of the Israeli–Palestinian +972 Magazine, tells me: 'We need a serious, honest commitment to fighting antisemitism, in a leftist fashion, from a left perspective, both internally where we find it in our ranks and also doubling down on fighting it on the right and not allowing the Israeli laundry machine to whitewash antisemitism on the right, as it has been doing.' But he also adds: 'I can feel in my bones, as I'm talking to you and saying we need to fight antisemitism, I hear those voices saying: "Oh you are just serving the Israeli narrative."' Some of those who think the left must tackle antisemitism anticipate a backlash from their allies, because talking about the issue has become such a right-wing thing.

I am reminded again of Naomi Klein's book *Doppelganger*, in which she writes about the left discarding important political issues the moment they are picked up by the right. Klein describes how the far right, which has effusively welcomed aboard her own personal doppelgänger Naomi Wolf, noticed society's understandable fears over big tech, information and privacy and responded with weird conspiratorial claims about what the tech was doing during the Covid era. To which the liberal reaction was to shrug and sneer. And so those reasonable fears over big tech were not actually addressed by the progressive side. Klein writes: 'Once an issue is touched by "them" [the far right] it seems to become oddly untouchable by anyone else.'

Documenting this, Klein realises that her doppelgänger, who she refers to as 'Other Naomi', represents something even worse than she had originally thought: 'A larger and more dangerous form of mirroring – a mimicking of beliefs and concerns that feeds off progressive failures and silences.' What progressives ignore, the right champions, distorts and claims as its own.

And once again we have moved away from the thing that is so often forgotten. The problem here is not simply that our political adversaries have claimed the cause of anti-antisemitism. It is that they are not really tackling anti-semitism at all. Instead, they are muddling the picture, if not being downright antisemitic themselves. Closing down criticism of Israel does not promote awareness of antisem-itism; rather, it degrades any meaningful understanding of it. The far right performatively Caring-A-Lot about anti-semitism is camouflaging all kinds of harmful views about Jewish people, while deplorably using Jewish communities as cannon fodder in attacks on other racialised minorities. For leftists, exposing the dangerous hypocrisy and cynical manipulation going on here is a good place to start. But it is not, on its own, going to be enough. We can only strip the Care-A-Lot veneer off the far right if we simultane-ously plug that gap, by genuinely and coherently talking about anti-antisemitism, linking it to our antiracism both intellectually and morally. After decades of ceding this space to the political right, those of us who consider ourselves to be antiracists need to substantively and emphatically take it back.

SIX

Skin in the Game

Through the summer of 2023, an American grand jury heard the trial of the Pittsburgh synagogue shooter. Five years earlier, on 27 October 2018, this gunman had carried out a deadly rampage at the Tree of Life synagogue. Members of a long-standing Jewish community had gathered for what should have been a regular Shabbat service, but instead were assailed by a heavily armed attacker who massacred anyone in sight. Eleven were killed and seven wounded, including five police officers. It was the deadliest antisemitic attack on US soil.

Over the three-month trial of the fifty-year-old terrorist, witnesses recounted the details of that day. The court heard survivor Jeffrey Myers, a rabbi at the Tree of Life congregation, who said that when the gunman attacked, he thought he was about to die and began to recite the *Shema*, a centrepiece Jewish prayer uttered in one's final moments. 'I thought about the history of my people, how we've been persecuted and hunted and slaughtered for centuries', he said. 'And about how all of them must have felt in the moments before their death, and what they did was recite Deuteronomy, chapter 6, verse 4, "Hear, O Israel, the Lord is our God, the Lord is One."' They heard Andrea Wedner, shot in the arm while her mother, ninety-seven-year-old Rose Mallinger, was killed right next to her. 'I kissed my fingers and I touched my fingers to her skin. I cried out "Mommy!"' she told the court. Shannon Basa-Sabol, an emergency services handler, described how she took a call that day from Bernice Simon, eighty-four, only to hear her shot dead while still on the line. Bernice's eighty-six-year-old husband, Sylvan, whom she had married at that same synagogue over sixty years earlier, was killed with her.

The Pittsburgh shooter, Robert Bowers, was found guilty on sixty-three counts and sentenced to death under a law the Trump administration had reintroduced, giving the US government the power to order the death penalty for federal crimes, and which current president Joe Biden has yet to revoke. His case showed that, while Bowers acted alone, the motives were not his exclusively. Reporting of far-right terrorism often paints the assailant as a 'lone wolf': someone who is not of sound mind and not a card-carrying member of any group. During Bowers's sentencing, his lawyers argued that the killer had acted out of individual delusions. But Park Dietz, a forensic psychiatrist and expert witness for the prosecution, explained why this was not the case. A seasoned analyst of far-right extremism, Dietz said: 'There's a consensus in psychiatry that if one's weirdo beliefs are shared by a large group, that's not a delusion.' Those beliefs, shared by sprawling groups and individuals worldwide, are what made Bowers seek out the Tree of Life in the first place. He had heard that the synagogue was affiliated with HIAS (the Hebrew Immigrant Aid Service), which works to help refugees. He thought this over 100-year-old Jewish-American organisation was facilitating the arrival of 'invaders... that kill our people'. And, Dietz explained, the killer's defence 'simply mistook every ordinary, widespread, white separatist belief as delusions because they were not familiar with them'. Bowers had gone down the online rabbit-holes of the far right and emerged a believer in the Great Replacement Theory. And this viral conspiracy was the source of his so-called 'weirdo' belief that Jewish-Americans were dispatching deadly invaders into the country.

The Great Replacement Theory is the racist conspiracy that white people are being 'replaced' by non-white, non-Christian immigrants and that this is all being secretly orchestrated in a plot to undermine Western societies. With uncanny frequency, its adherents tend to end up casting Jews – those eternal others – as the shadowy plotters in this scheme. And the theory has spread rapidly over the past decade or so, a chauvinism-steeped response to the changing demographics and social advancements of major Western nations. Replacement is intended to overwhelm and force white Christian populations across the West into a minority. According to this conspiracy, migration is not a product of the post-colonial period, the idea encapsulated by one of Britain's most influential thinkers on race, Ambalavaner Sivanandan, in the statement: 'We are here because you were there.' Nor are migrant populations present in Western Europe because they were invited to fill workforce gaps during the postwar period. It is not that people, for a whole host of reasons, have been forced to leave home countries in which they would have preferred to remain. Migration is not, according to replacement theorists, the inevitable consequence of wars (sometimes caused by Western interference) or persecution or environmental catastrophe or economic devastation. And it is not just the regular flow of humans that has taken place across countries for as long as people have had feet to carry them. No, immigration, according to this racism-fuelled theory, is a deliberate plan to replace white people in the West. If you see a refugee-friendly government policy, or even just one that sticks to international treaties, they see conspirators enacting a 'white genocide'.

The Great Replacement Theory is promoted across the far right's online ecosystem in countless articles, videos and podcasts. Just as Park Dietz explained in that Pittsburgh courtroom, the conspiracy is a bedrock of far-right subculture. Spend a short time in the mushrooming online world of the far right – rapidly coalescing networks that are often now described as the alt-right – and you will come across the Great Replacement Theory. You'll find slick videos with techno soundtracks and crowds of Black and Brown people attempting to get into Europe, or in refugee camps talking about wanting to do so. You'll see white Americans and Europeans describe their neighbourhoods as 'flooded' or 'swamped' by supposedly violent and criminal immigrants. You'll hear the viral influencers of the alt-right – a younger, better-dressed and internet-savvy iteration of the far right – endlessly warn that their countries are being overrun with migrants espousing repressive beliefs, all while liberals welcome them with open arms. Indeed, discussions of the Great Replacement Theory often include tirades against liberals, who are stupidly allowing it to happen while also refusing to have children in sufficient numbers to counter the demographic shift. One clip that keeps cropping up like a motif shows Syrian refugees arriving in Germany. At the height of the deadly Syrian civil war in 2015, the German government pledged to provide asylum to refugees, whose arrival at German train stations is greeted by locals bearing welcoming banners and hugs. It's a wholesome, heart-warming scene. But in the far-right world, it is spliced with clips of crowds crossing borders and claims of migrant violence, set against ominous music intended to sow fear. The Great Replacement Theory really took off around 2015, as Europe was going through what media reports typically referred to as its 'migrant crisis'. In reality, it was a crisis for the refugees, forced to leave war- and conflict-ravaged Syria, Iraq, Libya and Afghanistan. Most went to countries neighbouring their own, while some took perilous journeys to Europe, often by sea and in unsafe boats.

The Great Replacement Theory neatly ties together a set of bigoted beliefs, weaving them into an internally coherent worldview. It organises under one idea: the far right's hatred for migrants, Muslims, liberals, feminists and LGBTQ communities, because every one of those groups, according to the theory, contributes to a dangerous takeover of 'white' nations. Either you're a non-white migrant doing the replacement, or a white person welcoming refugees into European countries, or you're not staying at home in gender-conforming roles to have more white kids; in any case, you are part of the problem. And the reference to Jewish people, plotting behind the scenes, just keeps cropping up. It does not take long for someone to start blaming 'The Jews'.

In the years since the Pittsburgh synagogue shooting, we have heard a lot more about the Great Replacement Theory because the gunmen who carried out several murderous rampages around the world kept bringing it up. On 14 May 2022, ten people were shot dead and three wounded in a devastating supermarket attack in Buffalo, New York, by a nineteen-year-old who cited the Great Replacement Theory in a 'manifesto' he posted online. Eleven of the thirteen victims were Black. Among them was Andre Mackniel, fifty-three, who had popped into the store to buy a birthday cake for his son, who had just turned three. The youngest victim, thirty-two-year-old Roberta Drury, was out shopping for her brother's family. She had moved cross-state to Buffalo eight years earlier to help as her brother recovered from bone marrow surgery, part of his cancer treatment. Another victim of the deadly rampage, sixty-five-year-old Celestine Chaney, had gone to the store with her older sister and was meandering along the food aisles, as we all do. She had survived breast cancer and three surgeries for aneurysms, only to be shot dead while picking up ingredients to make strawberry shortcake. The white supremacist, who livestreamed his hateful killing spree on Twitch, had specifically picked Buffalo's Tops Friendly Market because it was in a predominantly Black neighbourhood. His so-called manifesto was a fusion of visceral and murderous hate for Black people entangled with rampant antisemitism, declaring: 'The real war I'm advocating for is the gentiles vs the Jews.' This terrorist called Jewish people 'the biggest problem the western world has ever had', claiming that 'they must be called out and killed'. An entire Black community was thrown into unbearable grief and shock and trauma, their lives horribly and irreversibly shattered by a terrorist who, in the midst of a racism-fuelled rampage, still somehow blamed 'The Jews'.

The Buffalo shooter claimed he was 'inspired' (a truly nihilistic take on the term) by the murderous attack on 15 March 2019 on two mosques in Christchurch, New Zealand. That grotesque act of terror left fifty-one people dead and dozens more wounded. Among those murdered while at prayer was the three-year-old Mucaad Ibrahim, who had in the chaos of the attack been separated from his father. The first and oldest victim was Daoud Nabi, a seventy-one-year-old refugee from Afghanistan. He had escaped the Soviet–Afghan War in 1979, bringing his young family to safety. The attack claimed the lives of people with heritage across several countries, including Syria, Somalia, Egypt, India, Pakistan and Palestine; people who had moved to New Zealand with hopes of security and a good life. People like twenty-one-year-old Talha Rashid, whose family had migrated from Pakistan ten years earlier; who had just got a new job and was hoping to soon marry. His father Naeem, a fifty-year-old teacher, had tackled the killer and thereby saved the lives of others, but was himself shot and died in hospital.

The morning before he carried out what would be the deadliest shooting in New Zealand's history, the gunman uploaded a seventy-four-page document full of Great Replacement racism and obsessed with the idea that non-white Muslims might become majorities in Western countries. He name-checked Anders Breivik, who murdered seventy-seven people, mostly teenagers, at a youth camp, in Norway's worst terror attack in 2011. Breivik too cited Great Replacement as justification, claiming he was saving Europe from a Muslim takeover facilitated by leftists (the youth camp he chose for his killing spree, on the island of Utøya, had been held by the Norwegian Labour party). In August 2019, a terror attack on Hispanic shoppers at a Walmart in El Paso, Texas left twenty-three people dead and dozens more injured. The shooter drove 700 miles to target this community, in one of America's worst hate crime attacks. He gunned down Mexican and Mexican-American shoppers of all ages: a fifteen-year-old boy, Javier Amir Rodriguez; a grandfather making a family visit; a couple who had just taken their dog to the groomer; another couple who died shielding their two-month-old baby son. In a message posted online minutes before the attack, this gunman declared he was 'defending my country from cultural and ethnic replacement' brought on by 'the Hispanic invasion of Texas'. Months before, a gunman targeted a synagogue in California on the last day of Passover, killing a sixty-year-old woman and injuring three other people. He admitted to setting fire to a nearby mosque a few weeks earlier. His online posts were filled with hatred of Jews and Muslims and migrants, and mentions of the Great Replacement Theory. 'I would die a thousand times over to prevent the doomed fate that the Jews have planned for my race', he wrote. Later that same year, a gunman failed to storm a packed synagogue in Halle, Germany, during a Yom Kippur service, though he killed two people outside the building. In footage of the attack, which he posted online, this far-right extremist railed against feminists, declining birth-rates and immigration, before declaring: 'The root of all these problems is the Jew.'

That each of these terror attacks targeted a different minority group while citing the same common enemy signals the urgency of tackling racisms collectively. It tells us that while we debate Jewish absorption into whiteness, for the far right 'The Jews' are at the heart of all things race-related, irredeemably embroiled and eternally, demonically complicit. It also speaks to the sheer folly of thinking we can tackle horrifically murderous racist ideologies without also confronting the constantly recurring violence of antisemitism.

'Jews will not replace us'

As the far right has gained political influence and moved from the margins into the mainstream, so too has the Great

Replacement Theory. It is in our political air supply. It is mentioned by French presidential candidates and American Republican loyalists. While not represented in Britain's Parliament, it is a stalwart of the far-right English Defence League, and the populist-right UKIP and its successor the Reform party, which by early 2024 reached around ten per cent support in polling. Politicians in Westminster and in parliaments across mainland Europe talk about 'hordes' and 'floods' of migrants, or in terms of an 'invasion', all of which plays into the Great Replacement Theory, because it entrenches far-right terminology and framing around immigration. A US poll taken by the Associated Press in May 2022 found that one-third of respondents believed that an effort is afoot to replace native-born Americans with new immigrants for electoral purposes. A 2023 UK poll by the Policy Institute at King's College London commissioned by the BBC found about the same number of Brits believed the same thing. In France two-thirds of those polled in 2021 by market research agency Harris Interactive thought that the Great Replacement would happen. Not everyone who believes this theory automatically thinks 'The Jews' are at the heart of it. Politicians and right-wing commentators may not even mention the bit about the plotting Jews, locating the source of the problem instead with liberals or 'elites'. But antisemitism, because of its centuries-long function in this context and for this very purpose, is all too often lurking in conspiratorial talk of plots by 'elites'. It is such an activating part of this conspiracy, like the yeast making the whole thing rise. And talk of 'shadowy elites' is so often code for 'The Jews' that, put together and regardless of whether direct reference is made, the theory is likely to end up there.

In his 2017 essay 'Skin in the Game', Eric K. Ward of Race Forward explains the function of antisemitism within far-right white nationalist movements. White nationalists, often interchangeably described as white supremacists, believe that white people are racially superior and that this elevated status should be reflected in law. Such views are the mainstay of the far right. Ward describes his lifelong exposure to the racism of white nationalists who harassed and abused him as he moved from state to state. He writes: 'As a Black man, I am regarded by white nationalists as a subhuman, dangerous beast.' And at the same time, from his earliest exposure to white nationalism, antisemitism was overt, everywhere, the fuel that racists and supremacists used to power virulent and often violent anti-Black hatred. Asked to define white nationalism today, Ward writes that he would respond the same way he would have thirty years ago: it is 'committed to building a whites-only nation, and antisemitism forms its theoretical core'.

Ward charts how the Great Replacement Theory builds directly on *The Protocols of the Elders of Zion*, that Tsarist-era work of fiction that depicted an international Jewish conspiracy to control the world. When American industrialist Henry Ford brought *The Protocols* to the United States during the 1920s, he printed half a million copies weekly under an adapted title that better denoted the subject matter: *The International Jew*. Versions of that same world domination conspiracy have popped up at various points in America's history ever since. Once you have, as in *The Protocols*, a blueprint for Jews nefariously controlling the world, it is possible to riff endlessly on the story. As Ward sets out, antisemitism grew more embedded into the racist myth-making of white nationalism precisely as American Jews were being absorbed into whiteness – because that is when bigoted conspiracists could start banging on about hidden groups and invisible powers. What's more, following the civil rights struggle that overturned many of the laws that had upheld white supremacy – including the Jim Crow laws – white nationalists found in replacement conspiracies a theory that made sense of this world-turning change. After all, how could African-Americans, the very people they thought inferior, have attained all this social progress? 'Some secret cabal, some mythological power, must be manipulating the social order behind the scenes', writes Ward. It had to be 'The Jews'.

The grain of truth distorted by this conspiracy is, of course, that some American Jews were involved in the civil rights movement. For instance, during the Freedom Summer of 1964, a campaign to raise the number of African-Americans registered to vote in the state of Mississippi, Jews made up roughly half the number of young white volunteers who joined the movement. Two of the three civil rights activists murdered in June that year by the Ku Klux Klan – James Chaney, Andrew Goodman and Michael Schwerner – were Jews from New York. The white nationalist explanation of who was behind what, as Ward notes, also made sense of the social gains of other groups deemed inferior by the far right: women and LGBTQ communities. And so, in a conspiratorial pattern carved through the ages, white nationalists see Jews, the eternal other, the insider-outsiders, as the ultimate source of every problem, the mobilising force behind every social justice movement. Fast-forward to the present day and you see the far right making accusations – often echoed by prominent politicians and commentators – about Jews bankrolling and orchestrating the Antifa antiracist political movement or Black Lives Matter. Given how frequently both Jews and people of colour are hit with the same stick, it seems borderline obtuse that these groups have not come together more robustly to fight back.

Released a year after Ward wrote *Skin in the Game*, Spike Lee's 2018 film *BlacKkKlansman* is a comedy-drama based on the true story of Ron Stallworth, a young, African-American police officer who infiltrated the Ku Klux Klan during the 1970s. Near the start of the film there's a ranting, piece-to-camera monologue from a fictional white nationalist which, for anyone who has dipped a toe into the online (dis)info-pools of the alt-right, will seem horribly familiar. This racist character, Kennebrew Beauregard, is played by Alex Baldwin, perhaps an in-joke since the actor also played former president Donald Trump on *Saturday Night Live*. In the role of Beauregard, he rolls through all the usual hateful accusations and conspiracies. America, he says, is under attack because of integration. The 1954 *Brown v Board of Education* decision, a milestone win for the civil rights movement which ruled that segregating kids at schools was unconstitutional, is in Beauregard's rant a decision 'forced upon us by the Jewish-controlled puppets on the US Supreme Court.' His tirade is drenched in vicious slurs against African-Americans and Jews, taking in communists and the civil rights movement, too. All of them were coming for the white American way of life. It was at its core: 'An international Jewish conspiracy.'

Spike Lee's film is a tour through the motifs of replace-ment theory seeded during the 1970s. It echoes Ward's analysis that, for white nationalists, it was simply unthink-able that the African-American community, long demeaned, disdained and subjugated, were actually making social and political gains. How could that even be possible? This is why we see the distinct racial stereotypes inherent to each bigotry dovetail so neatly into the Great Replacement Theory. Anti-Black racism is about domination and exploi-tation, denigrating and often sexualising people of colour (which can underpin all that weirdly obsessive alarmism over birth rates). But antisemitism is, at its heart, a con-spiracy about power. It is the racist imagining of a shadowy cabal of Jewish people manipulating and pulling strings for their own personal gain. Perhaps one reason that the Great Replacement conspiracy is proving so popular with the far right is that it serves them a perfectly mixed racism cocktail.

BlacKkKlansman introduces a fictionalised plot twist to the true story of the African-American police officer, Ron Stallworth; that is that the white police officer who works with him undercover on the KKK infiltration is a Jewish man named Flip Zimmerman. This Jewish cop meets the Klan in person as the necessary 'white' face of Ron Stallworth, who could not appear to the clan himself. At first, Zimmerman is not fully invested in the sting, which his colleague pulls him up on. 'You're Jewish', Stallworth says. 'Why you acting like you ain't got skin in the game?' Zimmerman replies that he was always just another white kid. But the more Zimmerman meets with the Klan, and the more exposed he is to their raging antisemitism, the more he is forced to confront a Jewish identity previously buried under a white-passing surface. A powerful portrayal of the Black liberation struggle amid relentless, routine and eye-watering racism, *BlacKkKlansman* carefully layers in the attendant antisemitism of white nationalism. We see Zimmerman making friends and common cause with Klan members who deny the Holocaust, loathe Jews and sometimes suspect he might be one. He narrowly escapes several traps set by one of his new racist buddies as a way of exposing his Jewishness. 'I never thought about it much', he tells Stallworth. 'Now I'm thinking about it all the time.' Landing in the middle of a Trump presidency, at a time when antisemitism was surging, the film was a painful reminder that Jewish people may pass as white, until they don't.

BlacKkKlansman ends with real footage from a white nationalist march in Charlottesville, Virginia in August 2017. Far-right groups had rallied to protest against the removal of a statue of Robert E. Lee, one of the leaders of the Confederacy era who fought to maintain slavery. A thirty-two-year-old anti-fascist protester, Heather Heyer, was killed and thirty-five more injured that day as a neo-Nazi drove his car into a crowd of counter-protesters. As they marched bearing tiki torches, white nationalists chanted: 'Jews will not replace us!' Carin Mrotz, the former director of Minnesota's Jewish Community Action who we first met scrubbing a swastika off a garage door, recalls how, for those unfamiliar with the replacement conspiracy, the chants about Jewish people were so incongruent that they were ignored or misheard, blurring into other chants of: '*You* will not replace us.' She tells me: 'A bunch of white racial justice activists completely missed it. If you are not aware of something, you will hear what you need to hear.' That's when Mrotz and her colleagues knew that they needed to be having a very different conversation about antisemitism.

Hydra-headed racism

Throughout history, racism has constantly cross-pollinated across continents, each version shaping and informing the characteristics of the other. While the Great Replacement Theory, currently viral in the far-right universe, is premised on the core racist theories of white nationalists through the ages, it has also evolved and rebranded, just like today's dapper-dressing alt-right. The theory has taken inspiration from contemporary European sources, themselves steeped in racial hatred for Muslims which has grown considerably in the years since 9/11. One of the most influential is French writer Renaud Camus, who coined the very term in his 2011 book *Le Grand Remplacement*. A lauded author of gay literature, Camus took a sharp political turn with his theory about the replacement of 'indigenous' French people by migrants from mostly Muslim countries, who arrive in France as 'conquerors' and 'invaders'. According to Camus, these supposed colonisers (many of them from the former French colonies of North Africa) plan to overwhelm Christian France by sheer demographics, turning it into a repressive Islamist state. He calls this 'genocide by substitution'. Needless to say, it is pure fantasy. Migrants now comprise around ten per cent of France's population, a rise of three per cent from the mid-1970s; hardly numbers denoting rapid increase, much less a full-blown takeover. In December 2023, a survey from Ipsos found that the popular perception of migration figures was higher than the actual numbers across ten Western countries including France, Britain, Germany and America. One might wonder what it is about our media and political conversations over immigration that is leading to such wildly inaccurate impressions.

Camus's new politics, including his support for Marine Le Pen and other far right figures, turned him into an outcast among old friends and he was dropped by his publishers. His book was never translated into English and sales in France were not significant, but nonetheless the Great Replacement Theory flourished within the far right's growing, global underground ecosystem. In interviews, Camus tells of an epiphany during the late 1990s when he visited medieval villages in southern France and saw Muslim women walking along the streets. 'You would go to a fountain, six or seven centuries old, and there were all these North African women with veils!' he told the *New Yorker* in 2017. That Muslims were strolling along old French village streets was, to him, a life-altering revelation. What others might view as a multicultural medley of past and present, Camus saw as reason to panic.

Camus has denounced the violent rampages of gunmen citing the Great Replacement Theory and claims his ideas are not antisemitic. On that second point the Anti-Defamation League agrees, stating in its explainer on the subject that: 'His initial concept did not focus on Jews and was not antisemitic.' Judging from appraisals of his book, it would seem more rooted in Islamophobia: how else to describe the idea that Muslims in France are destroying French civilisation and culture, or that this is in part down to Muslim communities having higher birth rates? In this it parallels *Eurabia*, an earlier prototype of the Muslims-are-invading genre. Written in 2005 by Gisèle Littman using the pen name Bat Ye'or, *Eurabia* is a luridly conspiratorial warning of Western countries falling under Islamic rule, in a supposed plot to destroy European civilisation. Once you declare that mostly Muslim migrants, depicted as backward, violent and uncivilised, are arriving in large numbers in Western countries in an orchestrated way, it begs the question: who is doing the orchestrating? And that narrative tends to blame, well, do I need to say it? It's a plotline as old as time, with pre-established archetypes, and the same characters playing the same roles in the same story. The Christchurch, Buffalo and Pittsburgh killers all cited the Great Replacement Theory. All mentioned Jewish people as secretly responsible for immigration. Who told them to put it all together that way? No one person or author. It is simply the way things get put together within the racist ecosystem of the far right. As Aurelien Mondon at the University of Bath explains, this ecosystem is infused with the antisemitism of 'the fantasised figure of the Jew, the person you might not see but who is trying to undermine us from within'. Within this world, he says, the 'elites' being referred to – whether cosmopolitan, metropolitan or liberal – are often read as 'The Jews'.

Few things illustrate this so well as the far right's obsessive demonisation of George Soros. Through his Open Society Foundations (OSF), he has contributed billions to democracy-building projects around the word. A ridiculously wealthy Jewish banker, a Democratic party donor and a supporter of liberal, environmental and migrant-friendly causes, Soros is like a walking antisemitism bingo card for right-wing conspiracists. And he has been the subject of hateful campaigns everywhere, not just in Hungary, as we have seen, but across America, Italy, Turkey and Israel. Jelena Subotić of Georgia State University has noted that Soros is a handy enemy for populist leaders who pin onto him whatever problem they want to rouse public sentiment over. 'While the attention is so often on Soros, he is but today's version of the antisemitic target onto whom the nation's ills are projected', she writes. 'Before Soros there was Rothschild, and before Rothschild there was Dreyfus. This is how transnational antisemitism operates – it fixates on Jews as agents of disturbance of the nation, as leading, designing or financing protest and dissent, all with the purpose of destroying a particular international order that populists want to preserve.' Soros, in other words, is today's perfect bogeyman and scapegoat. And in our current political landscape, it is immigration that so many hard-right leaders want to blame him for.

This was the thrust of the Hungarian leader Viktor Orbán's attacks, which cast Soros as the chief architect and financier of immigration into Europe. This message was repeated for years, across political speeches and broadcast ads. During the 2017 election campaign, Orbán's government papered the country with anti-immigration billboards featuring a giant image of the Jewish philanthropist and the strapline: 'Don't let Soros have the last laugh.' Several of the posters were graffitied with the words: 'Stinking Jew.' Winning another term in parliament, Orbán's Fidesz party passed a Stop Soros law in 2018, which criminalised the provision of help to asylum seekers. That same year, the Hungarian prime minister gave a speech outside Parliament. 'We are fighting an enemy that is different from us', Orbán told the cheering crowds. 'Not open, but hiding; not straightforward but crafty; not honest but base; not national but international; does not believe in working but speculates with money; does not have its own homeland but feels it owns the whole world.' Whatever the Hungarian leader might say to refute accusations of antisemitism, Jewish people have throughout time been demonised using this exact language.

In 2018, Israel's prime minister Benjamin Netanyahu who, as we have seen, is great friends with Orbán, picked up the baton of Soros-blaming, claiming that the Jewish billionaire was behind campaigns in Israel to prevent the deportation of African refugees. Netanyahu and other government ministers also claim that Soros backs anti-Israel organisations. In late 2023, the business billionaire Elon Musk accused Soros and the OSF of wanting to destroy Western civilisation. And the Israeli minister for diaspora affairs, Amichai Chikli, rushed to his defence. Chikli, whose portfolio includes combatting antisemitism abroad, posted to X: 'The Israeli government and the vast majority of Israeli citizens see Elon Musk as an amazing entrepreneur and a role model. Criticism of Soros – who finances the most hostile organizations to the Jewish people and the state of Israel is anything but anti-Semitism, quite the opposite!' This confounding distortion over what antisemitism is and who is doing it can go to incredible extremes. In 2019, the Trump confidant, former New York City mayor and Roman Catholic, Rudy Giuliani, said of the demonised Jewish philanthropist: 'Soros is hardly a Jew. I'm probably more of a Jew than Soros is.' So determined are these politicians to cement their self-appointed roles as arbiters of antisemitism that they will go as far as to deny someone's Jewish identity. Once again, we see that for these right-wing self-styled campaigners against antisemitism, it has little to do with Jewish people.

Meanwhile, Netanyahu's other good friend, Donald Trump, and his supporters have cranked up the volume of anti-Soros hate. Soros was one of the three Jewish figures that featured in Trump's 2016 closing election ads, which railed against 'those who control the levers of power in Washington and for the global special interests'. By 2018, right-wing commentators helped Trump push a fake story about Soros being connected to a migrant caravan of Mexicans walking to America. That summer, the British anti-immigration and Brexit figurehead Nigel Farage told Fox News: 'I really feel that Soros, in many ways, is the biggest danger to the entire Western world.' Later that year, a pipe bomb was sent to the home of George Soros, with others dispatched to Hillary Clinton, Barack Obama and CNN's New York offices.

As with the white nationalists who blamed Jews for the achievements of the civil rights movement (which some Jewish people supported but, needless to say, did not spearhead), there is an element of truth to the claims of Jewish involvement in helping refugees. Amos Schonfield, deputy director at HIAS+JCORE, a UK Jewish organisation that campaigns on refugees and racial equality, explains that helping migrants is a cause with which many Jewish people identify. 'We were once refugees', he says. 'And we understand what it was like to be vilified. You can look around the sector in the UK and the heads of refugee charities quite often have Jewish backgrounds.' Anti-immigration conspiracists have taken this kernel of truth, that Jewish people might empathise with refugees, and distorted it into evidence of their nefarious plot to undermine Western societies.

George Soros does help refugees. His Open Society Foundations pledged $500 million to projects and companies supporting migrants and refugees in 2016, while the organisation is committed to working on issues around the health and well-being of migrants, refugees and asylum seekers. Of course, so do other organisations, such as the Catholic charity Caritas, which has long helped migrants and displaced peoples and which does not seem to rile the far right quite like Soros. But the OSF's support for immigration provides those who demonise him with an element of plausible deniability. They can say: we don't hate Soros because he's Jewish; we just hate his liberal agenda! But the trouble with antisemitism is that it is hiding in plain sight. Antisemitic myths are deeply woven into Christian societies. Why else would Viktor Orbán's anti-immigration posters featuring Soros so quickly attract graffiti reading 'stinking Jew'? Why not just 'stinking liberal'?

This aspect of plausible deniability is particularly difficult because, as we have seen, many right-wingers cast themselves as the real defenders of Jewish people against spiralling antisemitism. In 2018 (a big year for the anti-Soros crowd), the *Daily Telegraph* ran a front-page story about Soros with the headline: 'Man who "Broke the Bank of England" Backing Secret Plot to Thwart Brexit'. Here was a Jewish financier – at the same time the subject of vicious antisemitic campaigns in Hungary and in the US – portrayed in a right-wing British broadsheet as standing accused of interfering in western democracies and now conspiring within domestic politics. But while the dog-whistling was pointed out by commentators and journalists at the time, the *Telegraph* refused to countenance that the piece had mainlined a classic antisemitic conspiracy. Which leads us to the question posed by the *New Statesman*: 'Do you have to stoke antisemitism knowingly in order to be responsible for doing so?'

Since then, the far-right networks spreading the Great Replacement Theory online have only grown in number and influence. The Covid-19 pandemic, with all the conspiracies that erupted over the virus – the masks, the lockdowns and the vaccine – was one giant incubator for antisemitism. As Aurelien Mondon explains, the pandemic lent itself to antisemitic theorising because it ticks all the right boxes: 'The idea of big government crushing our liberties, the WHO having so much power, the shady deals with big pharma, experimenting with bodies – what's in the vaccines? It was all ripe for the taking.' Meanwhile, people who would not normally lurk in far-right networks – anxious parents, authority-wary eco-hippies and bored lockdown teens – were suddenly extremely online and pulled into them as they searched for information about the pandemic. The Trump-supporting far-right conspiracy movement QAnon, with its millions of online members, was pivotal in driving Covid conspiracies worldwide. In *Going Mainstream: How Extremists are Taking Over*, Julia Ebner interviews J. T. Wilde, an anti-vax singer popular with the QAnon crowd. He starts talking about the people directing the global pandemic response including the vaccines rollout and tells her that the people 'running the show' were the usual people who run things: 'The people that were behind the money 100 years ago, are still behind the money. They are running the entire world.' Ebner writes that, while the musician had not mentioned any specific group, he also did not need to for a particular inference to be drawn by part of the audience. 'In my work with security and intelligence forces', she comments, 'I have witnessed how this kind of rhetoric can inspire hatred and violence against those who have historically been the most common scapegoat for conspiracy theories: Jews.'

Several QAnon conspiracies draw on coded antisemitism, steeped in familiar conspiratorial narratives to do with Jewish people supposedly snatching children and ritualistically drinking blood. These include the bizarre 'Pizzagate' conspiracy, the charge that Democratic party leaders, alongside Hollywood luminaries, are linked to a child-smuggling paedophile cult. One of the forms of child abuse this supposed cult is declared to be engaged in is harvesting a youth elixir chemical from their blood. Pizzagate came up during the 2016 US election and was resurfaced by QAnon with the chemical-harvesting twist in 2020. Whether deployed consciously or not, this is recognised by race-hate experts as a modern-day retelling of the medieval blood libel, those stories about Jewish people ritualistically using the blood of children. In an interview with the Jewish Telegraphic Agency, Eric Feinberg, vice president of content moderation at the Coalition for a Safer Web, which aims to combat online extremism, adds that references to the *Protocols* and to a 'Zionist Occupied Government' (or ZOG, a government controlled by Jews) are rampant all over QAnon forums. Millions of people are surfing amid all this multifaceted racism daily, filling up on fear and loathing of Muslims, migrants, Jews and Black communities, getting sucked in and riled up.

Sometimes the Great Replacement conspiracy is invoked by the same people who claim to be concerned about antisemitism, Israel or both. Republican politicians have castigated supposedly antisemitic pro-Palestine marches while spouting lines about the Great Replacement Theory. In late October 2023, the then British home secretary Suella Braverman called protests against Israel's war on Gaza 'hate marches' but had no problem using the language of 'invasion' to describe refugees, or with channelling elements of the Great Replacement Theory in a speech about immigration just a month earlier. Delivering a keynote speech to a right-wing think-tank, the American Enterprise Institute, in Washington DC, Braverman described irregular immigration as an 'existential challenge for the political and cultural institutions of the West' and then added: 'Just as it's a basic rule of history, that nations which cannot defend their borders will not long survive, it is a basic rule of politics, that political systems which cannot control their borders will not maintain the consent of the people, and thus not long endure.' All of which led to Braverman attacking the UN's Refugee Convention, signed in 1951 to protect people fleeing persecution – a direct response to the world's abject failure to help people trying to escape the Third Reich or the thousands displaced in the aftermath of the Holocaust. The antiracism campaign group Hope not Hate warned that Braverman's immigration speech, delivered in September 2023, used language and ideas that came 'straight from the Great Replacement Theory'. Meanwhile, in some cases the far-right obsession with the Great Replacement Theory drags Jewish people into the 'white' side of the equation, by claiming Jewish people everywhere and especially in

Israel are threatened by the so-called invasions of violent Muslims. They wield disingenuous philosemitism so as to be Islamophobic. Jewish people are being used as shields by the very people who, if not actually spouting antisemitic theories, are doing very little to stop them and, in many cases, deny those conspiracies are even about Jews to begin with. This has creepy resonances with the medieval elevation of Jews by kings and other leaders, again to be used as shields and to deflect blame. We are all being gaslit on so many levels. It is no wonder that we cannot come together to respond.

The allyship camp

Antiracism movements can end up siloed in a culture of scarcity – the idea that there is only so much concern for racism to go around – leaving us ill-equipped to join forces against the sort of Hydra-headed bigotry of the Great Replacement Theory. And yet the need to do just that could not be more urgent. As Ben Lorber has explained, far-right antisemitism is rallying people not just against Jewish minorities, but against all forms of social justice and democracy itself. 'It serves as an especially flexible and versatile scaffolding for sweeping attacks against progressive movements', he writes, 'and corrodes the foundations of robust democracy by convincing people that social movements arise not as organic expressions of real communities demanding rights and representation, but as the shadowy

work of subversive elites infiltrating the body politic.' This
is the point of antisemitism, after all: to confuse us over
where actual power lies and to dilute and repel our efforts
to confront the social, racial and economic injustices emanating from those real structures of power. Looking at
the online ecosystem built by the far right and seeing its
tenets spattered onto our political landscape, the sweeping
attacks that Lorber describes are all too clear. Antisemitism
is propping up a smorgasbord of bigotries, spanning wild
replacement theories and claims of child smuggling rings
and cultural takeovers and Islamic invasions, amid attacks
on refugees and liberals and feminists and the transgender
community. But at exactly the same time, spurious claims
of antisemitism are also used to attack Black Lives Matter,
post-colonialism, critical race theory, 'the woke' and, as we
saw in the attacks on those American university presidents
during a US House Committee hearing, a generalised
'elite'. The most virulent form of antisemitism today is
coming from the far right, bleeding into the mainstream
while, simultaneously, claims of antisemitism are used
to clobber every section of the progressive coalition. It's
another of the mind-bending distortions of far-right world.
This scattergun onslaught from seemingly contradictory
sources, and against sometimes overlapping parts of the left,
also explains why we struggle to formulate a rigorous and
unified response.

But I think there's another reason we are flailing in the
face of the far right's Hydra-headed racism. It relates to
how progressive movements understand antisemitism to

begin with. Several Jewish leftists I speak with express an awkwardness about discussing the antisemitism of the Great Replacement Theory within progressive spaces, fearing that this might be viewed as centring their own identity (what about all those deadly attacks on other racialised minorities?). Antiracism is rightly focused on dismantling structural racism, which requires an understanding of the ways that whiteness upholds and keeps those discriminatory systems in place. And leftist Jews who identify as white often talk about the need, foremost, for Jewish communities to develop an understanding of their own whiteness. But in doing so, however understandably, they are omitting something of their own experience of racialised depictions, something that is vital to antiracist movement-building. It's kind of like a progressive version of *BlacKkKlansman*'s fictional Jewish cop, Flip Zimmerman, insisting on living his life as just another white person. The trouble is that, just like Zimmerman, Jewish people have skin in the game. Whether or not that is visible or acknowledged. And as Eric K. Ward wrote, we can't combat far-right racism without talking about the antisemitism that powers it. He came to see antisemitism as 'so central to white supremacy that Black people would not win our freedom without tearing it down.'

Carin Mrotz, the former director of Minnesota's Jewish Community Action, told me that for decades, the organisation existed primarily to offer Jewish people, once the victims of oppression, 'a path to showing up as allies of those most directly targeted by oppression and injustice today'. But in the eruption of antisemitism in the US following Trump's 2016 election, she started to realise how limiting this was. As she wrote in 2021: 'By positioning ourselves only as allies in fighting white supremacy, we'd erased the ways white supremacy directly targets us as Jews. We'd allowed our coalition partners to ignore Black Jews, Jews of colour and working-class Jews. We'd failed to understand our community as stakeholders and turned ourselves into saviours … We'd also left our movement partners unprepared to support us when we needed it.' This racial and social justice group has made tackling antisemitism an essential part of its racial justice agenda. The group now has a combatting hate organiser on the team, working within progressive movements to build awareness of anti-Jewish racism and white nationalism.

Amos Schonfield tells me that Jews on the left tend to buy into the idea that Ashkenazi Jews are white-passing, relatively privileged and not a category of oppressed peoples. 'I present as a white, male, straight cis guy', he says. 'I am here providing allyship for other communities rather than needing it myself.' And so, when it comes to far-right antisemitism and the Great Replacement Theory, he explains, 'It is slightly disorienting to be in the camp of needing allyship.' But Schonfield acknowledges that this sort of thinking can hinder progressive movements. 'Solidarity is a two-way street only if I'm willing to centre that. If I'm not going to take up the space of being Jewish and of that being a part of my identity, how can I expect other people to notice?' What Schonfield and Mrotz and others are articulating is that when Jews show up in progressive movements *only* as white allies, rather than as a racialised minority that might also need support, it does a disservice in both directions. It is flattening and obscuring how we view Jewish people, and that ends up hampering an understanding of how racism works as a whole. After all, white-presenting Jewish people can be aware of having the privileges of whiteness, but also know that holding-privilege-while-Jewish is precisely what sets off white nationalists' antisemitism. None of that means anyone should give up on examining the mechanisms of structural racism, or how that relates to white Jewish people. But it does point to why Jews need to be able to show up as both white and not-white. We need the capacity within progressive movements to hold this contradiction. We need to create enough cognitive, political and emotional space to embrace all of it.

Conclusion

In the opening scenes of the documentary film *Rabbi on the Block*, Tamar Manasseh, a Black Jewish rabbi, leads a Yom Kippur memorial on the streets of Chicago's South Side. The Day of Atonement, the holiest of Jewish holidays, is a time for reflection over wrong-doings and seeking forgiveness. It's also a time to recite remembrance prayers for lost loved ones. For the past few years, Manasseh has carried out the Yom Kippur service on her neighbourhood street corner, with remembrance candles lit for those lost to street violence. Released in 2023, the film shows this ceremony taking place as a neighbourhood of African-American and Hispanic communities share painful stories of loss. One woman talks about her visiting brother being murdered in the streets, just before his eighteenth birthday. Another remembers her son, who was murdered in 2015 outside her home. One man honours his killed uncle, whom he describes as 'a ball of energy'. The rabbi administers hugs as she facilitates this service for mourning and pain, extending the Jewish day of atonement and remembrance to every person and every faith in that neighbourhood in an act of community and solidarity and love.

I'm not setting this up as a heartwarming conclusion to the story, of how everything would be fine if only we could just learn to get along. Manasseh really is an incredible and inspiring force for good. But as this documentary shows, her life's work of creating a bridge between Black and Jewish communities is anything but straightforward. It is filled with the pain of prejudices and ignorance, the difficulties faced by Black Jews within Ashkenazi Jewish communities, the barricades of misunderstanding that keep different minorities siloed apart in separate struggles. *Rabbi on the Block* shows the strength and value of true, deep allyship. But it also shows how very difficult it is to get there.

My hope for this book is that it sheds some light on why the subject of antisemitism has become such a horrible, divisive battleground, an ugly, distorted mess of claims and counterclaims; why it has torn progressive movements apart. What we have been struggling with is a jumble of contradictory, but separate and identifiable problems: a comprehension gap in understanding antisemitism as a live structure of racism; divisions over the way claims of antisemitism get deployed in our politics; confusions caused by the way we understand Israel, or the way different elements of the far right use both Israel and antisemitism. When we get right down to it, very little of our conversation is actually about Jewish people or their lived experiences, so much as it is about 'The Jews', as the antisemitic conspiracy and as the victims of it, and how both factors manifest in our society and in our political ecosystems.

But any light shed on our antisemitism battleground is just the start, a lamp lit to guide us on the road ahead. If one of the truths about antisemitism is that leftist movements of all kinds need to stop ceding the fight against it and start reclaiming it as an antiracist cause, the next truth is that this is one hell of a task. It demands copious, inexhaustible buckets of good faith because our entire political conversation is set up to obstruct that. The work must take place while bad-faith actors abound, while mainstream conversations throw us off track, while emotions are frayed, while baseless claims of antisemitism are directed at allies with growing frequency and while some in our own camp have fallen prey to conspiracies and rejectionism. We need to do it while the algorithms will subsume our efforts with polarised takes that overwhelm with clicks, shares and likes and while it seems we cannot carve out the time when faced with so many other urgent and still neglected causes. But we should be confident in the necessity of understanding and overcoming antisemitism right now – as the far right surges across the globe and as Israel, itself in the hands of a hardline right-wing government, wages an apocalyptic war on Gaza (ongoing as I write). And we need to act fast, precisely because of the wide-ranging harms unleashed by this battleground over antisemitism, as well as the actual antisemitism itself. Most of all we need to act because so many of our mainstream politicians have shown us time and again that, far from being able to tackle antisemitism sensitively and competently, they are a part of the problem, an active ingredient in the endlessly divisive confusion.

But far from the world of parliamentary politics, many are already reclaiming the fight against antisemitism as an integral component of broader antiracism efforts. In fact, this was one of the points made at the US House Committee on Education and the Workforce hearing in December, the one entitled 'Holding Campus Leaders Accountable and Confronting Antisemitism', resulting in the resignation of two university presidents. Speaking as an expert witness at the hearing, Pamela Nadell, director of the Jewish studies programme at the American University, said that campuses across the country were already deeply engaged in the challenge of dealing with antisemitism. 'The problem is they don't make the headlines, because they are not a bunch of protesters', she said. Nadell told the hearing that change was being driven by personal interventions. She cited examples of American universities where members of staff from the Israel studies and Middle East studies faculties did not agree with each other over politics but nonetheless wrote joint letters urging for campus discussions to be held in civil tones. It sounds small, but the fact that academics from these faculties could unite over such statements actually worked. It set a tone and led the way. They were teaching not just about their expert fields, but about how to responsibly disagree across fields of expertise.

Researching this book has put me in contact with countless individuals who, away from the sensationalist headlines, are already dedicated to this work, across different racialised minorities, including Palestinians, Israelis and many others. Whether it's setting up antisemitism awareness training for leftists or building Jewish movements that lean into religious and cultural practices of Judaism in rejecting the violent racism of the Israeli state. Whether it's community organising to create support in the aftermath of attacks on minorities, or left-wing groups building solidarity in the face of white nationalism and the Great Replacement Theory. Whether it is vital academic work to sharpen our analysis of different racisms in a de-siloed manner, or thoughtful definitions of antisemitism that provide clarity without trampling over Palestinian rights. These people and projects are many. They inform and inspire my writing. They fill me with hope. But now, they need your help.

Acknowledgements

Thanks to Andrew Gordon at David Higham Associates, who saw the potential for this book when it was a barely formulated idea and whose excellent guidance helped to develop this work from its beginning.

Thanks to the entire team at Oneworld for believing in and putting so much into this book. Cecilia Stein's invaluable advice, skill and encouragement kept the whole thing going, while she, Hannah Haseloff and Rida Vaquas vastly improved the book with their thoughtful editing. I am also grateful to Kathleen McCully for her brilliant copy-edits.

I will always be thankful to have worked with gifted and inspiring editors Maya Wolfe-Robinson at the *Guardian* and Don Guttenplan at the *Nation*, both of whom encouraged me to write about this subject in the first place.

A long list of academics, journalists and experts, far too many to mention here, read chapters of this book: thank you to every one of you; I hope you all know how deeply I value your generosity and careful attention.

For their friendship, encouragement, wisdom and support over many long conversations, huge thanks to Aditya Chakrabortty, Maya Goodfellow, Chris McGreal, Rachel Leah Jones, Samantha Ellis, Rachel Puttick, Francesca Klug, Marina Benjamin and Carinne Luck. And Faiza, Lisa and Anjula: you too have kept me going with your care and solidarity.

A book like this is simply not possible without the efforts of countless others: the many people willing to be interviewed, to share experiences, insights and expertise, or to think things through with me; the many whose extensive work and deep knowledge I have tapped into and learned from. It is a collaborative effort, driven and inspired by the sheer good fortune of being in conversation with a global community of people who passionately believe in and strive for a better world.

Finally, thanks and so much love to Anat, to Aboodi and to other family members who, throughout our disagreements, remain always in my heart.

Notes

All links were correct at the time of publication. References are provided for quotations, with the exception of tweets, and my own conversations and interviews.

Introduction

2 **'A graveyard for children'**: António Guterres, *Reuters*, 6 November 2023: www.reuters.com/world/middle-east/un-chief-says-gaza-becoming-graveyard-children-2023-11-06/.

2 **'All the indicators'**: Abdulqawi Ahmed Yusuf, *New York Times*, 28 March 2024: www.nytimes.com/live/2024/03/28/world/israel-hamas-war-gaza-news#icj-israel-gaza-aid-famine.

2 **'Does calling for the genocide'**: Elise Stefanik, US House Committee on Education and the Workforce hearing, 'Holding Campus Leaders Accountable and Confronting Antisemitism', 5 December 2023: www.c-span.org/video/?532147-1/university-presidents-testify-college-campus-antisemitism-part-1.

4 **'One of the things'**: Claudine Gay, ibid.

5 **'human animals'**: Yoav Gallant, *Guardian*, 9 October 2024: www.theguardian.com/world/2023/oct/09/israel-declares-siege-on-gaza-as-hamas-claims-israeli-strikes-killed-captives.

5 **'maximum damage'**: Daniel Hagari, *Guardian*, 10 October 2024: https://amp.theguardian.com/world/2023/oct/10/right-now-it-is-one-day-at-a-time-life-on-israels-frontline-with-gaza.

5 **'city of tents'**: Israeli defence official, *Sky News*, 12 October 2023: https://www.skynews.com.au/world-news/city-of-tents-israeli-defence-official-vows-every-building-in-gaza-will-be-destroyed-in-ground-manoeuvre/news-story/203242e24af1dd4757e0250001e7ed8a.

9 **'very fine people'**: Donald Trump, *Politico*, 15 August 2017: www.politico.com/story/2017/08/15/full-text-trump-comments-white-supremacists-alt-left-transcript-241662.

9 **'an enemy'**: Viktor Orbán, Hungarian prime minister, *Jewish Telegraphic Agency*, 15 March 2018: www.jta.org/2018/03/16/politics/hungarian-prime-minister-orban-attacks-enemy-speculates-money-election-rally-speech.

10 **'Louis Farrakhan, the leader of the Nation of Islam':** 'Louis
Farrakhan', Southern Poverty Law Center: https://www.splcenter.org/
fighting-hate/extremist-files/individual/louis-farrakhan.

10 **'causing degeneracy in Hollywood':** Louis Farrakhan, '2018 Saviours'
Day' address, Nation of Islam: https://media.noi.org/watch/saviours-
day-22518. **2:41**: Farrakhan talks about President Nixon believing
things about Jews that he did not have the 'balls' to say out loud.
2:42: Farrakhan continues: 'He [Nixon] talked about their grip on the
media, he talked about their grip in Hollywood, and how the Jews were
responsible for all this filth and degenerate behaviour that Hollywood
is putting out, turning men into women and women into men.'
3:32: 'Satan is going down and Farrakhan by God's grace has pulled the
cover off of that Satanic Jew. And I'm here to say: your time is up, your
world is through. And the good Jews, you'd better separate from these
satanic Jews, lest they take you down to hell with them, because that's
where they're headed.'

11 **Politics as a 'mirror world':** Naomi Klein, *Doppelganger* (London: Allen
Lane, 2023), p. 11.

12 **'Jewish friends of mine':** James Cleverly, *Telegraph*, 2
November 2019: www.telegraph.co.uk/politics/2019/11/02/
jewish-families-will-leave-uk-jeremy-corbyn-wins-general-election/.

1 The Colour Chart Conundrum

17 **'An absence of the negative consequences':** Reni Eddo-Lodge, *Why
I'm No Longer Talking to White People about Race* (London: Bloomsbury
Circus, 2017), p. 86.

21 **'People are really still antisemitic?':** from Carin Mrotz,
'Fighting Antisemitism Is a Critical Piece of a Racial Justice Agenda',
Forge, 15 February 2021: https://forgeorganizing.org/article/
fighting-antisemitism-critical-piece-racial-justice-agenda.

22 **'The fact the Jewish people themselves':** Robyn Autry, 'Whoopi
Goldberg Awkwardly Demonstrates How the Idea of Race Varies by
Place and Changes over Time', *Conversation*, 8 February 2022: https://
theconversation.com/whoopi-goldberg-awkwardly-demonstrates-how-
the-idea-of-race-varies-by-place-and-changes-over-time-176505.

24 **'The British historians wrote':** Eric Williams, *Capitalism and Slavery*
(Chapel Hill: University of North Carolina Press, 1944).

25 **'England was the first':** Geraldine Heng, 'England and
the Jews, before Shakespeare', 16 February 2022: www.

shakespearesglobe.com/discover/blogs-and-features/2022/02/16/
england-and-the-jews-before-shakespeare/.

26 **'the benchmark by which'**: Geraldine Heng, *England and the Jews*
(Cambridge: Cambridge University Press, 2018), p. 5.

26 **'The broad and pervasive'**: Christopher Browning, from George L.
Mosse, *Toward the Final Solution: a History of European Racism* (Madison:
University of Wisconsin Press, 2020), p. xxi.

28 **'the first permanent forcible expulsion'**: Geraldine Heng, *England's Dead
Boys: Telling Tales of Christian-Jewish Relations Before and After the First European
Expulsion of the Jews* (Baltimore: Johns Hopkins University Press, 2012).

30 **'The campaigns against Muslims and Jews'**: Ella Shohat, 'Rethinking
Jews and Muslims: Quincentennial Reflections', *Middle East Report* (178),
Sept–Oct 1992.

30 **'Antisemitism formed'**: ibid.

31 **'From the beginning'**: Ibram X. Kendi, *How to Be an Antiracist* (London:
Bodley Head, 2019), p. 40.

36 **'in the context of the overarching caveat'**: Tudor Parfitt, *Hybrid Hate:
Conflations of Antisemitism and Anti-Black Racism from the Renaissance to the
Third Reich* (Oxford: Oxford University Press, 2020), p. 42.

36 **'The linkages between Jews'**: ibid., p. 52.

37 **'the negroes of Africa'**: from Devin E. Naar, 'Our White Supremacy
Problem', *Jewish Currents*, 29 April 2019: https://jewishcurrents.org/
our-white-supremacy-problem.

38 **'different and apart'**: Parfitt, *Hybrid Hate*, p. 140.

38 **Marr 'argued that the despised blood'**: ibid., p. 166.

38 **'woolly matted hair'**: ibid., p. 51.

39 **'Anti-Jewish riots'**: Mosse, *Toward the Final Solution*, p. 122.

40 **'There are some streets'**: John Garrard, *The English and Immigration:
1880–1910* (Oxford: Oxford University Press, 1971), p. 50.

40 **'we were in a foreign country'**: ibid., p. 50.

40 **'unpleasant, indecent people'**: ibid., p. 51.

41 **'No-go' areas**: Paul Scully, Conservative MP for Sutton and Cheam,
Guardian, 26 February 2024: www.theguardian.com/news/2024/feb/26/
tory-mp-paul-scully-claims-there-are-no-go-areas-in-birmingham-and-
london.

43 **'Who knows but that'**: Mosse, *Toward the Final Solution*, p. xxxv.

43 **Not 'solely a matter of colour'**: W.E.B. Du Bois, 'The Negro and the
Warsaw Ghetto', *Jewish Life*, May 1952.

44 **'Race is the child of racism'**: Ta-Nehisi Coates, *Between the World and
Me* (Melbourne: Text Publishing Company, 2015), p. 7.

45 **'It took generations':** James Baldwin, 'On Being White and Other Lies', *The Cross of Redemption: Uncollected Writings* (New York: Pantheon Books, 2010), p. 136.

45 **'Precisely because race':** Emily Tamkin, *Bad Jews: a History of American Jewish Politics and Identities* (London: Hurst Publishers, 2022), pp. 59–60.

47 **'it's not about race':** Whoopi Goldberg, *The View*, 31 January 2022.

47 **'An American, perhaps especially':** Robyn Autry, 'Whoopi Goldberg Awkwardly Demonstrates How the Idea of Race Varies by Place and Changes over Time', *Conversation*, 8 February 2022: https://theconversation.com/whoopi-goldberg-awkwardly-demonstrates-how-the-idea-of-race-varies-by-place-and-changes-over-time-176505.

48 **'I feel, being Black':** Whoopi Goldberg, *The Late Show with Stephen Colbert*, 1 February 2022.

49 **'Don't write me':** ibid.

49 **'It is true that':** Diane Abbott, letter to the *Observer*, 23 April 2023: www.theguardian.com/theobserver/commentisfree/2023/apr/23/success-for-women-not-same-as-for-men-letters.

53 **'The ancient spirit left':** Tom Segev, *1949: the First Israelis* (New York: Henry Holt and Company, 1998), p. 156.

53 **'The danger we face':** David Ben-Gurion, 'Newly Released Documents Show a Darker Side of Ben Gurion', *Haaretz*, 24 April 2015: www.haaretz.com/2015-04-24/ty-article/.premium/the-darker-side-of-ben-gurion/0000017f-e564-dea7-adff-f5ff5e920000.

58 **'There's always this question':** Tamar Manasseh in *Rabbi on the Block*, dir. Brad Rothschild, 2023.

59 **'the identification of affinities':** Emma Dabiri, *What White People Can Do Next: From Allyship to Coalition* (London: Penguin, 2021), p. 13.

2 Whose Privilege Is It Anyway?

62 **'The Conservatives were (and are still) embroiled in accusations of Islamophobia':** Kiran Stacey, 'More than half of Tory members in poll say Islam a threat to British way of life', *Guardian*, 28 February 2024: https://www.theguardian.com/politics/2024/feb/28/more-than-half-of-tory-members-in-poll-say-islam-a-threat-to-british-way-of-life; Alex Forsyth, 'Islamophobia: Conservative Party members suspended over posts', *BBC News*, 20 September 2019: https://www.bbc.co.uk/news/uk-politics-49763550; 'General election 2019: PM apologises for Islamophobia in Tory party', *BBC News*, 27 November 2019: https://www.bbc.co.uk/news/election-2019-50576508.

62 **'specific examples of harassment'**: 'Investigation into Antisemitism in the Labour Party', Equality and Human Rights Commission report, October 2020, p. 3: www.equalityhumanrights.com/sites/default/files/ investigation-into-antisemitism-in-the-labour-party.pdf.

62 **'if the leadership had chosen to do so'**: ibid., p. 6.

63 **'piccaninnies' with 'watermelon smiles'**: Boris Johnson, 'If Blair's So Good at Running the Congo, Let Him Stay There', *Daily Telegraph*, 10 January 2002: www.telegraph.co.uk/comment/personal-view/3571742/ If-Blairs-so-good-at-running-the-Congo-let-him-stay-there.html.

63 **'letter boxes'**: Boris Johnson, 'Denmark Has Got It Wrong', *Daily Telegraph*, 5 August 2018: www.telegraph.co.uk/news/2018/08/05/ denmark-has-got-wrong-yes-burka-oppressive-ridiculous-still/.

76 **'What matters is'**: Stephen Bush, '*Jews Don't Count* by David Baddiel review', *The Times*, 5 February 2021: www.thetimes.com/culture/books/ article/jews-don-t-count-by-david-baddiel-review-p8pf9xhcz.

77 **'Hamas are the new Nazis'**: Benjamin Netanyahu, *The Hill*, 17 October 2023: https://thehill.com/policy/international/4261308-netanyahu-labels-hamas-the-new-nazis-alongside-germanys-scholz/.

78 **'Final Solution'**: Gilad Erdan, *Jerusalem Post*, 31 October 2023: www.jpost.com/international/article-770921.

78 **'The yellow patch'**: Dani Dayan, *Reuters*, 31 October 2023: www.reuters.com/world/israels-un-delegates-criticised-wearing-yellow-stars-symbol-pride-2023-10-31/.

81 **'I thought "Oh shit"'**: Bob Bland in *This is Personal*, dir. Amy Berg, 2019.

81 **'This is the rebirth'**: Kirsten Gillibrand, *Time*, 1 May 2017: https://time.com/collection/2017-time-100/4742711/ tamika-mallory-bob-bland-carmen-perez-linda-sarsour/.

82 **'I personally witnessed'**: Vanessa Wruble, *Vox*, 21 December 2018: www.vox.com/identities/2018/12/21/18145176/ feminism-womens-march-2018-2019-farrakhan-intersectionality.

82 **'noxious comments about Jewish people'**: Louis Farrakhan, '2018 Saviours' Day' address, Nation of Islam: https://media.noi.org/watch/sav-iours-day-22518. From **2:13**: Farrakhan talks about Jews in various nations of the world taking on the language and culture of the native population and running 'the money... the business.' From **2:15**: Farrakhan says he has Jewish friends, then adds: 'But when you know them and you're not afraid to say who they really are, they move to destroy you.'

82 **'powerful Jews'**: Louis Farrakhan, *CNN*, 28 February 2018: https:// edition.cnn.com/2018/02/28/politics/louis-farrakhan-speech/index.html.

82 **'Farrakhan has denied accusations of antisemitism':** Kathianne
Boniello, 'Louis Farrakhan files $5B defamation suit against ADL over
"false" antisemitism claims', *New York Post*, 21 October 2023.

83 **'I'm not an anti-Semite':** Louis Farrakhan, *BuzzFeed News*, 16
October 2018: www.buzzfeednews.com/article/josephbernstein/twitter-
wont-suspend-louis-farrakhan-for-tweet-comparing; Josefin Dolsten,
'Farrakhan's Anti-Semitic Tweet Gets Deleted After Twitter Policy Change',
Forward, 10 July 2019: https://forward.com/fast-forward/427327/
louis-farrakhan-s-2018-tweet-comparing-jews-to-termites-is-gone-after/.

83 **'transphobic, homophobic and patriarchal comments':**
'Antisemitism, Homophobia Promoted at Nation of Islam Celebration',
Anti-Defamation League, 4 March 2020:
https://www.adl.org/resources/blog/antisemitism-homophobia-
promoted-nation-islam-celebration. In a *Breakfast Club* interview, he suggested that women 'invite the rapist… invite the pervert' by not covering
up. See **1:01** of 'Minister Farrakhan FULL Interview at The Breakfast Club
Power 105.1 (05/24/2016)', YouTube, 24 May 2020: https://www.youtube.
com/watch?v=--xe7G4VnZE.

83 **'How can a Black woman be racist?':** Bob Bland, from John-
Paul Pagano, 'The Women's March Has a Farrakhan Problem', *Atlantic*,
8 March 2018: www.theatlantic.com/politics/archive/2018/03/
womens-march/555122/.

83 **'It's very clear to me':** Linda Sarsour, *Haaretz*, 21 November
2018: www.haaretz.com/us-news/2018-11-21/ty-article/
linda-sarsour-apologizes-to-womans-march-members-for-slow-response-
to-anti-semitism/0000017f-dc39-d3a5-af7f-febf94fa0000.

83 **'We regret that':** Linda Sarsour, 20 November 2018: https://drive.google.
com/file/d/17CInucXjr6UHdFwXpJ-XvP-Qc08k9qMn/edit.

85 **'In that most difficult period':** Tamika Mallory, *Newsone*, 7 March
2018: https://newsone.com/3779389/tamika-mallory-saviours-day/.

86 **'An organisation like the Nation of Islam':** Eric K. Ward, from
'Why Celebrities Keep Quoting Louis Farrakhan – Despite His
Antisemitism', *The Times of Israel*, 21 July 2020: www.timesofisrael.com/
why-celebrities-keep-quoting-louis-farrakhan-despite-his-anti-semitism/.

86 **'Watching Farrakhan bask':** Adam Serwer, 'Why Tamika Mallory Won't
Condemn Farrakhan', *Atlantic*, 11 March 2018: www.theatlantic.com/
politics/archive/2018/03/nation-of-islam/555332/.

87 **'We thought we were':** Rachel Timoner in *This is Personal*.

87 **'That's not my responsibility':** Tamika Mallory in ibid.

89 **'The complaint that antisemitism':** Ben Gidley, Brendan McGeever
and David Feldman, 'Labour and Antisemitism: a Crisis Misunderstood',

Political Quarterly, 91 (2), April–June 2020: https://onlinelibrary.wiley.com/doi/pdf/10.1111/1467-923X.12854.

94 **'Although the government':** Oku Ekpenyon, *BBC Front Row*, 3 May 2021.

96 **'It is important to memorialise':** Madge Dresser, 'UK Government Refuses to Fund Slavery Memorial Endorsed by Johnson in 2008', *Guardian*, 10 December 2019: www.theguardian.com/world/2019/dec/10/slave-trade-memorial-charity-uk-government-refusal-of-funding-boris-johnson.

3 Which Side Are Jews On?

100 **'one of the most intense':** Robert Pape, 'Israel's Military Campaign in Gaza Seen as among the Most Destructive in Recent History, Experts Say', *Associated Press*, 11 January 2024: https://apnews.com/article/israel-gaza-bombs-destruction-death-toll-scope-419488c511f83c85baea22458472a796.

102 **'We know too well':** Nelson Mandela, South African president, 4 December 1997: www.mandela.gov.za/mandela_speeches/1997/971204_palestinian.htm.

104 **'We must expropriate':** Theodor Herzl, from Rashid Khalidi, *The Hundred Years' War on Palestine* (London: Profile Books, 2020), p. 4.

105 **'The native populations':** Ze'ev Jabotinsky, *The Iron Wall*, 4 November 1923: https://en.jabotinsky.org/media/9747/the-iron-wall.pdf.

107 **'Such radical social engineering':** Khalidi, *Hundred Years' War*, p. 9.

113 **'Invasion is a structure':** Patrick Wolfe, 'Settler Colonialism and the Elimination of the Native', *Journal of Genocide Research*, 8 (4), 2006: www.tandfonline.com/doi/full/10.1080/14623520601056240.

113 **'settler colonialism pure and simple':** Patrick Wolfe, from Rachel Busbridge, 'Israel-Palestine and the Settler Colonial "Turn": From Interpretation to Decolonization', *Theory, Culture & Society*, 35 (1), 2018.

117 **'a discourse that folds':** Brian Klug, 'Speaking of Zionism', *Marxism 2017*, 8 July 2017.

118 **'victims of victims':** Edward Said, 'The One-State Solution', *New York Times*, 10 January 1999: www.nytimes.com/1999/01/10/magazine/the-one-state-solution.html.

118 **'The Europeans see':** Raef Zreik, 'When Does a Settler Become a Native?', *Constellations*, 23 (3), 2016, p. 359.

118 **'the "third party"':** Gil Hochberg, 'Remembering Semitism', *ReOrient*, 2 (2), 2016, p. 193.

119   **'a portion of a rampart of Europe':** Theodor Herzl, from Yair
 Wallach, 'The Racial Logic of Palestine's Partition', *Ethnic and Racial
 Studies*, 46 (8), 2006.

119   **'national conflict':** Yair Wallach, 'The Racial Logic of Palestine's
 Partition', *Ethnic and Racial Studies*, 46 (8), 2006.

109   Idith Zertal and Akiva Eldar, *Lords of the Land: the War over Israel's
 Settlements in the Occupied Territories, 1967–2007* (New York: Nation Books,
 2005).

124   **'European interests':** Hakem Al-Rustom, *The Arab and Jewish Questions:
 Geographies of Engagement in Palestine and Beyond*, eds. Bashir Bashir and
 Leila Farsakh (New York: Columbia University Press, 2020), p. 127.

124   **'the Holocaust':** ibid., p. 130.

124   **'Accounting for':** ibid., p. 127.

124   **Hitler 'applied to Europe':** Aimé Césaire, *Discourse on Colonialism*
 (New York: Monthly Review Press, 2000), p. 36.

125   **'the long European legacy':** Hochberg, 'Remembering Semitism',
 p. 194.

126   **'Europe's way':** ibid., p. 194.

126   **'For Europe':** Zreik, 'When Does a Settler Become a Native?', p. 359.

127   **'left-wing echo':** Lydia Polgreen, 'Restoring the Past Won't Liberate
 Palestinians', *New York Times*, 18 February 2024: www.nytimes.
 com/2024/02/18/opinion/israel-gaza-palestine-decolonization.html.

128   **'I don't care':** Iyad el-Baghdadi, from ibid.

129   **'We are stopping':** Donald Trump, *CNN*, 13 October 2017: https://
 edition.cnn.com/2017/10/13/politics/trump-values-voters-summit.

129   **'My country is':** Nigel Farage, *Independent*, 4 September 2014: www.
 independent.co.uk/news/uk/nigel-farage-says-britain-needs-to-stand-up-
 for-its-judeochristian-values-to-combat-homegrown-militants-9708082.
 html.

129   **'Europe's Judeo–Christian roots':** Hochberg, 'Remembering
 Semitism', p. 198.

132   **'Within this new':** ibid., p. 197.

132   **'In the new Europe':** Brian Klug, 'Unasking the Jewish Question',
 paper delivered to the Bruno Kreisky Forum for International Dialogue,
 November 2022.

133   **'I do not stop':** Marine Le Pen, *Atlantic*, 19 April 2027:
 www.theatlantic.com/international/archive/2017/04/
 marine-le-pen-national-front-jews-muslims/523302/.

135   **'The National Front is a party':** Roger Cukierman, *The
 Times*, 24 February 2015: https://www.thetimes.com/article/
 french-jews-turn-to-le-pen-after-muslim-attacks-w9ppmj5d9g7.

135 **'Unfortunately within the Jewish community':** Delphine Horvilleur, 'France's Star Female Rabbi Fights a Lonely Two-front Battle Against Antisemitism and Islamophobia', *Haaretz*, 23 May 2018: www.haaretz.com/jewish/news/2018-05-23/ty-article/.premium/frances-star-female-rabbi-fights-a-lonely-two-front-battle/0000017f-ef8f-df98-a5ff-efaf9de70000.

136 **'villa in the jungle':** Ehud Barak, 'Ehud Barak: the Military Mastermind Israel Loves to Hate', *Guardian*, 26 November 2012: www.theguardian.com/world/2012/nov/26/ehud-barak-quits-politics-israel.

136 **'We are part of the European culture':** Benjamin Netanyahu, *Guardian*, 19 July 2017: www.theguardian.com/world/2017/jul/19/eu-will-wither-and-die-if-it-does-not-change-policy-on-israel-netan-yahu.

137 **'It's very good':** Benjamin Netanyahu, 'A Day of Terror: the Israelis', *New York Times*, 12 September 2001: www.nytimes.com/2001/09/12/us/day-terror-israelis-spilled-blood-seen-bond-that-draws-2-nations-closer.html.

137 **'Israel, an embattled democracy':** Ariel Sharon, 'Speech by Prime Minister Ariel Sharon on September 11, 2002', *Haaretz*, 10 September 2002: www.haaretz.com/2002-09-10/ty-article/speech-by-prime-minister-ariel-sharon-on-september-11-2002/0000017f-db39-d3ff-a7ff-fbb9307f0000.

138 **'front line in the battle':** Amichai Chikli, 'Israel is on the Front Line of the Battle for Western Civilisation, Says Diaspora Minister', *Jewish Chronicle*, 17 November 2023: www.thejc.com/news/israel/israel-is-on-the-front-line-of-the-battle-for-western-civilisation-says-diaspora-minister-wk0gx8wb.

138 **'If we don't win now':** Benjamin Netanyahu, *Fox News*, 13 November 2023: www.foxnews.com/media/israeli-pm-netanyahu-warns-america-if-we-dont-win-now-then-europe-is-next-and-youre-next.

4 The 'New' Antisemitism

144 **'Like the Roman God':** Brian Klug, 'Interrogating "New Antisemitism"', *Ethnic and Racial Studies*, 36 (3), 2013, p. 10.

146 **'if we only begin':** Theodor Herzl, from Brian Klug, 'The Collective Jew: Israel and the New Antisemitism', *Patterns of Prejudice*, 37 (2), 2003, p. 118.

147 **'Let there be no mistake':** Abba Eban, from Anthony Lerman, *Whatever Happened to Antisemitism?* (London: Pluto Press, 2022) p. 47.

147 **'Clearly by the mid-1980s':** Lerman, ibid., p. 63.

148 **'united and galvanized many of America's Jews':** Tamkin, *Bad Jews*,
p. 92.

154 **'We see them':** Cynthia Hale, 'Black Pastors Pressure Biden to Call
for a Ceasefire in Gaza', *New York Times*, 28 January 2024: www.nytimes.
com/2024/01/28/us/politics/black-pastors-biden-gaza-israel.html.

154 **'People will say':** Tony Judt, 'The Way Things Are and
How They Might Be', *London Review of Books*, 32 (6), 25
March 2010: www.lrb.co.uk/the-paper/v32/n06/tony-judt/
the-way-things-are-and-how-they-might-be.

155 **'Attempts to equate':** Max Hastings, 'A Grotesque Choice', *Guardian*,
11 March 2004: www.theguardian.com/world/2004/mar/11/race.
pressandpublishing.

156 **'Israel has been':** Reut Institute, 'Building a Political Firewall Against
Israel's Delegitimization', March 2010.

157 **'Because Israel's delegitimization':** ibid.

158 **'There's only one word':** Chuck Schumer, *Washington Post*, 5 March
2018: www.youtube.com/watch?v=ju1wz87Slz4.

159 **'I have the right':** Alan Leveritt in *Boycott*, dir. Julia Bacha, 2021.

159 **'appalled that a newspaper':** Barry Block, ibid.

160 **'written primarily to help':** Kenneth S. Stern, written testimony, United
States House of Representatives Homeland Security Committee on
Countering Violent Extremism, Terrorism, and Antisemitic Threats in New
Jersey, 3 October 2022: www.congress.gov/117/meeting/house/115162/
witnesses/HHRG-117-HM00-Wstate-SternK-20221003.pdf.

162 **'The vast majority':** David Feldman, 'Antisemitism and Criticism of
Israel', Council for the Defence of British Universities, 6 February 2024:
https://cdbu.org.uk/antisemitism-and-criticism-of-israel/.

162 **'was not drafted':** Kenneth Stern, 'The Problem with Defining
Antisemitism', *New Yorker*, 13 March 2024: www.newyorker.com/news/
persons-of-interest/the-problem-with-defining-antisemitism.

162 **'frequently casting aside':** David Feldman, in ibid.

163 **'It is likely in practice':** Geoffrey Robertson, 'IHRA
Definition of Antisemitism is Not Fit for Purpose', *Doughty Street
Chambers*, 13 August 2018: www.doughtystreet.co.uk/news/
ihra-definition-antisemitism-not-fit-purpose.

165 **'contributing to the atmosphere':** Dima Khalidi, 'Chilling and
Censoring of Palestine Advocacy in the United States', *On Antisemitism:
Solidarity and the Struggle for Justice* (Chicago: Haymarket Books, 2017) p. 182.

167 **'The backlash in the arts world':** 'Artists "Cancelled" as Israel-Hamas
War Reverberates beyond Battlefield', *Financial Times*, 7 December 2003:
www.ft.com/content/32aa026c-7534-4e3a-a995-8c15d07abd7b.

167 **'an exponential increase'**: Radhika Sainath, 'When Posting about the Israel-Hamas War Costs You Your Job', *The Cut*, 30 October 2023: www.thecut.com/2023/10/israel-hamas-war-job-loss-social-media.html.

167 **'This stifles free expression'**: 'Speaking out on Israel/Gaza Must Be Allowed: UN Experts', *UN*, 23 November 2023: www.ohchr.org/en/press-releases/2023/11/speaking-out-gaza-israel-must-be-allowed-un-experts.

171 **'All our choices'**: Jonathan Glazer, '"We Refute our Jewishness and the Holocaust Being Hijacked": Jonathan Glazer Calls for End to Gaza Attacks at Oscars', *Guardian*, 11 March 2024: www.theguardian.com/film/2024/mar/11/zone-of-interest-international-film-oscar.

171 **'To stand on German soil'**: Yuval Abraham, 'Israeli Director Receives Death Threats after Officials Call Berlin Festival "Antisemitic"', *Guardian*, 27 February 2024: www.theguardian.com/film/2024/feb/27/israeli-director-receives-death-threats-after-officials-call-berlinale-antisemitic.

172 **'It became an empty accusation'**: Bassem Youssef, *France24*, 27 March 2024: www.france24.com/en/tv-shows/t%C3%AAte-%C3%A0-t%C3%AAte/20240327-anti-semitism-has-become-a-comical-accusation-comedian-bassem-youssef.

173 **'When antisemitism is everywhere'**: Brian Klug, 'The Myth of the New Antisemitism', *Nation*, 15 January 2004: www.thenation.com/article/archive/myth-new-anti-semitism/.

173 **'The repetition of'**: Susan Neiman, 'Germany on Edge', *New York Review*, 3 November 2023: www.nybooks.com/online/2023/11/03/germany-on-edge-israel-palestine/.

179 **'heard about this thing'**: Stern, 'Problem'.

180 **'Even if they reject'**: Yair Wallach, 'Jewish Progressives Are Deeply Critical of Israel, yet Inextricably Tied to It', *New Statesman*, 29 November 2023: www.newstatesman.com/ideas/2023/11/jewish-progressives-relationship-israel.

182 **'Play the ball'**: Mehdi Hasan, *Win Every Argument: the Art of Debating, Persuading and Public Speaking* (London: Macmillan, 2023), p. 74.

182 **'Calling your opponent's ethos'**: ibid., p. 64.

184 **'How do I deflect'**: Alissa Wise, 'Building Toward the Next World', *On Antisemitism: Solidarity and the Struggle for Justice* (Chicago: Haymarket Books, 2017), p. 208.

5 With Friends Like These

188 **'for the Jewish people'**: John Hagee, *New York Times*, 23 May 2008: www.nytimes.com/2008/05/23/us/politics/23hagee.html.

188   **'the LGBTQ community':** Hagee tweeted on 10 September 2022 that 'The only marriages God will ever recognize is [sic] between a man and a woman': https://x.com/PastorJohnHagee/status/1568676936519667713. He also claimed that Hurricane Katrina was 'the judgment of God' acting in response to a planned gay pride parade in an interview in 2006: 'Pastor John Hagee on Christian Zionism' *Fresh Air*, NPR, 18 September 2006: https://www.npr.org/2006/09/18/6097362/pastor-john-hagee-on-christian-zionism (from **22:40**).

188   **'although he apologised for the latter':** 'Pastor Hagee Apologises; Donohue–Hagee Meet', *Catholic League for Religious and Civil Rights*, 24 June 2008: https://www.catholicleague.org/pastor-hagee-apologizes-donohue-hagee-meet/.

188   **'I am horrified that':** Hadar Susskind, *NBC News*, 15 November 2023: www.nbcnews.com/news/us-news/divisive-pastor-john-hagee-criticism-role-march-israel-rcna125346.

188   **'One can support Israel':** Emily Tamkin, 'Why Televangelist John Hagee Was a Shocking March for Israel Speaker', *MSNBC*, 15 November 2023: www.msnbc.com/opinion/msnbc-opinion/john-hagee-march-for-israel-antisemitism-rcna125291.

190   **'I know you all think':** Yali Hashash, 'How White Christian Zionism Is (Re)shaping Israel', *Emor*, 23 February 2023.

190   **'We've been evangelised':** ibid.

191   **'God promises Abraham':** Mike Pence, 'God's Plan for Mike Pence', *Atlantic*, January/February 2018: www.theatlantic.com/magazine/archive/2018/01/gods-plan-for-mike-pence/546569/.

191   **'Islam not only condones':** John Hagee, from Steven Gardiner, 'End Times Antisemitism', *Political Research Associates*, 9 July 2020: https://politicalresearch.org/2020/07/09/end-times-antisemitism#_edn58.

192   **'unwaveringly supported':** Tristan Sturm, 'Religion as Nationalism: the Religious Nationalism of American Christian Zionists', *National Identities*, 20 (3), 2018, p. 300: www.tandfonline.com/doi/full/10.1080/14608944.2016.1255187.

193   **'one of the largest':** Ben Lorber and Aiden Orly, 'Why Did an Antisemitic Christian Zionist Have the Chutzpah to Declare that He'd Be Leading a Holocaust March?', *Religion Dispatches*, 27 April 2022: https://religiondispatches.org/why-did-an-antisemitic-christian-zionist-have-the-chutzpah-to-declare-that-he-would-be-leading-a-holocaust-march/.

194   **'Israel is God's prophetic clock':** John Hagee, *Baptist Standard*, 20 November 2023: www.baptiststandard.com/news/faith-culture/evangelicals-see-israel-hamas-war-in-light-of-end-times/.

194 **'The supporters of Israel'**: Benjamin Netanyahu, *Christians United for Israel Conference*, 17 July 2017: https://cufi.org/issue/netanyahu-says-israel-has-no-better-friends-than-us-christian-zionists/.

195 **'We have no better friends'**: Benjamin Netanyahu, *Times of Israel*, 3 January 2019: www.timesofisrael.com/brazil-applauds-netanyahu-bolsonaro-bromance-new-ties-with-jewish-state/.

195 **'the backbone of'**: Ron Dermer, *Haaretz*, 10 May 2021: www.haaretz.com/us-news/2021-05-10/ty-article/.premium/israel-should-focus-outreach-on-evangelicals-not-u-s-jews-former-envoy-says/0000017f-e0b9-df7c-a5ff-e2fbcc410000.

195 **'They are able to'**: Hashash, 'How White Christian Zionism Is (Re)shaping Israel'.

197 **'We're seeing prophecy'**: Robert Jeffress, 'Robert Jeffress, Pastor Who Said Jews Are Going To Hell, Led Prayer at Jerusalem Assembly', *New York Times*, 14 May 2018: www.nytimes.com/2018/05/14/world/middleeast/robert-jeffress-embassy-jerusalem-us.html.

197 **'You can't be saved by'**: ibid.

197 **'Jerusalem is where'**: John Hagee, *Associated Press*, 15 May 2018: https://apnews.com/article/9d744cfd08544820b5e5de64d9cd02f1.

198 **'The bedrock of support'**: Frank Schaeffer in *Praying for Armageddon*, dir. Tonje Hessen Schei, 2023.

200 **'We expect God'**: Boyd Bingham in *'Til Kingdom Come*, dir. Maya Zinshtein, 2020.

201 **'It's from Christians'**: Yael Eckstein in ibid.

203 **'looks like an effort'**: Lee Fang in *Praying for Armageddon*.

203 **'the Christian Zionists have'**: Stephen Walt and John Mearsheimer, from Sturm, 'Religion as Nationalism', pp. 300–1.

207 **'The Jewish people'**: Donald Trump, *Washington Post*, 17 December 2021: www.washingtonpost.com/politics/trump-jews-israel/2021/12/17/12f68c2c-5f50-11ec-ae5b-5002292337c7_story.html.

207 **'Some would argue'**: Maya Zinshtein in *'Til Kingdom Come*.

208 **'You don't want to hear'**: William Bingham III in *'Til Kingdom Come*.

209 **'We're not antisemites'**: from Szabolcs Panyi, 'How the Alliance with Israel Has Reshaped the Politics of Victor Orban', *Direkt36*, 30 September 2019: www.direkt36.hu/en/az-izraeli-szovetseg-ami-atirta-orban-politikajat/.

210 **'It was possible to launch'**: Andrew Heisler, *Times of Israel*, 20 July 2017: www.timesofisrael.com/decrying-netanyahu-betrayal-hungary-jews-say-pm-ignoring-them/.

210   **'Orbán's praise in 2017 for the nation's wartime leader':**
Philip Stephens, 'Viktor Orban's Hungary crosses to Europe's
dark side', *Financial Times*, 13 July 2017: https://www.ft.com/
content/2032f1c2-66e5-11e7-8526-7b38dcaef614.

211   **'that has penetrated every level of society':** Zsofia Kata Vincze,
from Joshua Leifer, 'Tapping the "Hidden Spring" of Antisemitism in
Orban's Hungary', *+972 Magazine*, 12 October 2018: www.972mag.com/
tapping-the-hidden-spring-of-anti-semitism-in-orbans-hungary/.

214   **'the dinner table test':** Sayeeda Warsi, *Guardian*, 20
January 2011: www.theguardian.com/uk/2011/jan/20/
lady-warsi-islamophobia-muslims-prejudice.

214   **'Many scholars in the area':** Ruth Wodak, 'The Radical Right and
Antisemitism', in *The Oxford Handbook of the Radical Right*, ed. Jens
Rydgren (Oxford: Oxford Academic, 2018), p. 1.

215   **'vital to the construction':** Jelena Subotić, 'Antisemitism in the Global
Populist International', *British Journal of Politics and International Relations*,
24 (3), 2022, p. 465.

215   **'It is plastic':** ibid., p. 463.

216   **'as long as we support':** Susan Neiman, from Henry Mance,
'Philosopher Susan Neiman: "I Hate the Words Pro-Israel and Pro-
Palestinian. I'm Pro-peace"', *Financial Times*, 6 November 2023: www.
ft.com/content/8840d3d8-151f-4f2e-a831-2857c3515c41.

216   **'a natural friend':** Subotić, 'Antisemitism', p. 469.

217   **'the West's first line of defence':** Geert Wilders, *Haaretz*,
18 June 2009: www.haaretz.com/2009-06-18/ty-article/
dutch-anti-islam-mp-israel-is-wests-first-line-of-defense/0000017f-
e347-df7c-a5ff-e37f2b470000.

217   **'frontline of Islamic extremism and jihad':** English Defence League,
from Nigel Copsey, 'The English Defence League: Challenging Our
Country and Our Values of Social Inclusion, Fairness and Equality', *Faith
Matters*, 2010, p. 18.

217   **'preserve our own Judeo–Christian civilisation':** Geert Wilders,
from Hannah Rose, 'The New Philosemitism: Exploring a Changing
Relationship between Jews and the Far-Right', International Centre
for the Study of Radicalisation, 2020, p. 11.

217   **'our Judeo–Christian culture':** Nigel Farage, ibid., p. 11.

218   **'To all the Jews of France':** Benjamin Netanyahu, *Forward*,
13 January 2015: https://forward.com/israel/212614/
french-jews-feel-conflicted-about-israels-call-for/.

218   **'If 100,000 Jews leave':** Manuel Valls, *Atlantic*, 10 January
2015: www.theatlantic.com/international/archive/2015/01/

french-prime-minister-warns-if-jews-flee-the-republic-will-be-judged-a-failure/384410/.

220 **'from 500,000 to 2.3 million followers':** Steven Lee Myers, Tiffany Hsu, 'Riding Rage Over Israel to Online Prominence', *New York Times*, 11 April 2024: https://www.nytimes.com/2024/04/11/business/media/jackson-hinkle-israel-gaza-misinformation.html.

221 **'The obvious question is':** Julia Ebner, *Going Dark: the Secret Social Lives of Extremists* (London: Bloomsbury, 2020), p. 176.

221 **'Supported by the co-existence':** Hannah Rose, 'The New Philosemitism: Exploring a Changing Relationship between Jews and the Far-right', International Centre for the Study of Radicalisation, 2020, p. 22: https://icsr.info/wp-content/uploads/2020/11/ICSR-Report-The-New-Philosemitism-Exploring-a-Changing-Relationship-Between-Jews-and-the-Far-Right.pdf.

222 **'Once an issue is touched':** Klein, *Doppelganger*, p. 93.

6 Skin in the Game

225 **'I thought about':** Jeffrey Myers, *Jewish Telegraphic Agency*, 30 May 2023: www.jta.org/2023/05/30/united-states/911-dispatcher-and-rabbi-take-the-stand-on-first-day-of-pittsburgh-synagogue-shooting-trial.

226 **'I kissed my fingers':** Andrea Wedner, *Jewish Telegraphic Agency*, 14 June 2023: www.jta.org/2023/06/14/politics/defense-lawyers-in-pittsburgh-synagogue-shooting-trial-will-not-call-witnesses-or-present-evidence.

226 **'There's a consensus':** Park Dietz, *Jewish Telegraphic Agency*, 12 July 2023: www.jta.org/2023/07/12/politics/is-antisemitism-always-delusional-the-pittsburgh-synagogue-shooters-punishment-could-hinge-on-the-answer.

227 **'simply mistook':** Park Dietz, *Jewish Telegraphic Agency*, 10 July 2023: www.jta.org/2023/07/10/united-states/pittsburgh-synagogue-trial-expert-says-antisemitism-and-white-suprema-cism-not-delusions-spurred-shooter.

227 **'We are here':** Ambalavaner Sivanandan, from Reni Eddo-Lodge, *Why I'm No Longer Talking to White People About Race* (London: Bloomsbury Circus, 2017), p. 9.

231 **'The real war I'm advocating':** Payton Gendron, *Times of Israel*, 15 May 2022: www.timesofisrael.com/manifesto-attributed-to-buffalo-shooting-suspect-pushes-antisemitic-conspiracies/.

232 **'defending my country':** *Associated Press*, 4 August 2019: https://apnews.com/article/immigration-shootings-us-news-ap-top-news-his-panics-df6dc60f37664833ba3b953927ef835d.

233 **'I would die':** *Forward*, 28 April 2019: https://forward.com/fast-forward/423381/

alleged-poway-synagogue-shooter-lives-with-his-parents-and-thinks-jews-are/.

233 **'The root of all'**: *New York Times*, 21 February 2020: www.nytimes.com/2019/10/09/world/europe/germany-shooting-halle-synagogue.html.

235 **'As a Black man'**: Eric K. Ward, 'Skin in the Game', *Political Research Associates*, 29 June 2017: https://politicalresearch.org/2017/06/29/skin-in-the-game-how-antisemitism-animates-white-nationalism.

235 **'committed to building'**: ibid.

236 **'Some secret cabal'**: ibid.

241 **'You would go to a fountain'**: Renaud Camus, from Thomas Chatterton Williams, 'The French Origins of "You Will Not Replace Us"', *New Yorker*, 27 November 2017: www.newyorker.com/magazine/2017/12/04/the-french-origins-of-you-will-not-replace-us.

242 **'His initial concept'**: '"The Great Replacement": an Explainer', *ADL*, 19 April 2021: www.adl.org/resources/backgrounder/great-replacement-explainer.

243 **'While the attention'**: Subotić, 'Antisemitism', p. 467.

244 **'We are fighting'**: Viktor Orbán, *Guardian*, 5 December 2020: www.theguardian.com/world/2020/dec/05/george-soros-orban-turns-to-familiar-scapegoat-as-hungary-rows-with-eu.

245 **'He is hardly'**: Rudy Giuliani, *New York Times*, 24 December 2019: www.nytimes.com/2019/12/24/us/politics/rudy-giuliani-george-soros-jewish.html.

245 **'Trump's 2016 closing election ads'**: 'Donald Trump "Donald Trump's Argument for America" | Campaign 2016', *Washington Post*, 6 November 2016: https://www.washingtonpost.com/video/politics/team-trump-donald-trumps-argument-for-america-campaign-2016/2016/11/06/218f32d4-a443-11e6-ba46-53db57f0e351_video.html.

246 **'I really feel that Soros'**: Nigel Farage, *Fox News*, 20 June 2018: www.youtube.com/watch?v=7gXsOvcs_Ks&t=137s.

247 **'Man who "Broke the Bank of England"'**: *Daily Telegraph*, 8 February 2018: www.telegraph.co.uk/politics/2018/02/07/george-soros-man-broke-bank-england-backing-secret-plot-thwart/.

247 **'the question posed by the *New Statesman*'**: 'The Telegraph's George Soros story follows in the footsteps of the alt right', *New Statesman*, 8 February 2018 (updated 9 June 2021): https://www.newstatesman.com/uncategorized/2018/02/telegraph-s-george-soros-story-follows-footsteps-alt-right.

248 **'In my work'**: Julia Ebner, *Going Mainstream: How Extremists Are Taking Over* (London: Ithaka, 2023), p. 182.

250 **'hate marches':** Suella Braverman, *Guardian*, 30 October 2023: www.
theguardian.com/politics/2023/oct/30/uk-ministers-cobra-meeting-
terrorism-threat-israel-hamas-conflict-suella-braverman.

250 **'existential challenge':** Suella Braverman, *Independent*,
26 September 2023: www.independent.co.uk/news/uk/
suella-braverman-conservative-home-secretary-european-convention-
on-human-rights-britain-b2418856.html.

251 **'It serves as':** Ben Lorber, 'Taking Aim at Multiracial Democracy',
Political Research Associates, 22 October 2019: https://politicalresearch.
org/2019/10/22/taking-aim-multiracial-democracy.

253 **'so central to white supremacy':** Eric K. Ward,
'Skin in the Game', *Political Research Associates*, 29
June 2017: https://politicalresearch.org/2017/06/29/
skin-in-the-game-how-antisemitism-animates-white-nationalism.

Conclusion

260 **'The problem is':** Pamela Nadell, US House Committee
on Education and the Workforce hearing, 'Holding Campus
Leaders Accountable and Confronting Antisemitism', 5
December 2023: www.c-span.org/video/?532147-1/
university-presidents-testify-college-campus-antisemitism-part-1.